Simon Temp..

UNDRESSED FOR DINNER

The story of a family trying to lead an
ordinary life in an extraordinary place

With Best Wishes
Simon.

HAYLOFT PUBLISHING
CUMBRIA

First published in Great Britain 2013 by Hayloft Publishing Ltd.,
This revised edition, 2016.

A CIP catalogue record for this book is available from the British Library

ISBN 978-1-910237-22-9

Designed, printed and bound in the EU

Cover illustration © Henry Jenkins – www.Henryjenkins.co.uk
with additional illustrations © Emily Bennett

Hayloft policy is to use papers that are natural, renewable and recyclable products and made from
wood grown in sustainable forests. The logging and manufacturing processes are expected to   conform to the environmental regulations of the country of origin.

Hayloft Publishing Ltd, 44 Appleby Road, Kendal, LA9 6ES, (registered office)
L'Ancien Presbytère, 21460 Corsaint, France (editorial)

www.hayloft.eu

For both our Dads who would have enjoyed being part of the story.

For my Mum who made the story possible.

For my gorgeous wife Wendy and our incredible children, Oliver and Emily, who are the story.

ACKNOWLEDGEMENTS

We have welcomed tens of thousands of guests to the castle and every one of them has helped to make it what it is. To list them all would require another book, so this story is a thank you to every single one of them.

There are many others who have played a pivotal role on this incredible journey. They are also too numerous to mention individually but in particular: Sarah and Denis for inspiring us; my aunt, Tish and her late husband Ray for supporting us by being our first ever paying guests; Andrew and Allison who came into our lives for our first Christmas at Augill and have been at our side ever since; Miranda and Graham for teaching me how to hang wallpaper and showing me why balancing a paint pot on the stairs is never a good idea; Charles and Elaine who have been the sort of friends who are always there in a crisis; Clive and Jo for their quiet support and free labour; Father Mark for his irreverent spiritual guidance; Jenny Morgan for showing Oliver that the world is his oyster; Bill and Jenny who have been a constant part of Augill life, substitute grandparents to Oliver and Emily and the best of neighbours; Buzz and Gloria who are each much more important parts of our lives than their fleeting mentions suggest; all our wonderful staff, past and present, who look after us as well as they do the castle and without whom none of what we do would be possible.

Having done what we have and got where we are, this book would not have been possible without the support and encouragement of Wendy who made me take time out to write it; Jacqui and Martin at Les Mimosas who gave me a room and left me in peace to write and took me out when I'd had enough; Miranda who read the first manuscript and was brave enough to give me truly unbiased critical feedback; Dawn, my publisher, editor and sounding board who made sure my words made sense; Henry who came up with such great illustrations for the cover; Emily who drew such a wonderful family portrait for the chapter headers.

FOREWORD

After over 30 years of the Lake District Book of the Year Awards, now part of the Lakeland calendar, an icon of English culture and the only regional literary award in the whole of the UK, I have to say that almost all the entries over the years have been er... safe, traditional, nice, well spoken, you could take them anywhere and they would not let you down or shock the curate.

Simon Temple-Bennett, in his entry in 2014, could not have been more different. The judges, all sensitive souls, were rather taken aback. His book was so contemporary it hurt. On page 16, there were four fucks in sixteen lines. Modern life, eh?

Personally, I was a bit jealous, that he could find a compliant publisher willing to accommodate all these rude words. I do a column in the *Sunday Times* and also *Cumbria Life* and I am not allowed to be so rude in public.

I also write a column in the *New Statesman*, where I can write anything. On the other hand, who reads the *New Statesman*?

Simon is an off-comer to Cumbria, so probably didn't know how polite and well bred we are, at least in print.

In 1997, he and his wife bought a wrecked Augill Castle in the Eden Valley, and turned it into an award-winning hotel. He describes a row with his mother, who put up some money, but then thinks she is being excluded. He appears to have a Basil Fawlty temper and attitude to life, and his guests. He is very funny on locals – though they were probably not amused – and also on his problems with the Tourist Board and on foot and mouth.

It is not a literary book, as such, but he has one very nice literary device – having conversations with his dead father.

It's 'Carry on Hotelier' – racy, funny, you want to read on. Some of the stories I could not quite believe were totally true, but it's all good fun and excellent stories. There are not many funny books coming out each year in Cumbria, which would explain why it won our award as Book of the Year. It should appeal to all modern Cumbrians – as long as they don't mind the language.

Hunter Davies

PREFACE

When we bought Augill Castle in 1997 we were young and naive with an optimism that could be tempered by nothing. We planned to open a few rooms for bed & breakfast and live an idyllic rural family life.

Twelve years later, with a business much bigger than either of us imagined – the castle is now an award winning place to stay of international renown with fifteen bedrooms – the reality of raising a young family and running a business under the same, often leaking, roof, sharing our home with guests from around the world and weathering a fair amount of personal tragedy gave rise to a blog – Simon's Life In A Country Castle.

So well received were my humorous, and occasionally emotional outpourings that I felt encouraged to turn them into a book.

The first edition of *Undressed For Dinner* was published in December 2013. The story of a family trying to lead an ordinary life in an extraordinary place, it is a story which lurches from hope to disappointment, joy to heartbreak, triumph to disaster and back again but most of all it is a story with a sense of humour, reminding us that life should never be taken too seriously.

We don't sell a contrived, polished, overly manicured version of country house living. A stay at Augill Castle is much more the real-deal – a shared experience where guests are invited to find a sense of belonging, to relish the freedom from rules and codes of conduct – as one reviewer put it, to kick off their wellies by the front door without causing a scandal. It is a quintessentially English experience and consequently slightly chaotic and sometimes just plain bonkers.

Undressed For Dinner is, likewise, slightly bonkers and some friends have questioned my sanity in committing often very personal feelings and events to paper. True, it is, at times, painfully honest but writing it was a cathartic experience.

In 2014 it was judged Lakeland Book of the Year, a significant departure, I think, from the award's hitherto staple of worthy tomes but testament to the fact that many people could relate to the story and the daily struggle to make sense of life that so many of us have in common, no matter what path we tread or tune we choose to dance to.

That, combined with a sell-out of the first print run, was encouragement enough for me to write a sequel, *Stop For Breakfast*, published in summer 2016, continuing the story where *Undressed For Dinner* left off. To coincide with the publication of *Stop For Breakfast*, this new edition of *Undressed For Dinner* has been released with minor amendments and a new foreword by the founder of the Lakeland Book of the Year award, Hunter Davies.

Hunter describes the story as 'so contemporary it hurts'. I don't know about that – I didn't set out to write a book to break literary moulds, just to record an honest and entertaining account of a true story. For that reason there are some naughty words because real life is full of expletives, given voice or otherwise but in my defence, if a defence is needed, the page on which he highlights so many fucks is the page bearing the story of our son's birth on a gurney in a broken-down ambulance in a pub car park at 3am with the only other available ambulance 40 minutes away. What else would anyone say?

This is a tale with many characters. The most important people in our lives at Augill appear as themselves; my way of saying thank you. Others are composites of the worst and best bits of many people we have met along the way. A few are just plain fantasy. Which are which you, dear reader, must decide as, for my part, running a place such as Augill Castle can be such a surreal existence at times that the edges between reality and imagination have become somewhat blurred.

To find out more about staying at Augill Castle and becoming part of the story visit

www.stayinacastle.com

How Did We Get Here?

Harriet and Gordon booked their house party about a year ago and, unlike some house party guests, have been a delight to deal with. When asked what was the occasion they simply said it was a regular get together of like-minded friends. We thought no more of it.

We had been given carte blanche to devise the menus and choose the wines. 'All they want is for everything to be natural,' Wendy says.

'It's so good of you to welcome us into your home in such an open hearted way,' enthuses Harriet.

'Well, it's what we do,' Wendy smiles back, sweetly.

We have also been asked to find them an open-minded trio of musicians.

'Open minded?' Wendy asks, slightly quizzically.

'You know – the sorts that don't mind our unconventional ways,' replies Gordon.

When Wendy recounts this conversation I roll my eyes. Why on earth didn't she press them for more details of what they meant?

'Their taste in music is none of my business,' she harrumphs but I'm convinced there's more to their unconventional ways than we're privy to. It's more than a bit of after-dark Bob Dylan.

We don't ask many questions of our guests and sometimes the results can be alarming.

'You should have asked more questions,' I am complaining as the day of their arrival draws closer. 'They could be a cult or something. We may be brainwashed into joining a mass suicide.'

'Oh don't be so ridiculous Simon,' Wendy snaps.

We have laid on a magnificent afternoon tea and at three o'clock Harriet and Gordon arrive. They are clearly very excited about the prospect of sharing the castle with just their friends.

'It's very special,' says Harriet. 'Obviously we like privacy and it's not often you come across somewhere so lovely and welcoming and luxurious. We've ended up in some very basic places in the past.'

'Nothing basic here,' I reply, still deeply suspicious.

By four-thirty everyone has arrived and are gathered in the music room hungrily devouring the tea.

'What a lovely bunch,' Wendy says and I have to agree. They do seem to be the sorts of people we thoroughly enjoy looking after. By six-thirty everyone has disappeared upstairs to get ready for the evening ahead and we are making the final preparations for dinner. In line with the guests' requests for 'simple and natural' we have sourced everything on the menu from within a fifty mile radius of the castle, most of it organic.

The band arrives to set up and I am keen to find out what discussions they have had about music. But the reply to my enquiries leaves me puzzled. 'They don't want anything out of the ordinary, just mellow and laid back. That's what they said.'

'No unconventional requests?'

'Nope.'

There's movement in the upstairs corridor. It sounds as if everyone is coming down for pre-dinner drinks.

I go through to the hall to greet them at the bottom of the stairs and as Harriet and Gordon come round the landing towards me I am momentarily frozen to the spot before fleeing to the kitchen.

'Wendy,' I demand my wife's attention, 'what exactly did these people tell you when they booked this house party?'

'Oh for God's sake, Simon, can you drop it. They're perfectly normal,' comes her frustrated response.

'What did they say?' I persist.

'They wanted somewhere quiet, private and natural, they're naturalists,' she replies with a slowness with which one might address a child's persistent questioning.

'Natural! Naturalists! They're bloody naturists,' I whisper hysterically. 'They're all coming downstairs stark naked.'

Wendy drops her spoon. Faye, who has been working with us for so long and shared so many of our memories that we can no longer see her as anything other than family and who had thought she'd seen it all, drops her composure and screams while I try to regain mine.

'OK, so they're wearing shoes and she's got a pashmina around her shoulders.'

'Well,' Wendy says slowly, 'we must just act as if everything is normal.'

'Normal?!' trumpets Faye and another of our girls.

'Go and serve them some drinks, they might appreciate not having to bend over to get their own mixers out of the bar chiller.'

Now I dislike serving at the bar at the best of times and I look at Faye who usually jumps at the chance but she's suddenly very busy chopping carrots and avoids my gaze. As I make my way towards the library I'm wondering whether I should offer our guests cocktails. Straight up or on the rocks?

'Oh stop being so puerile,' I tell myself. I need not have worried about the bar. By the time I get there everyone is getting stuck in and seems quite self sufficient. In the Music Room two men are warming their backs in front of the open fire. I am sure I am imagining a slight whiff of burning hair.

Keen to get everyone to the table, as bare torsos are going to be a hell of a lot easier to deal with than the full monty, I have thrown a few extra logs on the dining room fire.

Once seated a semblance of normality returns and we marvel at how relaxed everyone is and how quickly they make us feel at ease. And by main course it all seems perfectly ordinary (although we feel it best to banish Holly from under the table given her indiscriminate Labrador appetite and propensity for planting her head in people's laps).

'Do you think they were expecting us to take our clothes off?' asks one of our waitresses.

'I don't think I've done a risk assessment for cooking in the buff,' I reply. 'And anyway, we're cooking sausage and two bean casserole. We wouldn't want a mix up.'

'We're not really?' one of them gasps.

'No, that would just be too deliciously ironic... if only we'd known.' I'm feeling far less scandalised than I imagine I should.

After dinner I confide in Gordon that we'd got it wrong and that we had no idea they were naturists until I saw them coming downstairs.

He stiffens momentarily but soon relaxes when he realises that we're not bothered now we've got used to the whole thing.

The band have taken a little time to come around to the idea. They were outside when everyone appeared for drinks and so are only now being confronted by the reality of the situation.

'Shall we start off with a bit of swing?' asks the band leader and I simply cannot resist replying, 'don't ask me, the answer my friend is blowing in the wind.' We fall about.

The rest of the evening goes much as any house party and it's all very good natured. Having always been ready to strip off on the beach should the opportunity arise, I am almost tempted to join in until Wendy reminds me that the staff may never be able to look me in the eye again. The guests enjoy plenty of banter with the staff and the band and by bedtime we are congratulating ourselves on dealing with such an unexpected situation so well.

Unfortunately we forget to warn the breakfast staff and next morning the phone ringing in her ear is the last thing Wendy needs after the night before.

One of the girls has come to work and is concerned that there are four people on the top lawn doing Tai Chi.

'They haven't got any clothes on,' she exclaims, 'do you know who they are?'

'It's alright, they're guests,' I reassure her.

'Oh that's alright then,' she replies, clearly relieved, 'I was just worried they were trespassing.'

How did we get here? The naturists have gone to bed, ironically more covered up now than while they were having dinner. We'd got into a conversation late in the evening and they had asked us, how did we get here, to where we are, to having made what we've made, done what we've done?

It's three in the morning. It's the hour of the unfortunates; those of us who don't have the tidy structure of a nine to five existence, who have to work when everyone else is sleeping – or playing.

Tucked up with family, entwined with lovers, working purposefully at a job that keeps the whole country going or stoned, pissed out of their head, at home or homeless, few people actually see with any clarity, actually stop and look at 3am. But for a hotelier the hours between night and morning are a familiar time. For me, it's peace, a time for winding down, collecting thoughts.

Reflection. How did we get here? It is a time for planning. But who could have planned that we'd end up with our home full of naked strangers? And where do we go from here? It is the hour of dreams and the hour of ghosts.

I am suddenly awoken from my reverie. I hadn't noticed him coming in and now he is standing just across the hall looking at me with a half smile. It's a long time since I've seen that smile.

I should be surprised, I don't expect to see anyone at this time of night. And I should be more than surprised to see him.

I: 'I didn't see you come in. Have you been there long?'

He: 'Long enough. You looked so peaceful I didn't want to disturb your thoughts. You like this time of the night.'

It's a statement from someone who no longer needs answers.

I: 'Yes. It's the clarity. Everything's sharper and clearer.'

He: 'It's a fine place.'

He's softly spoken. And his presence is soft too, unassuming. Perhaps that's why I hadn't noticed him before. I know he's been here before. It's been a while though I feel I should remember.

I: 'Fancy a snifter before bed?'

He always liked his drink and he chuckles. That chuckle.

I pour a brandy for me, I gesture the bottle towards him but he declines. He examines me a little closer now and I him. His face has changed since the last time I saw him and he looks younger, relaxed, at peace with himself and the world.

I: 'You look better than the last time I saw you.'

He: 'Hardly surprising.'

Suddenly anger grips me and takes me by surprise. He senses it and stiffens, ready for an onslaught. I aggressively pour him a drink and it sloshes up and over the sides of the glass and spills. I push it towards him. He doesn't look right without one.

I: 'Where the hell have you been?'

He: 'What could I have done?'

I: 'Support, encouragement.'

And my hand squeezes the brandy glass so hard it shatters. He moves forward to look at the damage and then shrinks away, still wearing that half smile of self satisfaction that I remember so well.

He: 'Never was very good with blood.'

I: 'Were you ever very good at anything?'

I regret saying that before I've even finished spitting the words at him. But he's well beyond hurt now.

He: 'Well you've turned out alright so I got something right.'

I: 'Well it'd have been a lot bloody easier if you'd been around. You can't take much credit.'

Although I know, in truth, that he's the reason for everything.

I: 'You might have left some instructions – what's an eighteen year old supposed to do with no father? Mum was never any good with money was she?'

Another chuckle.

He: 'You don't take after your mother in that respect thank goodness.'

I smile as I wrap a tissue around my hand and tidy up the shards of glass. But it's a bitter smile.

I: 'Fat lot you know then, I rather think I inherited your talent for projecting a champagne lifestyle image on a lemonade budget.

Anyway, what makes me angry is that you did it to yourself. You abused yourself and it killed you. How selfish is that?'

He deflects the criticism.

He: 'So, how's it been?'

I: 'Busy. And hard, bloody hard. I'll tell you about it if you've got the time.'

He: 'Oh I've got all the time in the world son, I can stay for as long as you like.'

And I am physically taken back.

I: 'Christ, if only you'd said that once before you died – just once.'

He: 'I know I didn't give any of you the time you deserved and I know...'

I: 'No!' I cut him off sharply, 'if only you'd once called me son.'

CHAPTER ONE

June 1998, 3.30pm on the day of our first guests' arrival. I am at the top of a ladder fixing curtain poles when a car draws up and out they climb. Wendy runs in, flustered, excited and downright terrified. She's been downstairs getting dinner ready and now wants to know how long it'll be before the room is ready.

'Give them some tea and cake,' I say, more optimistically than I feel. Forty minutes, two crumbly holes in the wall, several knarled rawl plugs and no functioning curtain pole later, Wendy is back. 'They've eaten the cake and drained a second pot of tea.'

'Well give them some more or offer them a tour of the garden.' From my vantage point I can see them trailing out of the front door having clearly plumped for a tour of the garden (via the lavatories, which aren't properly finished either, no doubt, after all that tea) but it doesn't take long as we haven't actually got around to tackling the garden yet so it's more a tour of rampant neglect.

By five o'clock Wendy has taken matters in to her own hands, has broken out the spirits and is playing rousing tunes on the piano. By the third round of *Roll out the barrel* or *Annie Get Your Gun* or something similarly music hall, I'm done. It was the extra push I needed and the guests are grateful to at last have a bed for the night.

As I leave the room, I give the newly hung curtains a cursory glance, willing them to stay that way until Sunday afternoon, after which they don't warrant a second thought.

The rest of the weekend goes well. Our first paying dinner guests don't keel over clutching their stomachs, there is no need for more music hall ribaldry around the piano and the fire alarm doesn't go off in the middle of the night (or while we're cooking). It's a warm weekend and by Sunday morning the castle is full of fresh air, sunlight and happy people, the windows are slung wide open and all seems right with the world.

We are outside bidding farewell to two of our guests when suddenly there is a roar of indignation from the first floor where another of our now long suffering guests is standing at the open window being enveloped by tumbling curtains. We look on with a mixture of amusement and horror, the whole scene unfolding in painful slow motion, as he instinctively reaches up to protect himself from the falling curtain pole and the towel around his waist falls to the floor.

As a hotelier it is often necessary to think on one's feet which usually means act first and repent at your leisure. But I'm at a loss, frozen to the spot. It is Wendy's quick thinking that lightens the moment and saves the day. From inside the music room comes a sudden and rousing rendition of that old favourite *I've got a lov-er-ly bunch of coconuts.*

As with so many other guests with whom we have shared such pivotal moments in the development of the castle, these become firm friends and the following Christmas they send me a brand new power drill.

A steady stream of guests throughout the summer takes our minds off the imminent arrival of our first baby. And, if starting up a new business and waiting for a baby aren't enough, Wendy decides we should invest in a dog.

'You simply can't have a country castle without a dog,' she says.

It's a *fait accompli*, as if I hadn't guessed, as some friends have one puppy left from a litter of black labradors.

Holly joins the family and would become more of a potent symbol of what Augill really is than any amount of clever marketing. She becomes the embodiment of the Augill magic: happy, laid back, ever welcoming and ever so slightly mad.

Only as we are wallpapering room number four, me up a ladder, Wendy reaching over her tummy with an extendible pasting brush, do we realise it's actually the glorious 12th, our baby's due date.

The pregnancy has, to be fair, taken something of a back seat. It's not been without its angst: Wendy has already miscarried twice so with every unexpected twinge, at each ante-natal visit there has been a fear of the worst, a constant threat that our hopes will crumble, that our dreams will come crashing down only to have to be rebuilt again from scratch. But since everything has so far gone to plan we have become more relaxed.

We try ante-natal classes in Penrith but lose interest after we are asked to join hands with everyone else in the garden, breathe deeply and move rhythmically backwards and forwards in a circle while our teacher, for want of a better word, sighs 'in, out, in, out.'

I can only think it is a tantric form of the hokey cokey but apparently we are supposed to be as one, recreating a contracting womb. I am further disillusioned when my enquiries about what we do with the baby once we get it home are met with a blank stare. Apparently, once we've given birth to the thing we are completely on our own. Incredible. Even owning a pig requires a license.

Two weeks after the twelfth our midwife insists Wendy should go to hospital to be induced. We duly comply because we are still young and foolish and believe all doctors, nurses and midwives are professionals and know what they're doing and should be trusted to do it properly.

The birth is a shambles and sixteen hours of labour later finds us with a half born baby in a pub car park on the edge of the Lake District. It's 3.15am.

So long has Wendy been in labour that our baby is becoming distressed (not to mention Wendy and me). A decision is taken to move her to the general hospital in Lancaster in case further intervention is required. An ambulance is called. But half way between Kendal and Lancaster it breaks down and we find ourselves stranded outside a pub waiting for rescue. At 3.45am there is no chance of a stiff drink though God knows everyone needs one, and when the second ambulance arrives the gurneys are incompatible.

'You'll have to get up and walk to the new ambulance Wendy,' says the midwife in a matter-of-fact sort of way.

'I need to push,' wails Wendy.

'It's coming,' I scream.

And somewhere between the ambulances, with Wendy doubled up in pain, me screaming because I don't know what else to do and the midwife still trying to monitor the erratic foetal heartbeat with a mobile monitor, the baby begins to crown.

'Fuck,' I cry.

'Fuck', sobs Wendy.

'Jesus Christ,' whispers the midwife who bundles everyone into the new ambulance and then screams at the driver to get us to the hospital.

'Not until you've got your seat belts on,' replies the jobs-worth.

'Just put your fucking foot down now,' screams the midwife, and then, 'In all my years, in all my years...'

'...this is a fucking nightmare,' I complete the sentence.

It takes ten minutes to reach Lancaster during which Wendy doesn't know whether to push or not, the midwife tries to reassure her but her anxious tapping and readjusting of the heart monitor does little to reassure me. At the same time she is swearing at the driver to get a bloody move on.

By the time we reach the hospital everyone is on standby. Wendy is rolled straight off the ambulance towards a delivery suite where a whole gaggle of midwives, paediatricians and anaesthetists is waiting. It's not a bad turn out given the hour. But they're too late. It's over. She doesn't need them.

With one final push the baby slides out and, were it not for the quick actions of a paramedic who catches him, would have landed on the floor square in the middle of the corridor. The umbilical chord has been so tightly wrapped around his neck that the baby is completely blue.

For a split second the world freezes. The assembled professionals are gripped by a collective inertia as they watch the scene unfold in Hollywood slow motion: Wendy letting out one final piercing scream as she pushes, the baby emerging at full velocity, the paramedic lunging towards the business end of the gurney, hands outstretched.

Not for the first time I am rendered inarticulate. 'Fuck,' is all I can manage.

Our midwife is similarly dumbstruck. 'Fuck,' she mutters.

I know it isn't supposed to happen this way but then I don't know how it is supposed to go either. It's the enduring theme of everything that we have, and will, do together. Blind faith.

In a jumble of emotions, thoughts and mixed metaphors, that split second seems endless – slow motion has become a freeze frame. As I look round Wendy lies exhausted and spent on her trolley, the midwife is ashen and in front of us, in the arms of the paramedic crouched on the floor lies a limp, motionless baby still attached to his mother.

Blood, goo, confusion, terror. I don't know where to look or what to do. And then there's a wail. My boy is wailing, filling his lungs and everyone else is breathing with him.

I: 'And there I am, a father. And guess what? I'm angry. I don't have a father of my own to ring and say 'you're a grandad', to ask 'how did it feel when it happened to you?

And then I'm even more pissed off when I remember that even if you had been there you'd have been useless anyway.

And I'm angry that you've made me feel angry without even being there when all I should be feeling is happy and elated (according to the books).'

He: 'You wanted that perfect father figure to be there holding your hand?'

I: 'I don't know about holding my hand, I wanted some moral support.'

He: 'You had friends.'

I: 'Oh don't be so bloody obstinate, I needed blood, family, bonding... you know all those things you obviously forgot about when you took on the job of being a father.

'Were you even there when I was born?'

He: 'Well, in my defence we weren't encouraged to get involved in births back then.'

I: 'Were you even at the hospital?'

He: 'No.'

I: 'Where were you?'

He: 'Do you need to ask?'

I: 'Yes. Where were you?'

He: 'At the White Hart.'

I: 'Getting pissed with your mates. So the die was cast before I was even born.'

He: 'Well I can tell you now how I felt when you were born.'

I: 'Can you remember?'

He: 'I was scared, I was confused, I felt totally clueless.'

I: 'Obviously nothing much changed.'

He: 'Listen, throw cheap insults at me if it makes you feel better, but think about this: What has changed is you. You are not me, you are you in spite of me and that is all you need to focus on. Let go of the anger or it'll eat you. It's already eating you.'

It is ironic that a new mother can be induced but that there is no induction into being a new mother. There is no maternity leave when you work for yourself so Wendy opts to stay in hospital for the full five days. She learns how to bathe our new son, how to breast feed and how to change a nappy. And that's it. We return home to the castle on bank holiday Monday where a full house of guests are desperately waiting to meet the new arrival and as we cook dinner he is handed around the dinner table.

They all want to know about the drama of the birth while clamouring to hold the baby and we appreciate for the first time that this is how it is going to be. Everyone is going to want a piece of us and a piece of our children.

Quite suddenly we realise just what we've taken on. Not just a castle, but a lifestyle. We're selling a lifestyle. We are Augill and Augill is us. It feels good and it terrifies. How would things have turned out if we'd realised that twelve months earlier?

CHAPTER TWO

The rain is pouring down the steps into our basement restaurant in Mayfair. The chef is having a hissy fit about the size of his lamb shanks and two of the bar staff are in some sort of lesbian stand-off. Our loyal customer base has deserted us for the next best thing to open up just down the street. Again. They'll be back, of course, but I'll resent them just a little bit more than I did last week.

A year we've been here but it feels like a decade. The business is not what it seemed. The books had been well and truly cooked, the staff are mutinous, the other partners conspicuous by their absence and I am just about to turn thirty. It's not a good time.

But it is the perfect time for Wendy, my new but already long suffering wife to tell me she has found us a way out of London to a new and eminently more fulfilling life.

Images of sun drenched vineyards, shady olive groves and long sleepy lunches that have been a constant backdrop to all my dreams flood into focus. I imagine happily bobbing back and forth to the village for bread each morning in my battered old Citroen 2CV. Relishing the challenge of taking on *Monsieur le facteur* and his errant ways, his preference for breeze blocks over local building materials, his idiosyncratic French plumbing ideas and being able to negotiate a beautiful farmhouse renovation out of him nonetheless. I imagine a small crystal blue swimming pool in which our children (Wendy has always maintained she wants six) and all their sun-kissed friends will play, with multi-lingual laughter bouncing off the sweet chestnut woods clinging to either side of the valley, mingling with the far-off bleating of our goats grazing on wild thyme and rosemary. And I imagine, as I glance at the mucky London street water still trickling down the stairs, bringing with it an occasional fag end, a climate of long languorous summer days and star-filled nights where the prospect of storms bringing water flooding into the house is welcomed with excitement and laughter.

We had talked about this dream ever since we were first together. Two years after we met we took a holiday together and ended up in a little southern French village in Languedoc. From the moment we arrived in Roquebrun as two impressionable, ridiculously in love young things it had a hold on us. And the place we stayed was even more spellbinding. Les Mimosas, a handsome merchant's house in the middle of the village was run as a *chambre d'hôte* by Sarah and Denis la Touche, a couple from new Zealand who themselves had fallen in love with the place while on a French road trip, with a charm and lightness of touch that drew us in. The simplicity of the bedrooms, the sweeping grey stone staircase with its distressed green balustrade, the floor to ceiling windows opening on to vineyards in one direction and the honey coloured houses of Roquebrun tumbling down the hillside to the banks of the River Orb in the other. Breakfast and dinner on the terrace under a canopy of vines. Drinks in the village bar under the shade of the plane trees, swimming in the river beneath the town bridge, everything was as in our dream.

As if to complete that dream, when we returned we were engaged to be married and we told each other one day we would be there, in Roquebrun, at Les Mimosas or somewhere similar.

When we first had the opportunity to buy into the London restaurant we went straight to Les Mimosas to talk about our plans with our friends. Together we pored over recipes, tried out ideas in the kitchen, talked long about the seasonality of food and devised menus that made our mouths water and our tummies rumble. It was the inspiration we got from Les Mimosas and Sarah's cooking that persuaded us we could do it.

Of course, what we really wanted was what they had but that was out of our reach financially and, anyway, it wasn't for sale. You can lust after someone else's dream but can you buy it from them? 'One day' we told each other, over and over, 'we can be here, doing this. Give London a couple of years. If we can make a go of it in London we can do it anywhere.' That would turn out to be truer than either of us could ever have imagined.

Oh Wendy, our saviour of the senses. Tell me more about bringing our dream to life.

'It's a castle in Cumbria,' she says.

'Umbria!' I exclaim, almost unable to contain my excitement and love for this woman who shares my wanderlust and my frustration with modern life and is willing to take this big plunge into the deep blue Mediterranean off the heel of Italy; who is by my side in the quest for a life less ordinary, who will go with me to Italian evening classes to translate our French country fantasy into something even more exotic, a southern Italian idyll.

'No, darling, Cumbria. It's somewhere near Scotland.'

The rain outside has stopped but suddenly everything seems very much blacker as she presses a set of property details into my hand.

'Near Scotland? The land of perpetual midnight?' I grew up in Somerset and Wendy in Africa. I can't believe I've heard correctly.

'It's a castle Simon, and look, it's the same price as that house in Chiswick we've just looked at.'

There is no denying that this castle is a lot of bricks for the money compared with a two bedroomed end of terrace in West London. But, castle or not, I am deeply unimpressed as before my eyes the olive trees, the swimming pool, the goats and their lovely cheese wrapped up in the freshly baked baguette I have just returned home with in my 2CV, via the village bar, are all washed away on a cascade of soggy fag butts and dirty London gutter water.

'Well can we at least go and have a look, it can't do any harm can it?' Wendy pleads, perhaps not yet fully understanding my despondency. We need a weekend away.

To date, weekends away for this happy young couple have always involved warm sunshine, good food and drink and invariably, a foreign accent. God knows what the food and drink will be like, I have no idea if the sun even rises above the horizon that far north but at least there will be foreign accents. I acquiesce.

And that is how two twenty-somethings come to be sitting in a rural lane in Cumbria staring across the fields at a Victorian castle asking each other, 'who the hell do we think we are that we can even consider this?'

It's July 1997. We have been married for a year, already suffered two miscarriages and struggled to get the little bistro restaurant in London on its feet (having naively gone into partnership with a group of businessmen we didn't know who have turned out to be nothing short of a West End episode of *The Sopranos*). A six hour drive has brought us to Augill Castle, a fully castellated, turreted Victorian folly in the Eden valley at the foot of the North Pennines, one mile outside the sleepy by-passed village of Brough, three miles from the slightly more vibrant market town of Kirkby Stephen. It is late evening and the castle is glowing in the golden sun, its square tower and round turrets almost apologetically protruding from a cloak of ancient English woodland that has been there much longer than this nineteenth century edifice.

A light mist is forming over the fields, unusual for July but it has clearly been raining and steam is rising from the tarmac in front of us. Timidly we navigate our way down the bumpy, potholed, tree lined drive and park on the gravel in front of the castle. The gardens are completely overgrown after what looks like a good three or four years of neglect. There are hints of structure underneath the weeds – stone terraces, paths not quite obscured by encroaching grass, a few herbaceous plants straining to make a statement above the invasion of nettles, bind weed, ground elder and grass. Even the gravel directly in front of the castle is matted with grass suggesting that there have been few visitors to the place over the last couple of years.

We approach the front door and almost before we have rung the bell a larger than life character beckons us in with one hand, nursing a large glass of Noilly Prat in the other.

'This is what keeps me sane in this God awful place,' she tells us, gesturing towards the glass with her spare hand. Her sales pitch clearly needs some work.

We have barely stepped across the threshold before we are being whisked around the castle on a tour. Coupled with her ill-disguised disdain for the place, it is enough to tell us the owners cannot get rid of the place quick enough (later confirmed, as we would discover that the large lady of the house had told anyone who would listen during her nine month tenure of Augill that when it comes to castles, 'big is not always beautiful'. She tells us the family had bid for the castle nine months earlier at auction without really realising what they had bought until they moved in. They were, in truth, accidental owners of a castle.

The castle had been empty for three years, had 137 burst pipes which they fixed but the dry rot, wet rot, floorboards and parquet floors warped by damp and the hideously overgrown garden and fifteen acres of grounds hadn't been touched.

Between the plaster and the wallpaper throughout the castle large fungi are growing. Their solution has been to sellotape the wallpaper over the growths. The cast iron fireplaces are orange with rust as are most of the radiators and everywhere smells unloved. As we gaze in awe at the intricate plaster ceiling mouldings we are, at once amazed they have not crumbled and fearful they may yet come crashing to the floor.

'We've got several people interested,' our host tells us which we struggle to believe, 'so we're going to go to sealed bids.' And with that, after less than an hour we are back out in the garden, the door shut firmly behind us.

'She's not taking us seriously,' says Wendy dispiritedly.

'I'm not taking us seriously,' I reply. 'This is madness.'

We stay the night in a B&B in the village and our landlady tells us that several people have indeed been to look at the castle. 'It has a chequered history. People have been coming with fancy ideas of turning it into a hotel and such like. It'll never work.' But while she clearly sees the place as exactly what it is, a folly, she is presumably happy for the punters to keep coming with their unrealistic plans as it seems she is putting most of them up while they're here.

That night we sit up into the early hours in our little attic room going over and over what it is we are thinking of in even considering taking on such a monumental project but try as we might to yield to reason and rational thought, we have both fallen under the spell of the castle and have succumbed to our first taste of what would later define the very success of the place: The Augill Magic.

As with most grand plans, the ideas form before the practicalities have ever been worked out. By the time we return to London we decide we can renovate the place, get it working as a B&B and sell it on in a couple of years' time at a profit (after all, the present owners' guide price is giving them a handsome £100,000 premium with no effort at all so we'll surely be quids in). We just have to find the money to buy it.

> *I: After you died Mum had said to me, 'If you ever find the project of a lifetime I'll support you, whatever it takes.' I don't know whether she really thought I'd take her seriously.'*
> *He: 'I know she thought I should have supported her better, given her more financial freedom but I was scared she'd leave me if I did.'*
> *I: 'Oh spare me the self-pity.'*

Since being widowed my Mum has lived a solitary life, one of those corporate wives who suddenly found she had no identity of her own once the prop of her husband's arm had been taken away. She has lurched from one curious house purchase to another, happy to renovate and titivate and then, bored, eager to move on.

'You know you said if I ever found that once in a lifetime opportunity?' I ask her on the phone the next day.

'Yes,' she says as slowly as a single word can be, bracing herself.

'Well can you come on a trip next weekend, we've got something to show you. It really is better you see for yourself because if I try to explain you'll think us mad.'

There is less talk in the car as the three of us head north than there had been the weekend before and much more opportunity to take in the landscape through which we are travelling. Anyone who has ever travelled on the M6 north of Lancaster and encountered for the first time the Lune Gorge flanked by the Howgill Fells, almost too perfect, their folds soft and rich enough to take a bite out of, looming in front and above them, understands how that journey to Cumbria sealed our fate before we even reached the castle. That it wasn't raining may have helped as it was only much later that we would come to understand just how much rain can fall in one place.

'Heaven's gate,' Mum whispers almost inaudibly as we follow the motorway which clings to the side of the fells before dropping down into the valley. 'Have I died and gone to heaven?'

Having visited the castle and been entertained by the owners, who are now taking us more seriously with our older benefactor in tow,

Mum, Wendy and I stay overnight in a nearby pub.

And that evening there are tears. And tantrums.

Tears over the baby we'd already lost three months after we were married. And the one we lost three months after that. Tears because we wanted a family not a castle. That these might be only the first tears of many scares us.

I: 'That Mum hadn't a clue about what she was doing and was just so desperate to be part of something. Tears of guilt that I was using her because of that. Tears of anger that you'd left her so vulnerable, that you weren't there to calm the turbulent mix of emotions that were driving our thought processes. And tears of absolute terror.'

He: 'And if I had been there, would it have made a difference?'

I: 'Of course it would. You know it would. If you'd have been around we'd never have even seen the place. You were no risk taker. If you hadn't died I'd still be on some mundane career ladder trying to make you proud with every promotion or modest pay increase and probably failing with none of us knowing what we were really capable of. And of course it would have made a difference because if you hadn't died she wouldn't have had the money.'

He: 'So you wanted me to be there to tell you something you knew I'd never say and let you do something you knew would never have been possible if I hadn't died? A bit of an impossible ask really.'

I: 'I know, I know. But as soon as you died your reality was replaced by an ideal and it was the ideal I wanted that night. Not you. I wanted a perfect father to take control. I resented the lack of a perfect father. All I had was the fantasy and a memory which didn't live up to that fantasy and it wasn't enough.'

Eventually the tears give way to some rational thought and we talk again long into the night. I know that Mum will do anything to be part of something again and I know that I am using her for that. She knows it too. But neither of us wants to confront that discomfort, a decision which will not stand us in good stead. The ball is squarely in her court now and I'm not holding out for a quick outcome. Life doesn't work that way. Does it? After all, she'll have to sell her house, resolving first that it is the right thing to do for her to move north with us, effectively putting her security at our disposal. It's a monumental decision.

The following Monday evening I receive a phone call.

'Hi it's me.' Mum sounds excited, an emotion with which she has never been overly familiar. 'I went to the estate agent to ask about marketing my house and the receptionist said she's been looking for a house in my road and has made an offer.'

'Cash?'

'It's sold.'

I ponder that if fate's fickle hand has already robbed us of our babies, a father and a husband, then maybe fate is dealing us a new hand of cards to entice us all back to the table.

Two weeks later we are back at the castle clambering over the battlements. We have called in a surveyor to check out the roof, the footings, the electrics and the central heating.

'Surely,' we tell each other, 'one of those will be so hideously expensive to put right that we can walk away with our heads held high and say it wasn't to be.'

The surveyor calls me over to the battlements at the front of the castle. I'm expecting the worst.

'Look, I'm worried Simon,' he looks me straight in the eye. Does my heart sink or swim? Whether because he is about to tell me the place is a pile of trouble or because it's not he looks serious and I've always felt uneasy about serious. 'Are you and Wendy sure you know what you're taking on? I mean, how old are you, twenty-nine, thirty?' First I willed him to find a problem because I'm shit scared, now I'm praying there's nothing wrong.

'I've been much more thorough than you asked,' he continues and what I hear, maybe fancifully, is a tone that suggests he is looking out for us because there is obviously nobody else to, 'and the truth is, apart from some dry rot which is no more than anyone could expect to find in any Victorian house, and a couple of settlement cracks, the place is sound.'

It's all I can do to stop myself toppling off the turret.

The castle is already sucking us in.

He continues, 'but it's a huge undertaking. I mean it still needs gutting, frankly. You've got enough to buy it but what about funding the renovations?'

'Well, we need to be careful but we have done some pretty comprehensive costings,' I lie.

I'm hardly about to admit that we haven't really thought that bit through and that, in fact, we won't have a spare penny once we've actually bought the place. A mortgage with no proven business history for the place is out of the question.

As I talk I'm pretty sure he can smell something and knows that up here it isn't dog shit. But as we will learn later, business planning is just bullshitting by a different name and there never will be enough money to complete any of the projects we start.

At the end of the following week our sealed bid has been accepted having been 'the most acceptable of the several we received'. Yeah right!

'Can you complete by mid-September?' asks the outgoing chatelaine of Augill.

'We haven't even got a solicitor,' I confide in Wendy and they want to be out in four weeks' time. A pin in the Yellow Pages puts us in touch with Charles, a thoroughly affable solicitor in Carlisle who would turn out to be so much more than just a solicitor. From our first discussion with him when he asks again 'are you sure you know what you're taking on?' he will become almost a substitute father, an invaluable source of wisdom for us both, although he would never realise it.

Our fate is sealed and we are fairly sure we are glad of it. Now, only time will tell.

CHAPTER THREE

On September 18 a very large removal truck arrives outside our very small rented house in West London. The street has probably never seen anything quite as large since it is capacious enough to swallow the entire contents of at least three of these little Georgian terrace houses. Nets, or more accurately, in most cases wooden slatted blinds, are twitching.

A passer-by asks casually where we are moving to. Even more casually I reply, 'a castle in Cumbria.' He looks at me, looks at the house we are emptying and shuffles off, saying to himself, 'idiot, I was only being polite. No need to be sarcastic.'

I smile. This sort of reaction is not a million miles from some of the things our family and friends have said when we have told them our news; hardly surprising given that it's not every day you hear of friends moving into a castle.

My grandmother is less concerned about the castle and more worried about the weather and the people.

'I thought they wanted to start a family,' she tells Mum on hearing the news, 'they'll never get pregnant up there, it's far too cold.' And later she continues, 'Well they'll not get me up there, it's full of blacks.'

I try to reason with her when I hear about her concerns. 'But Nanny, you lived most of your life in north London. It's full of immigrants.'

'Jews dear, Jews. Not blacks. Totally different.' And there's nothing more to be said.

The truck is already more than half full of the contents of Mum's house but there is plenty of room left, even though our house is definitely over-stuffed. But there's a problem.

'Nobody told us about the piano mate,' says one of the removal men casually as he passes me, carrying something or other purposefully as if ready to fill the truck with everything else, leaving behind the piano because he hadn't been told about it. That the baby grand fills almost half the ground floor suggests it isn't us that forgot about it.

'Oh dear,' I say in a non-committal sort of way as if to suggest that it really isn't my problem. There is a silent stand-off for a few moments and then I add, 'well we booked you because your firm specialises in the removal of pianos. Here is the piano,' I point towards the front door, 'here is the lorry,' I swing round to indicate the large vehicle with 'International Removers for over 100 years' written in bold letters on the side, 'where is the problem?'

There turns out not to be a problem as the truck is carrying the required equipment for the transport of the piano. 'It's just that pianos usually cost more, that's all,' I'm told.

Several hours and cups of tea later the packing is nearing completion when there is a phone call.

'Hello, this is the Environmental Health Department at Hammersmith & Fulham Borough Council.' I feel momentarily sick thinking that, on this of all days, there surely can't be a problem at the restaurant and then I register that it's not the same borough. The restaurant is in the City of Westminster. I can't begin to imagine what the council wants with us on the day of our departure. A few months earlier we received a letter from them informing us that following a complaint from a member of the public we were liable to prosecution because a shrub in our front garden was overhanging the pavement and causing a hazard. It was hardly a triffid, snapping at people, taking chunks out of their thighs as they passed by but the complaint obviously brightened up someone's day at the town hall. We had sorted out the problem by moving the offending shrub, which was in a pot, a foot backwards. Now it is in the back of the removal lorry.

'We have received a complaint that you are blocking the light to your neighbour's property.'

'What?' I can hardly believe what I'm hearing. 'I beg your pardon?'

'Apparently you have parked a large vehicle in the street which is obscuring the sun from your neighbour's windows. If you don't remove the vehicle we will be obliged to investigate further and you may be liable to prosecution.'

Somebody hasn't enough to occupy themselves. I can't decide whether it's the neighbour or the council official.

'Don't bother yourselves,' I say, extremely irritated, 'we're leaving.'

And as we depart an hour later I see our neighbour, to whom we never spoke in over a year of living there, watching us. I give her a goodbye gesture which I know I should feel ashamed of but don't. Please Lord let the Cumbrians be friendlier than this.

But it's a prayer in vain. As we would find out in years to come, neighbours are neighbours, good and bad, friendly and hostile wherever you are. Although we are moving to a castle in the country we are buying just the main building. The rest of the estate has been carved up and we are taking on six sets of neighbours, some of whom would prove to be our greatest allies as well as our most formidable challenge.

And now another thought is niggling at my conscience. As I watch the removal van disappear in the direction of the M1, with its proclamation of 'The North' hanging in icy blue across the carriageway, and with the front door of our beautiful little West London cottage now closed for the last time, I wonder how it is that we aren't heading south, across the Channel towards the dream we've already dreamt a hundred times.

Wendy has travelled up to Cumbria with Mum ahead of the removal lorry whilst I remain in London at the restaurant (we would not be selling that business for another year), planning to meet them in Cumbria later the next day.

On my arrival at the castle I take a moment to survey what we have bought. It's not a classical beauty in any sense and not the sort of building I'd be drawn to ordinarily, but it's quirky. There is a central square tower maybe fifty feet high, little round turrets on all the corners of the building, arched windows, lots of battlements and acres of leaded windows. It's a lot to take in. Just as I am losing myself in thoughts of why anyone would have built such a place, let alone why anyone would subsequently want to buy it, Wendy comes running out and throws herself into my arms.

'What have we done, what have we done?' she sobs into my breast.

'Woah, woah, what's this all about?'

Wendy is trying to catch her breath as she speaks. 'Oh, we arrived in the early hours and bedded down on the floor in our... our sleeping bags and when we woke up the bags were drip... dripping with water – I could wring the water out of them... and it stinks... and it's so cold and and...' She can hardly get her words out, '...and it's not the plan. It's not what we planned.'

'Stop now. We'll put the heating on constant and in a couple of days it'll feel like a different place.'

'There's no gas, I've already checked,' she wails.

'Alright, alright, we'll light the fires. All of them.'

I manage to calm Wendy down but inside I'm worried. Really worried. She is supposed to be the optimist in this partnership, we're both hankering after something completely different from what we've got and we're not talking to each other about it. She's right, this isn't what we had in mind as our next step on from London. Only two months ago we hadn't even set eyes on the place. And, as if to echo Wendy's sobs, I ask myself plaintively, echoing earlier conversations, 'Are we sure we know what we've taken on?'

I step across the threshold now as owner and it feels very strange. I am a first time buyer and I've got a castle. This is not the first rung of the property ladder, this is the top – higher than the top of Jack's beanstalk and from here there's a hellishly long way to fall.

Stripped of what few sticks of furniture the previous incumbents had it is a truly bleak place. The Tudor oak panelling in the hall is covered in a white bloom, the parquet floor is so wet that the wood blocks have curled up and the nails fixing them to the floor have rusted through. In several places the floor feels terrifyingly spongey and I am sure that whatever is holding it up from underneath isn't going to be doing so for much longer. The wallpaper in the drawing room is covered in black mould and mushrooms are growing out of the walls before our eyes.

'Fuck,' because what else is there to say? It certainly isn't the south of France. It'll take a lot more than a coat or two of whitewash to cover that lot up.

'How the hell didn't we notice all of this?' I ask myself as I run my hand across the wall and watch my fingertips turn black.

On the mantelpiece there's a note underneath a half empty bottle of Noilly Prat.

'Jeeze, she couldn't even leave us a full bottle?'

'No that was me,' Wendy apologises behind me. 'I needed something when we got here and I couldn't find any gin. At least the tipple she left is French. Read the note.'

It hardly lightens the mood.

Dear Simon, Wendy & Mary

Welcome to Augill. We arranged to have the place thoroughly cleaned from top to bottom. Hope they have done a good job...

Then there are a few practical notes about the boiler, bins and stop-cocks.

We hope you will be as happy here as we weren't. The neighbours are an odd bunch, some worse than others but you'll find that out for yourself. The nearest decent sized supermarket is 21 miles away but the Coop in Kirkby Stephen stocks the basics and can get in any type of alcoholic drink you want if you give them notice. You'll need it. Luckily you can be in civil-isation in Newcastle in a little over an hour (unless the road is closed by snow).

The plumber is called Joel and he lives in Warcop. You're going to need him.

A chap called Reg professes to know all about the grounds and the boundaries but he doesn't give up his secrets lightly. Hope you have more success with him than us.

If there's anything else, we've moved to The Lighthouse Keeper's bun-galow, Leafy Lane, Yarmouth, Isle of Wight.

I look at Wendy and as she tries heroically to raise a smile I wrap my arms around her (for comfort but mostly for some warmth) and whis-per in her ear. 'What the hell...'

Through in the billiard room (which we have already grandly re-named the music room since we refused to buy the previous owners' full size billiard table and have put our baby grand piano in there instead) the entire contents of Mum's house and ours, bar the bed-room basics covers less than half the floor. Mum is busily unpacking her collection of Lladró porcelain figures (which I have always despised) and arranging them on the piano oblivious to the fact that we have yet to assemble any beds or locate our clothes and toiletries.

'I just thought I'd cheer the place up a bit, make it a little more homely,' and then she shuffles off towards the kitchen.

'A week,' I proclaim. 'A week is what we have to get this place looking habitable with what we've got.' And it's true. A week is what we have before I have to be back at the restaurant and Wendy has to be back at work at her recruitment agency. There is a heavy silence as we try to take in the enormity of it all.

'Tea everyone,' and we turn to see Mum approaching looking like Mrs Overall from Acorn Antiques with a tray of steaming mugs.

'I would have done that,' says Wendy.

'No, no dear, it's no trouble. I know how to make tea. Like to be useful.'

Wendy draws breath then exhales slowly.

I wonder if the castle itself may be the least of our problems. We may be in for a rough ride if one big chatelaine has just made way for two.

We haven't been at the castle for more than a few days before we are receiving callers keen to introduce themselves and to find out more about the new 'off-comers' at the castle.

Among the first to appear are Martin and Clarissa Blanchard-Cafferty. They are typical of several high-minded northern families who consider themselves self-styled nobility but, having never actually enjoyed title or the privilege or status that attaches to it are in fact no further out of the trough than the rest of us, bar the bank account at Coutts & Co.

Within minutes of their arrival they manage to let us know that the castle was once part of their family estate in such a way as to leave us in no doubt that they resent the fact that a couple of very young southern upstarts have got their hands on the place.

And their parting shot is carefully designed to make us feel instantly and completely inadequate.

'So very useful to have some new young blood in the valley,' making us sound like a couple of prize heifers. 'It'll be the place for parties...'

and then, having paused for effect, 'if you can ever make a go of it –
nobody else has. Toodles.'

Subsequent local enquiries reveal that they farm in a gentlemanly
sort of way, do a lot of shooting and spend a large chunk of the coldest months in sunnier climes. They have two children, Jenny and
Rupert. Jenny lives in London and is, her mother maintains, an investment banker. Local opinion holds that she is so dim witted that the
real truth is she probably sells ISAs and savings accounts in the High
Street Kensington branch of Barclays. Rupert is an artist living in a
Hebridean croft with what his mother describes as a very close friend
from boarding school. 'They have such a lot in common. Inseparable.'
But she does, she admits, worry about where he's going to find
romance in such a desolate place. There are no prizes for guessing
what the locals think of that liaison. It is one thing to allow your dogs
to roger one another out on the moors but quite another to condone
that sort of thing among one's own offspring. Sexual enlightenment
has a long way to travel before it reaches the Upper Eden valley.

Hot on the heels of the Blanchard-Caffertys comes Reg. I still don't
know Reg's surname. He conforms to the widely held stereotype, in
later years confirmed by our new young Conservative MP that all
Westmorland farmers wear their trousers held up with baler twine.
His head permanently sports some form of headgear, changed in deference to the weather, but he never goes out bare-headed. He has been
looking after estate matters for more years than anyone, including
him, can remember and is keen to continue his relationship with the
castle and its new owners. I can instantly see the advantages of keeping Reg on-side (which is apparently something the previous owners
failed to do. Having told him that he had a legal obligation to divulge
everything he knew about the place he just clammed up and told them
nothing).

After an hour in his company I can appreciate that he is probably the
only one who understands anything about the intricacies of the estate
boundaries, the idiosyncrasies of the neighbours and the convoluted
negotiations that lie behind the various land use agreements. The
trouble is, I have difficulty understanding everything he says, he being
Westmorland born and bred and I suspect he has a similar problem
with my clipped southern vowels. I quickly resolve that I should

research the dialect so that I may better communicate with him and I hope, although seriously doubt, that he might do the same.

By the end of our first week at the castle we reflect on how we have encountered both extremes of the social spectrum and, somewhat complacently, imagine that this should set us in good stead for any other local personalities that may come our way.

It won't be long before we realise that nothing was ever going to have prepared us for the diversity of characters that live in this wild part of northern England.

Since moving in in September we have submitted a planning application for change of use of the castle to a country house hotel, sorted out the dry rot, got ourselves an architect and spent every weekend travelling up from London after closing the restaurant on Friday night, returning on Sunday evening.

We work like stink during these short weekends, clearing the garden, cleaning the castle. In fact doing whatever we can to make the place more commodious while we wait for a planning decision. Either side of the hard work we pass the time on the long journeys to and from London planning how it's all going to work. But after the talk, in the quiet times, there's a phrase that spins around in my head and won't go away.

Are you sure you know what you're taking on?

We have a commitment from the bank to lend us £45,000 to get the business going. Out of that we've got to redecorate anywhere that anyone paying is likely to see, renovate at least three bedrooms, create three bathrooms from scratch, equip a kitchen and market the place and we must undertake to have a buyer for our share of the London restaurant within a year. Nothing like a bit of pressure.

Each week our disdain for the remnants of our life in London grows and, although unable to leave any earlier on Fridays, we find ourselves returning later and later each Sunday. We are living Monday to Friday in a bedsit in Shepherd's Bush, W12, just half a mile but a whole world away from our extravagant little Georgian cottage in Ravenscourt Park, W6. Whoever would imagine that a simple number could make such a world of difference?

Our landlady, one Mrs Bakowski scrutinises every coming and going at the front door via CCTV and herself lives, sleeps and washes in one room, the kitchen, in order to maximise the number of tenants the house can accommodate. The Victorian terraced house, once a handsome three or four bedroomed villa, is split into eight bedsits. Ours, apparently is the luxury apartment as it has the bay window at the front. In fact the bay window, and just the bay window, is the sitting area with the rest of the room accommodating a shower, toilet, kitchen and twin beds of different heights. It's all open plan and surely breaks every building regulation in the book.

'Life is hard,' Mrs Bakowski crackles at anyone unfortunate enough not to be able to get from the front door to their flat without being collared, in a thick nicotine scarred eastern European croak.

'The fuck it is,' one fellow tenant remarks to us on a rare occasion when we failed to avoid contact with each other and passed on the stairs.

The rules are onerous. No visitors after 9pm. No wet towels on the radiators. No showers or baths between 11pm and 7am. No music after 9pm. No washing to be hung out of the windows to dry. Rent payable in cash every Friday WITHOUT FAIL. No cheques. No credit. So it is no wonder that by the Monday before Christmas we are setting off back to London at 4am with the intention of by-passing Shepherd's Bush altogether and going straight to work.

Negotiations with my business partners about how I can take a more hands off role in London aren't going well since it becomes apparent that none of them actually knows how to run a restaurant. Nevertheless I plan not to return to London every week from New Year. There is no way they are going to buy me out having fleeced me into the partnership in the first place and pocketed my cash, so a compromise deal is struck and it is agreed that the restaurant should be sold. Wendy has negotiated flexible working terms for the new year too but not without a fight.

All the time we have been commuting Mum has been holding the fort at the castle which proves something of a challenge. While she is making good progress with the neighbours in the six households which share the Augill estate, nobody will talk to her about anything technical or involving money.

'Is Simon about?'

'No, can I help?'

'No, it's men's business.'

It's never meant to be derogatory – it's just always been the way of things in common with most rural communities.

Having been on her own for five years, this does not go down well and having had three months of it it's taking its toll. As we discuss our arrival for our first castle Christmas together she is bristling.

'There are things to discuss, things I need to say. When are you planning to be here?'

'Christmas Eve. Calm down, we've got things to tell you too.'

Christmas Eve and our adventure can begin full time. But plans have a habit of tripping you up.

By Christmas Eve a storm has set in and is advancing up the country. We leave London at around five hoping to reach the castle at about midnight but the weather is tracking our progress north. With the rain horizontal, it's painfully slow and by the time we reach Yorkshire there are large bits of tree blowing across the A1 in front of us. We press on.

At midnight we reach Scotch Corner, that curiously named junction on the A1 at the top of Yorkshire, with another 120 or so miles till Scotland, which promises so much but is actually just a roundabout, a hotel and a service station. For us it heralds the beginning of the home stretch, the turning onto the A66 which takes us all the way across the Pennines to the castle.

But not tonight. The road is closed due to the dangerously high wind. Naively we decide to navigate the back roads across the moors without a thought for the fact that if the main trunk road is closed, there may be double trouble ahead by any other route. Still, the turkey is in the boot and it needs to be in the oven tonight.

The weather worsens and the branches flying in front of us threaten to give way to entire trees. The car begins to stutter. Water has been blowing into the front grill and it sounds and feels as if the engine is about to pack up. Ahead we see the lights of a village flickering through the storm and, common sense, so lacking when we turned down this road, tells us we must stop.

Middleton-in-Teesdale might be as remote a settlement as it is possible to find in these parts of the North Pennines. Tucked into a deep dale with just one way in and one way out, it can best be described as one of those places which is always, perhaps a little reluctantly, trying to catch up with the rest of the world. A green surrounded by white painted posts and chains dominates the village and I am sure I can make out the silhouette of some pillory stocks standing in the middle of the grass. They look to be in good working order.

'We'll have to stop here, it's madness to go any further,' I tell Wendy.

'Where are we? We can't stay in the car, it's freezing,' she wails.

'I'll find a room. Look there's an inn over there. Wait here.'

I can't make out the name of the inn from where we are as the sign is being blown horizontal but by the reception I get when I walk in 'The Slaughtered Lamb' wouldn't be inappropriate. I can't be sure that mingled with the whistling wind, the fretful creaking of the trees and the repeated squeak of the swinging inn sign I don't hear the howl of a werewolf.

There are maybe a dozen men at the bar and as they all fall silent and turn to stare in unison I almost choke on my words. A couple stand up and cross their arms and I am half expecting someone to tell me it is pointless to resist and for the two of us to never be heard of again.

'I know it's late and Christmas and all,' I am stuttering like an idiot, 'but umm, have you got a room for the night? It's just that we have nowhere else to go... and my wife's pregnant.'

You can hear a pin drop and then all of a sudden the inn comes to life. Although they are unaware of it, these strangers are the first people to hear our news. Given the location it's probable that at least some of them are sheep farmers too, although calling them shepherds might not be the best approach given our delicate predicament.

'Oh,' I remember quickly, 'and can we put our turkey in your fridge?'

The landlady takes us and the turkey in hand and as we are shown to our room I say, 'you are an angel.'

She looks me squarely in the eye. 'Don't ham it up any more son,' and grins. 'Happy Christmas.'

As we're lying in bed half an hour later I make a mental note to remember that that's exactly how you make an entrance in a country inn after midnight: On Christmas Day, with a pregnant wife. Donkey optional.

The next morning the inn is quiet. We are the only overnight guests, which explains why the heating is not on. But the morning has dawned crystal clear as often happens after a storm and as we drive over the Pennines the Eden Valley is laid out ahead of us like an endless green patchwork, everything wet but sparkling under a sapphire blue sky. And we feel unburdened by anything other than the weight of our untold news.

How we managed to conceive running a restaurant, commuting weekly to a castle, sleeping on two different height twin beds, too frightened to move for fear of infringing one of the house noise rules, baffles us still. But however it happened, we are bursting with excitement and when we arrive at the castle it's all we can talk about. Mum is the first to know (other than the innkeeper and his wife... and the customers... and I suppose half of Teesdale by now) and of course, is overjoyed and clearly puts any smouldering issues out of her head for the time being.

We feel safe in the knowledge that all is well. We have had a scan and have a picture of a real healthy baby to hand around.

'So, what do you want to talk about Mum?' we ask after the baby hysteria has abated.

'Oh it's nothing, it can wait.' But she seems distracted and I know that whatever it is, it won't be able to wait for long.

Chapter Four

I feel completely put upon. Taken for granted. You've just left me to rot up here.'

This is a bolt from the blue. We knew Mum had something to say but we weren't expecting this.

'Where the hell has this shit come from?' I ask, angrily, indifferent to the possibility that this is not the best way to speak to one's mother, especially when she has just helped you to buy a castle.

'I've been abandoned here for three months, having to deal with everything including some real tits who've treated me as a second class person and you two just don't let me in when you come home. You're all lovey-dovey like you don't need anyone else. You're so bloody independent as if nobody else matters. Selfish and self-absorbed.' Oh God, and now she's crying.

> *I: 'Which is something I've seen her do only once before – when I found her on the edge of the bed the morning after you died, clutching a lapful of blood stained sheets.*
>
> *'Although the sound of her gentle sobbing from behind a closed door haunted my childhood.'*

But the tears don't dissolve the knot of resentment that has gripped my stomach at this ridiculous and unreasonable outburst.

'How dare you say we've abandoned you? You knew the deal,' I say with just a small pang of guilt because I'm not sure she really ever did. None of us really knew what to expect.

'Are you sure you know what you're taking on?' It's ringing in my ears.

'We've been working our bloody arses off trying to make enough money to get this project going.'

'I know, I know,' she sobs pitifully, 'but you could have asked me for more help. I've felt useless and unimportant.' And then it all snaps in to focus.

'Oh I see, this isn't really about us then, it's about you. You think we've taken all your money and haven't made you feel important enough, is that it? Should we have been grovelling at your feet every time we came back up from London?' That hurts as I mean it to and I can see the knife go in deep as she winces and pulls herself up, bristling for a fight now.

He: 'You always had a vicious tongue, even as a child. I told you so often enough.'

I: 'Hah, that's calling the kettle black. The way you spoke to me most of the time was pretty vicious, you practically spat the words out. I learned everything from you.

'Don't suppose you remember the time you screamed at Mum that she would have been nothing if you hadn't dragged her out of the gutter.'

He: 'You heard that?'

I: 'We heard it all, saw it all. The screaming, the taunting. You were too drunk to care.'

He: 'Your mother was going to leave me that night.'

I: 'For another man? She'd never have done it, you know that, that night or all the other nights too, although, who could blame her?'

He: 'But she didn't. She didn't because of you and your brother not because of me. She always put you first, always.'

I: 'She always put everyone before herself. Don't forget how she nursed you at the end despite herself. I remember hearing her wretching in the toilet after she'd cleaned out your wounds; wounds that wouldn't heal because you refused to stop drinking and refused to take care of yourself. God, she was a saint. All so you could go down to the pub with your dignity intact while she was left to clean up all your blood and pus.'

I turn to Wendy who is sitting next to me. Her face is ashen and she is neither moving or making a sound. A single tear is rolling down her cheek.

'Well what do you make of this revelation?' I ask her with more than a slight note of sarcasm and too much venom. But she doesn't have a chance to answer.

'Oh Simon, don't be like that. I just mean, you both are so together that you don't let anyone else in, everyone says so.' It's a cheap shot and Mum knows it. She looks away into the distance as if a sudden commotion outside in the garden has caught her attention.

'Everyone says so? Oh for God's sake that's the sort of thing a thirteen-year-old says when they're losing an argument. I'm not going to apologise for having a strong marriage. We're bloody well going to need it if this place is going to work out. I just don't understand what this is all about.'

But in truth I do understand how she is feeling because we have the sort of marriage, a real partnership of two equals that she never did. Now she's so close to it she can't comprehend what she's part of.

'I just want to be included, consulted more, that's all. You don't understand. I have people calling and asking me questions that I can't answer because I don't know.'

'We don't know most of the fucking answers. We're making it all up as we fucking go along.'

'Simon!' And suddenly she's Mum taking control and I'm her little boy.

'Sorry.'

Wendy jumps to her feet. 'I'm making tea,' she says.

'No, I'll do it,' Mum says.

'No! I'm making the tea.'

After Wendy leaves the room we sit for a long time in silence, Mum sitting opposite is still surveying the imaginary action going on in the garden over my shoulder.

I'm not given to acts of spontaneous emotion, Wendy once having described me as being as demonstrative as a stick insect. I get up, casually stroll over to the sofa where my mother is sitting and put my arm around her. It feels awkward, unnatural, but I know it is the right thing to do because she melts into me, sobs a couple of times and then stops, breathing heavily but slowly.

'It's good to talk,' I say after a while, 'perhaps that's what's missing.'

'I just want to feel that I'm not a nuisance, that I'm not in the way.'

Is that how she has felt for most of her life?

He: 'She was evacuated from London during the war, you know that?'
I: 'Yes, she told us. Many times.'
He: 'She was three-years-old and she went to live with her grandmother in South Wales. She was made to go to chapel three times on Sundays, wear rags in her hair, she was separated from her brother and sister and only saw her parents on occasional weekend visits.
'She didn't return home until she was seven.'
I: 'You've become very understanding and empathetic.'
He: 'Ah, the benefit of ultimate hindsight.'

'Mum, we wouldn't be here without you, you've been holding the fort, we've been getting pregnant. It all starts now, all of it.'

'Tea and crumpets,' Wendy announces just before entering the room and we straighten up.

Much of the rest of New Year's Day passes with us feverishly making plans for the castle, the guest rooms and the baby.

But, although we don't realise it straight away, there has been a subtle shift in our mother-son relationship borne out of a frankness that neither of us had afforded each other before and with which we both remain habitually uncomfortable plus the realisation that two women cannot share one man. It would prove in the years to come to be the undoing, the slow unravelling, of what was once a very intimate - though never demonstrative - relationship. And Wendy? She will find herself facing up to the truth, uncomfortable as it is because she has spent her life trying to please – that she will never be able to please everyone, not in this household anyway.

On the recommendation of our surveyor we engage an architect. Roddy is an affable enough chap of the old school. He is semi-retired, relatively cheap and very low-tech. This an advantage financially as we have a tiny budget for an enormous job. In all other respects he probably isn't the best man for the job. It turns out, he specialised in designing hospitals. An advantage if we feel the need to turn the castle into a mental hospital and commit ourselves at a later date.

Ironically in later years two of our greatest friends and allies would turn out to be Charles and Elaine, a structural engineer and a conservation architect and there are undoubtedly aspects of the castle's interior design which would have been a little more imaginative had they been on board from the start, but for now we make do with Roddy's practical, and cheap (he is only charging us half his usual fee) input. He tells us he is discounting because he admires the efforts of two such young people in bringing such a lovely old building back to life which I cynically interpret as a roundabout way of saying, 'Are you sure you know what you're taking on? You're going to need every penny you can lay your hands on.'

Roddy's initial designs give us ten letting bedrooms and the floor plan looks alarmingly like a wing of a private hospital. He also gets a little hung up on wheelchair turning spaces. As the bedrooms are all on the first floor it's back to the drawing board when we remind him there is absolutely no budget for a lift.

After re-visiting the drawing board together several times, we alight on a plan for six letting bedrooms, cleverly utilising as much of the existing plumbing as possible from the apartments into which the castle had been carved up.

They're big bedrooms, palatial bathrooms, lots of space.

'It's not very commercial,' is Roddy's final observation.

'It's a disused castle in the arse end of nowhere,' I reply, 'what's commercial got to do with it?'

Planning permission comes through at the end of January. We never really considered the risk of buying the place without planning permission. We had written advice from the planning officer which, with a little imaginative reading between the lines, we convinced ourselves told us that the local authority would be only too happy to have someone with a plan take up residence.

I'm still running the restaurant from a distance and taking a modest salary (which goes a lot further in Brough than it did in Mayfair) and Wendy is working full time, splitting her days between home and offices in Telford, a commute of a mere 150 miles each way. Having the planning permission in writing is the first real tangible sign that we're planning to make our livelihood out of this place. By mid-March builders have been contracted and we have an opening date of early May at which time we plan to have three letting bedrooms ready.

'Do you think we ought to have some sort of business plan?' Wendy asks absent mindedly one evening while we are flicking through TV channels.

I snort. 'We did a business plan when the bank came to visit and agreed to lend us the forty grand.'

'That wasn't a business plan, it was bullshit.'

'Same thing,' I say, 'as I told Roddy, it's a castle in the back of beyond. We're not in the Lake District, we're not in the Yorkshire Dales. Our best bet of picking up passing trade is if they close the A66 because of snow.'

'Fuck,' Wendy is still jabbing at the remote control.

'You could say that, it wouldn't be the first time.'

The truth is there was never any real plan other than to escape the suffocation of London. That done, everything else is instinct and would always remain so.

By mid-April it is clear that the deadline is not going to happen. We're not even close. We seem to be the only ones surprised. There are no walls, no functioning electrics and only the barest of first fixings in the bathrooms. Apparently nobody had factored in the builders' ten day long shut down for Easter which, inexplicably, puts the project back at least three weeks. Rather like a classic builders' bum, the builders' Easter break extends way beyond what is decent.

Not for the first time do we reflect on how different it all could have been if that removal lorry had turned south rather than north.

Sure, the builders in France are just as unreliable, maybe more so, but in our idealised version of French country life nobody cares because everyone is *laissez faire* and there is no problem that can't be put right over a glass of pastis or a bière. And wouldn't it be easier to do it all ourselves in France?

Back in reality, a further delay of ten days in delivery of sanitary ware then puts the plumbing schedule back five weeks. I struggle to come to terms with this new mathematics of take a delay, double it and add a random figure and grow increasingly frantic.

Our foreman's attempts to calm me down are little help. 'Stop stressing, it won't make the job happen any quicker.'

'Well what the hell will then?' I bellow back at him.

But when eventually the baths, toilets and basins arrive we are totally unprepared for the stress that comes as part of the delivery and once again those words are ringing in my ears, 'are you sure you know what you're taking on?'

There is an unwritten law that professionals such as doctors, teachers, solicitors and architects know what they're doing and should be trusted to do it properly. That particular law is an ass. In years to come we will have first hand experience of all these professions letting us, and themselves, down.

First up: The architect.

Roddy, it rapidly becomes apparent, cannot project manage. He is clearly more at home in the public sector where deadlines exist to be moved, budgets are there to be exceeded and it takes five people to do what one person does in the real world. The builders are running rings around him and, by extension, us and I feel powerless to intervene. After all, this is my first property. To me a noggin is a children's Viking character rather than part of a timber partition and a breaker is something you might seek out on the back of a surfboard, not an electrical component.

We are, however, blinded by our excitement at seeing things coming together and today the first of our cast iron claw footed baths is being fitted. By tonight we could be having a bath in our first new bathroom.

Or perhaps not. There's a problem. The bathroom floor has a five inch slope from one end of the room to the other, nobody has taken this into account and all the water is now sitting at one end of the bath resolutely keeping its distance from the plughole in the middle.

Wendy is the first to discover what has happened and she is incandescent. Too timid to stand up to a pregnant woman in full fury (and wisely so) the builders are standing in a semi-circle listening silently to Wendy's colourful thoughts on their incompetence when I walk in. Gently but firmly I manoeuvre her out of the room and as we go, spit over my shoulder at the builders, 'just get it sorted.'

They do but in the recriminations that follow the architect blames the builder and vice versa and in the end it all turns out to be my fault for specifying the wrong bath, a bit like the wrong leaves on the railway or the wrong sort of snow for the snow plough.

By late May things are still dragging on and pressure is required so we place a classified ad in the *Daily Telegraph*. 'Stay in a castle in

Cumbria' is all it says together with a telephone number.

We are inundated with enquiries and eventually I take a booking for the first weekend in June. It does the trick and the next ten days are mayhem as I continually remind plasterers, tilers, electricians, plumbers and carpet fitters that if we don't have three bedrooms open on time nobody gets paid.

That we open in time for summer is a mixture of luck, tenacity and sheer hard work. That Oliver arrives healthy is a blessing. We are at last beginning to realise what we have taken on and as our first summer turns to autumn we are feeling just a little smug.

Happy guests, new baby, exciting plans. And we start to take advantage of some of the perks that running a small hotel brings.

One of those perks is an invitation to a wine tasting event. The latest is at a large country house hotel in North Yorkshire. We arrive with friends at around ten-thirty for a day of wine tasting punctuated by a wine-matching lunch. It's still early to be drinking wine so we have prepared ourselves with bacon butties. The event is taking place across three or four rooms each filled with tables groaning with bottles of wine and champagne.

We make a bee-line for the nearest champagne. The bubbles invigorate us and there is no stopping us until lunch. Wendy berates me for helping myself to too big a glassful at one table where there is nobody to serve. I explain that it is necessary to have a little more in the glass in order to release the maximum aroma. She gestures towards the spittoon. I walk on. As she is still breast-feeding, Wendy is reluctantly being abstemious and has volunteered to drive so I return the gesture towards the spittoon. She reminds me that, as I should be aware by now, she is not in the habit of spitting and if she can't swallow she'd rather not bother. She has, she says, come for the lunch.

There is, of course, always a downside to any pleasure, and here it is the inevitable wine bore who really doesn't know when to stop and sounds as if he has swallowed a whole *Roget's Thesaurus* and far too much of his own self importance.

Long before it's time for lunch, I am starting to feel a little faint and feel the necessity to sit down and so we take a seat in the library for a seminar on the very latest thing, bio-dynamic wine making. Monty someone-or-other is something of a trailblazer in this field and his presentation is fascinating, made even more enjoyable by bottles of organic wines which are being passed around the room to taste (closely followed by a makeshift spittoon made out of a plastic funnel set in the top of a tragically empty Bollinger magnum). By the third tasting bottle, the spittoon has bypassed our row. It seems rude not to swallow as we are told these wines are so cutting edge they are not yet available on the open market. I confess I am unsure what bio-dynamic means and I'm finding it increasingly difficult to follow what's being said. I am confused as I am sure at the beginning of the talk someone said wine has been made bio-dynamically since Roman times. Not very cutting edge.

Behind us is the wine bore. He's hogging the spittoon having clocked that we have no need for it and is slurping mouthfuls of wine around his mouth much more noisily than anyone could consider decent. He opens up a discussion about the complexity of the wines and how they should fall apart on one's palate rather than wait until they hit the gut. I'm starting to think that rather than falling apart in my gut the dozen or so wines already in there have started a fight. Then, predictably it's all grassy nuances, hints of hedgerow, the essence of the *terroir* and overtones of the lunar eclipse. I'm starting to taste a more than subtle undertone of irritation and a strong whiff of bullshit. I'm keen to ask a question about the phases of the moon and how they affect the pruning of the vines but I can't seem to formulate the sentence. In fact, any attempt at words seems to result in nothing but a warm dribble from the corner of my mouth. Wendy decides it is time for lunch.

It seems a very long walk to the restaurant. When we arrive we are among the first there and hope that nobody thinks we have only come for the free lunch. Wendy has, of course, but the rest of us are here for the free wine. The waitress brings a jug of water and then two glasses of wine each. We are supposed to identify the two wines and then rate each against the food. This goes on for three courses. The food is delicious and so is the wine. Wendy is being very sensible and, as we are eighty miles from home where Oliver is with Mum on a strict ration of expressed milk, has not given in to temptation.

Needless to say, her glasses of wine do not go to waste.

We have tasting cards to fill out and by the end of the lunch I have drawn a whole family of flying pigs on mine which three of us agree makes a valuable contribution to the debate about which wine went best with each course. Wendy disapproves and one of our friends thinks better of showing her the blue elephant he has drawn.

On our way back to the tasting rooms the corridor seems to have got even longer, perhaps because Wendy is steering me towards the far end of the largest room where coffee is being dispensed. Ten minutes and a long latte later I feel partially restored enough to notice that as we're one of the first parties to finish lunch, the room is almost empty and the wine tables are all unattended.

Wendy reminds me that we must be professional and that we are here to network and research new wines. This is so very unlike her and I can only put it down to her new found sense of responsibility and the fact that she may not want Oliver to get too drunk from his nightly milk fix.

I remind her that I have a clear strategy for the rest of the afternoon which is to find easily quaffable wines for summer in the garden and as I've already had to explain once today assessing a wine's quaffability requires a good measure in the glass to appreciate the full complexity of aromas and flavour notes. She mutters something which sounds like 'boxes of chocolate and fudge' but I can't be sure. It might have simply been 'bollocks'.

On a serious note, we do find some seriously drinkable whites and roses and then, oh manna from heaven, right in front of us is an unattended bottle of vintage champers retailing for £120. In a pincer movement worthy of the British Army, three of us have poured three glasses before anyone notices. But it is a disappointing drink. The bubbles are just too big and as the room is now filling up again we notice that we are among only a few clients who have stayed all day and among all the fresh faced afternoon arrivals we are shown up for what we are. But, in this business you get out when you can and we've thoroughly enjoyed ourselves, met some new contacts and found some great new wines and I always maintain that a few aches, even in the head, at the end of the day denotes a good day's work.

'You're drunk,' accuses mum when we get home.

'I am not drunk,' I interrupt indignantly, 'I'm just very tired, it's been a busy day.'

'Just like your father.' But I'm too weary to take offence.

CHAPTER FIVE

In early 1999 Wendy seems withdrawn. She admits to feeling detached but is reluctant to say why.

Not for the first time Mum is unable to contain her frustration over her relationship with Wendy and her feeling that she has lost part of her son but not gained an equal share of her daughter-in-law and in my mother's black and white world that just doesn't add up.

One of our original six neighbours has moved and we managed to buy his cottage which Mum has made her own. But we rarely have time to visit her there and Mum's sense of isolation grows.

'Why won't she talk to me? I'm not trying to replace her mother but she's so distant sometimes,' she asks me repeatedly. And then to drive home her message, adds, 'She can be so cold.'

'Mum, she won't even open up to me sometimes. Give her time, it's been a hell of a year, it's been a hell of a few years - she's been pregnant for most of the time.'

Wendy was just fifteen when her mother died after a long battle with cancer. If there is ever a better or worse age to lose a parent, fifteen is maybe about as bad as it gets. Her memories, of course, are dominated by the long years of cancer treatment. Her mother had the long lingering sort at a time when surgeons were keen to cut first, and often, and ask questions afterwards. The result: sickness, more sickness, new hopes dashed and the inevitable affect all of that has on the whole family.

When someone in a family gets cancer, everyone gets it. It takes over as the driving force of the family, saps it of energy and invades every facet of domestic life. Understandably a child very soon begins to idolise a dead parent and the effect is that, as they grow older without the reality of flawed and imperfect parenting, they create an image of something that matches their ideal and so the loss grows greater.

Now, as we begin to plan for Oliver's christening later in the spring, Wendy seems to need a maternal hand more keenly than ever.

'I wrote to my Dad and he didn't reply.' Wendy is speaking blankly as if nobody should really hear what she says. We are watching television and I click it off.

'When, what did you write?' I ask gently.

'Before Oliver was born. I wrote and asked if he'd come, if he'd be here with us when we brought him home. But he never answered.'

'Perhaps he didn't get the letter.'

Wendy chooses to ignore that possibility, perhaps because she needs there to be a villain in this tale. 'Mum would have come, she'd have dropped everything and come.'

'Would she? Do you know that for a fact? You're his daughter too. He probably didn't get the letter.'

'He did.' And she flicks the television back on.

'Well he's coming to the christening and he'll be so smitten with his grandson we won't be able to keep him away,' I continue over the TV babble.

Wendy has never had an easy relationship with her father. Always craving parental affection which he is ill equipped to give, she finds it hard to accept, or perhaps even to acknowledge, that he too has lost someone very special.

But it is a good relationship too. They banter, laugh, communicate but always in the present, always for the moment and both steadfastly avoiding reference to the past.

The christening is just a few weeks away. It's going to be an important celebration because we will be getting our significant friends and family together at the castle for the first time. Wetting the head of the baby and the castle simultaneously.

Wendy's father Mike and stepmother Buzz are flying in from Africa and the timing of the christening has been adjusted to take account of Mike's chairmanship of the golf seniors who are just completing a tour of South Africa. He last saw the castle in its unfinished state just under a year ago and was heard to exclaim as he dodged the holes in the floorboards to get to his room, 'I just don't know what they've taken on – it'll never be finished.' and then turning to Buzz, he adds, 'are they sure they know what they've taken on?' But at the same time he was incredibly supportive and encouraging, clearly excited by the project as an emotional stakeholder rather than just a bystander.

Being the only father we have left between us, we are both, of course, desperately excited to show him that we did get it finished and looking forward to that parental seal of approval that, for us at least, can only really come from a Dad. Mike brings the extra kudos of having worked in banking all his life and having been instrumental in brokering finance for some of Africa's great entrepreneurial success stories so his is an endorsement which carries some weight.

It's going to be a big day. In a sense the crowning of all we have achieved so far. But for now we have our first Easter to cater, with the added complication that I am on crutches from a ladder fall in January when I took my full weight on my heel bone and split it in three. I have mastered the art of propping myself against the cooker with one hip while swinging a hot pan through 180 degrees without causing myself or anyone else further injury.

Oliver has been watching all of this for months from his clip on high chair which is now permanently attached to the end of our huge oak kitchen table. In fact, such a permanent and contented addition to the kitchen's fixtures and fittings is he that we don't notice him a lot of the time and he happily busies himself unless he's made an unpleasant smell or is crying for something to eat.

Such is the scene on Maundy Thursday as we prepare for a full house of Easter guests eager to chill out for the long weekend and be well fed and looked after. To help with this onslaught of demands, Wendy's brother Clive and partner Jo, are travelling up to help. They have become stalwarts, enthusiastic conscripts in this unlikely battle with common sense and so hard do they work whenever they visit that they are dubbed 'the Slaves from Bath'.

We have gone to town with personalised chocolate Easter eggs for each guest, an extravagant menu and even some evening entertainment courtesy of a musician friend who needs an Easter refuge from an unhappy home life.

One day, we muse, we may be doing well enough to have some staff but for now the castle is staffed by any family or friends gullible enough to offer to help. So far we have had garden weeding weekends, cleaning conventions and painting parties.

Wendy is in the office rustling through paperwork. When we started out at the castle we didn't formally assign each other different tasks or areas of responsibility but she seemed to fall naturally into the admin role and I wasn't going to stop her so now the office is her domain.

She comes through to the kitchen where Oliver is hammering on the table and I am balancing against the cooker, both in companionable silence. She seems irritated. 'I've had this really obnoxious South African guy on the phone three time already wanting to speak to you and he won't tell me what it's about. You know what they're like – it's man's business.' Wendy is no feminist but she doesn't like being treated like a second class associate in what is an equal partnership.

'It's probably advertising,' I tell her. And that's an area of the business that she has been more than happy to delegate to me. We think no more about it as at that moment there is a squelchy noise from behind us. Oliver has dropped his hammer, dropped off to sleep and his head has fallen forward, face squarely planted in his bowl of gruel.

An hour or so later Wendy comes through again, 'he's on the phone again and he's insisting on talking to you.'

'Doesn't he know it's Easter? Tell him I'll call him back when I'm not up to my elbows in chocolate.'

'It's a South African number.' It makes Wendy uneasy. I tell her I'll make tea and then I'll call him.

Another one of my new found talents is being able to carry two mugs of tea in one hand while walking with both crutches in the other. A few minutes later I'm triumphantly making my way towards the office.

Out of nowhere comes a cry the like of which I heard just once before when we lost our first baby. A wave of blind panic washes over me as the mugs crash to the floor and my crutches clatter away behind me.

I'm running. There's no pain even though I'm putting weight, and it's full weight, on my broken heel for the first time. I can't think about pain. Not my pain.

'No, no no, it's not true, no!' is all I can hear from the office and when I get there Wendy's face is grey, drained of colour, of life, but at the same time twisted with the sort of black emotion that we hoped we'd never see again after Oliver was born.

As I stumble into the office Wendy falls silent. Everything seems monochrome as if some malign presence has sucked all the colour out of the room. She looks in my direction but not at me, rather through me, and as in an old black and white movie, the phone falls in slow motion from her hand and dangles helplessly, twisting slowly on its chord just above the floor.

'What's happened? What's going on?' I demand. But Wendy doesn't reply. She just stares, eyes not even blinking. Then I hear a disembodied voice from the telephone receiver and instinctively pick it up without thinking that I may not want to know what news is at the other end.

'Hello?'

'Simon, I'm so sorry, I thought you'd have heard by now, it's all over Nairobi.'

'What?'

'A car accident in Johannesburg. Oh Simon, I'm sorry. Mike's dead.'

That fucking South African, why didn't I take his call? Why didn't he make me take that call? Then at least she'd have heard it from me.

The following hours are a blur. Wendy cannot take it in and she can think of nothing other than going to bed. I find myself seeking consolation on Mum's doorstep.

'Such a lovely man', she says, 'always the good ones. Is Wendy coming over?'

'She will when she's ready.'

But she doesn't and this begins to rattle Mum. 'Why isn't she coming? She needs to be with people, why isn't she coming? I'll go and get her.'

'Oh for Christ's sake, Mum, shut up.'

She looks utterly crestfallen. She wants to share, she wants to be part of someone else's loneliness rather than be lost in her own anymore. But for now it's Wendy who's lost. On her own in her own void.

It may not be where she chooses to be, but she can't get out and Mum won't be allowed in.

> He: 'She was surrounded all her life by people who needed her but whose need she didn't invite.'
>
> I: 'Yes, and with Wendy she had a chance to be needed by someone who could fill the void of the daughter she'd had to give up when she was young. But when it came to it she wanted to be needed by the one person who didn't need her because Wendy had learnt to become self sufficient.'
>
> He: 'Your mother saw that as rejection.'
>
> I: 'You know, from that day I knew something was going to have to change. It was the first time I realised that Mum had to be looked after too, to be fed emotionally and I wasn't sure I could do it.'

Over the next twenty four hours news of what actually happened filters through. The South African turns out to be the friend with whom Mike and Buzz were staying and it is he who tells me that Buzz was driving and that Mike was killed instantly in a side-on collision. Buzz is in a critical condition, unconscious in a Johannesburg hospital.

He apologises to me for not having been able to get the news to me before Wendy found out and we joke briefly about how getting past Wendy was never that easy.

And although he is full of sympathy and able to answer most of our questions, it all seems too unreal: something that has unfolded at the other end of another continent just can't feel real.

'They were on their way,' Wendy reflects and then corrects herself, 'he was coming to see Oliver, now he'll never see him. All because of his stupid golf. Why didn't he come when I wrote? It can't be real.'

But it is. And 24 hours later what is even more real is the arrival of a castle full of Easter guests. And Wendy's brother Clive. We've been unable to contact him. So when he arrives at lunchtime on Good Friday morning full of the joys of family togetherness someone has got to tell him.

Our guests allow us the space to come to terms with what has happened and keep a low profile. They are surprised when we tell them on Saturday morning that dinner is on as usual.

'Are you sure?' asks one incredulously. 'I mean, you're on crutches,

Wendy and Clive have just lost their father...'

'Yes, but what's the alternative? There's nothing to be gained from moping around and Wendy wants it. Your job,' and I address the whole table of guests, 'is to take our minds off it all.'

And they do. And so does Oliver who, blissfully ignorant of what's going on around him, yet again becomes the focus of everyone's attention because death, however tragic or unexpected is only ever part of the story.

CHAPTER SIX

Between Easter and the christening we fly to Kenya for Mike's memorial service. In Nairobi Cathedral it is standing room only and there is even a crowd outside the door. It brings home painfully to us all what we have lost. But the mood is far from sombre. Although the pain is still raw, it's a celebration of a life full of character, good humour and generosity. Oliver is there with us and he provides a welcome focus for everyone's attention – the new generation still to be damaged and broken by everything in life.

Back home a couple of weeks later Oliver's christening is, by contrast, a muted affair. Everywhere: in church, at the table, in the photographs is an empty space, or maybe a shadow of what should have been.

> I: 'Losing a parent before their job's done is like having a promise broken. Being left to get on with it on our own is like some sort of betrayal. But I felt sadder for Wendy when Mike died than I did when you died.
>
> 'I'd already put him on a plinth. I thought he was a God - the perfect father that you weren't because I only saw the good bits, the safaris, the lunch parties, the humour, the charming vulnerability.'
>
> He: 'And there's a big difference between dying of cancer and being killed in a car crash.'
>
> I: 'Big difference. No closure. There's still no closure. Even now it's as if he's going to walk back through the door. You don't suppose... No, stupid.'
>
> He: '...That when someone is taken in an accident they never quite leave?'
>
> I: 'Yes, that's exactly it.'

He: 'You may just have something there, because there are things left unsaid.'

I: 'But everyone dies with things unsaid.'

He: 'Yes, but not everyone dies without the opportunity to say those things if they want to. An accident, a sudden death, takes away the chance to make your peace if you want to.'

Things can only get better. Guests continue to come and tell us not to change a thing. We do, of course, because what they can't see is that there are some pretty big cracks which have just been papered over for the sake of expediency. For the first time I start to really understand the realities and practicalities of what we have taken on: A lifelong project which will swallow more cash than we can ever generate. But we love it. We love the place and we love the people, visitors and locals, mad as many of them are.

Maddest among them is Reg. He has been a life-saver on many occasions and since we moved in has cleared a fallen tree from the drive, dug us out of the snow, made sure we meet the right people with regard to fencing, hedge-laying, drainage and roofing repairs. He has steered us away from most of the people who would wish us ill and always with a wisdom and worldliness that utterly belies the fact that he has never strayed outside old Westmorland.

Today he is here to talk about sheep and I am ready to surprise him. Reg is a complex character. But a man of infrequent words. I say infrequent rather than few because when he does open up it is as if a field gate has been left open and a flock of Herdwick sheep have made a bid for freedom. However, much of what does come out on these occasions remains a mystery to me as I have only the slightest grasp of local dialect. This is unfortunate for me, though not for Reg who, I suspect could not give two damsons whether I have understood a thing he says or not.

But, not to be beaten, I have bought myself a slim but, I hope, invaluable tome: *A Dictionary of Cumbrian Dialect*. Flicking through its pages fills me with the hope that next time Reg's gate opens up I will be able to grasp the basic meaning of at least some of what he says and, perhaps rather too ambitiously, further fancy that I might be able to respond in an appropriate manner.

Now, a couple of basics that I have missed come in to play to scupper my plan for a new north/south entente cordiale. Firstly, unbeknownst to me, there is really no such thing as Cumbrian dialect, Cumbria being a wholly manufactured bureaucratic creation of the 1970s made up of the ancient counties of Westmorland, where we live, Cumberland, which might as well be another country, together with Furness, formerly part of Lancashire and therefore definitely foreign, (there are palm trees growing on the promenade of Grange-over-Sands). So speaking to someone like Reg, who was born and bred in Westmorland, in a West Cumberland dialect is like trying to order a Chinese takeaway in Russian. Secondly, what is printed phonetically on the pages of my dictionary bears less than a passing resemblance to anything emanating from Reg's mouth. Actually, by the sound of most of it, I think it comes up directly from his gut.

What's more, Reg views us with a mix of suspicion and curiosity. To him we are exotic creatures imported from another land. We are at once as fascinating but out of place to him as a couple of peacocks in a hen house. He is enthralled that I have a past as a journalist – something that is a galaxy away from everyday life in Westmorland – and that a couple of barely thirty-somethings could have found a castle and made a life in it just amazes him.

Nevertheless, with blissful disregard of these hurdles, I greet Reg over the gate of one of our fields. He is surrounded by sheep. Great. He will be feeling relaxed in his favourite company. These are perfect conditions for a discourse. I am not disappointed as Reg is in a talkative mood but he may chalk up what happens next as one of the more memorable, if not intelligible conversations of his life.

'Now then,' I open.

'Now then.'

'It's an alreet sort of morning.'

'Aye, that it is, not so bad.' He understands, so it's all going quite well so far.

'How's the sheep coming? Ready for tupping?'

'Aye alreet but I'm reedy for ma bait, howst bairden fettle?'

'Um…' I have the book in my pocket but realising I can't just whip it out for a furtive look I can only resort to 'Aye.'

'Ah sin tha an Border crack an deekaboot. Thas famoose.'

'Umm, aye.' Oh dear, my deception is unraveling.

Then things take a bizarre twist. That simple three letter word uttered uncertainly twice in a row is all the encouragement Reg needs to have some fun and he leads me headlong into a linguistic maelstrom.

'Thoo's lookin like thas bin thrang wid al yan screeves. Ist tha gay thrang?'

What? Surely he's not asking after my sexuality? Is a gay thrang some sort of alternative tackle sold under the counter at the farm supplies shop? I know Reg and I don't share the same taste in shirts, but isn't this going a bit far?

In a panic, because I have clearly bitten off more than I can chew, a particular phrase which stuck in my head for reasons I can momentarily not recall comes to mind. I blurt it out without a thought to its meaning or relevance. 'Ah knacked me cleppets when ah landed an yon yat.' Then I do remember with a dreadful sinking feeling that my phrasebook was written with tongue in cheek.

Reg looks at me with a mix of unease and silent amusement, perhaps thinking I am trying to explain a) why I wouldn't be wearing a

_____

*The conversation translated as:

'Hello'

'Hello'

'Nice day'

'Yes'

'How are the sheep, are they ready for breeding yet?'

'Yes, but I'm ready for some lunch (which I have brought with me in a handy box packed by my wife because Westmorland men don't make their own lunch), how is your little one?'

'Um, yes'

'I saw you on the local TV news, you're famous,' (a reference to a local news item about the castle)

'Umm, yes'

'It looks like you've been busy, judging by all the cars, have you been busy?'

'I caused some injury to my testicles (a term usually reserved for referring to a ram or tup's business assets) as I landed incorrectly when jumping a gate'.

'Mmm, any chance of a cup of tea? You're a great chap but there's something seriously wrong with your communication skills.'

pair of gay latex thongs on such a sunny morning or b) I am, but it was a mistake as they're chafing terribly.

'Mek us a cuppa scordy, ya'r sec a gran' fella but there's summat wrang wid ya'r dialeect.' Reg roars with laughter which brings with it a wave of relief even though I still have no idea what's going on. By the way he is now heading for the kitchen I gather he is asking me for a cup of tea and resolve to quit while I'm ahead. We revert to our status quo of Cumbrian versus Home Counties and somehow understand each other much better (* see next page for translation).

Over tea Reg offers to help me out in the grounds on a regular basis noting that I'm struggling to keep on top of things by myself and I willingly accept on the condition that he doesn't purposefully try to bamboozle me with words and phrases I don't understand.

He grins, 'would ah do such a thing ta thee?'

Somehow, a few hours with Reg makes the world a more contented place. It puts everything into perspective.

As if to continue my education into Westmorland life I have been invited to join a day's shooting the other side of Kirkby Stephen by Richard Gilbert-Standish, whose wife Selina had met Wendy at a WI meeting. Wendy had been dragged along, kicking and screaming if the truth be known, under the false impression that you are nobody in the county if you're not in the WI. Selina latched on to her as soon as she entered the room and having giggled, gossiped and been generally disruptive throughout the bramble jelly making demonstration and subsequent blind tasting they became, if not close friends then certainly good occasional company. Richard and I have less in common (other than acquaintance with Reg, and Richard howls when I recount my experiences and promises to take me in hand on that score) but Selina and Wendy have started their own WI branch - Women Inebriated with the tag line, Always a Hoot.

I think I am supposed to feel honoured at being invited into such hallowed territory as a family shoot but in fact I am just shit scared. I have never fired a shotgun in my life. Nevertheless I feel it is a good skill to master and who knows where it might lead.

The day of the shoot dawns cold, wet and misty. I arrive at the designated meeting point in my rather battered but eminently practical family estate car and park up alongside half a dozen Land Rovers all with excited but very well behaved dogs in the back. I am so glad I haven't brought Holly as I cannot be sure that once retrieved, she would actually return with any birds I shoot and since I am even more unsure that I am going to actually hit any birds she'd be seriously under-employed anyway.

Of course, being a typically proud young man, I don't want to seem wet behind the ears so, when asked if I have shot before, I simply nod. Then, realising my folly, I add, 'but it was some time ago, so if you wouldn't mind re-familiarising me.'

There are knowing glances and smirks and after that they all have the measure of me. I get a quick run down on how to load the cartridges, the use of the safety catch and how to hold the gun but as we set off up the hill I sense I am already being given a wide berth.

Ten minutes later and despite the miserable weather I am breaking into a sweat. The gun is heavier than I had anticipated and I am wearing far too many clothes. I notice that everyone else is dressed in greens and browns while I am wearing a bright yellow skiing jacket. I don't know whether this is really significant and certainly nobody has commented so I just have to be content that if the mist comes down any further and we get lost, mountain rescue will probably find me first.

Suddenly there's a rumpus in the trees to my left and shouts of 'mine' are coming out of the gloom all around me followed by several double-barrelled boom-booms.

The beaters have put up some birds and the rest of the guns are tracking them across the sky. By the time I have fiddled with the cartridges and the safety catch, the sky is clear and the dogs are in search of the quarry.

There's much back slapping and self congratulation all round among the other members of the party and I resolve to be better prepared next time. I don't have to wait long.

Again there's a lot of noise and then the birds are flying up into the sky in front of us, to the side and behind. I am completely disorientated, waving my shotgun left and right, up towards the sky and I shoot at something but miss completely. I am almost knocked off my feet by the rebound of the gun, then I hear a shout from my right, swing round and my shotgun goes off straight in the direction of Selina who is unpacking lunch.

She is standing a good two hundred yards away from me and I have no idea if shot even travels that far but before I can register what has happened, as I fall backwards I see her fall flat on the ground. I've either killed my host's wife or she was taking no risks and dived for safety.

'Oh shit,' I shout. 'Oh shit,' but nobody else seems to have noticed what has happened. I turn to see if anyone is coming to help my victim but nobody is.

When I turn back towards the scene she is back on her feet and striding towards me in what can only be described as a purposeful manner and I find myself repeating to myself, 'oh shit, shit, shit.'

She has the sort of face that is inscrutable. Neither smiling nor scowling, rather hewn into a perma-pose by a lifetime of days in the wind and sun and too many sloe gins. All I can tell for sure is that she isn't limping and half her skull has obviously not been blown away.

I am frozen to the spot and when she reaches me it's all I can manage to make eye contact.

'We don't tend to point our guns in the direction of other people, Simon, it's a bit alarming.' My whole body relaxes and I am sure she sees my shoulders slacken. She gently takes the gun out of my hand and explains the best way to hold it and the area in front and to the sides where it is generally considered safe to shoot.

'Luckily,' she says kindly, 'I was far too far away to have been killed but the odd piece of shot could have done some damage.'

I like to think that a lesser man would have given up in shame at this stage but I carry on manfully with Mrs Gilbert-Standish keeping a wary eye on me from a safe distance. By the end of the day I definitely feel I've got the hang of handling the gun but my aim hasn't improved. As I am presented with a consolation brace of birds to take home I wonder whether it really was my dismal aim that resulted in a personal tally of zero or whether it was the yellow jacket scaring the birds in the wrong direction. I'm inclined to go with the latter.

I: 'And yes, you know what I'm going to say, if only you'd been around to teach me to shoot. But, you know what? I'm beginning to understand something.'

He: 'What's that?'

I: 'You wouldn't have taught me to shoot. I'd never have asked and you would never have offered because you'd already decided I was a mummy's boy who wouldn't be interested or any good at that sort of thing.'

He: 'That is not true. I was harsh on you as a boy but as much because I was jealous as anything else.'

I: 'Jealous? Jealous of what?'

He: 'Of your relationship with your mother. You were so close. Sometimes it was sickly. The private jokes, the larking around.'

I: 'Well you were practically absent, drowning your sorrows or soothing your stress with beer or whatever it was you did.'

He: 'And part of that was because, rather like your mother felt with you and Wendy, I couldn't break in. I know it was all a vicious circle, I could have made more of an effort, but I didn't have particularly good parents as role models did I?'

I: 'Didn't you?'

He: 'Well, of course, you never met your grandfather.'

I: 'How history repeats itself.'

He: 'Quite. He was an eccentric and a drunk. He was never around during the war because of his secret communications work for the War Office and after the war his brilliant mind which wasn't really wired for normal everyday life went to waste. He slowly drunk himself into oblivion.'

I: 'Hmm, history really does repeat...'

He: 'Tut tut. But that was also to do with a sense of abandonment.

'Because he was like that I turned to my mother as role model. But your grandmother was a lousy mother and a terrible wife. When she wasn't dancing her way through the war she was sleeping through it. And not alone. She was in love with an American airman called Irving. My father knew about it but could do nothing. He was shut out.

'I was drilled to call him Uncle Irving.

'Do you remember that picture of your grandmother, me, the airman in uniform and the shiny new pedal car?'

I: 'Yes, I found it in Nanny's things after she died.'

He: 'Guilt. That was a gift of pure adulterous guilt. I was told not to tell my father where it had come from but of course he knew. It must have been like a stab to his heart every time he saw it.

'I used to be left at home with a neighbour watching out for me. I'd cry myself to sleep wishing for my mother to come home. Once a stray bomb fell a few streets away. I was in the bath and the tiles fell off the wall. My father was dead drunk and my mother was across town partying. I was six.'

I: 'So you resented my relationship with Mum.'

He: 'Parents damage their children. It's what we do. They aren't perfect for more than a second after they're born. We call it character building but it's damage really. We're all damaged and all we can do is make the best of what we've got left.'

I: 'I never realised.'

He: 'Does it help?'

I: 'Of course it helps. This is exactly what's missing without parents. Points of reference. Context.'

He: 'Mmm, I'm sorry then... And by the way... the shooting? I'd have probably got someone else to teach you. That was my way after all. Delegate responsibility wherever possible.'

CHAPTER SEVEN

With a second successful summer under our belts and the initial horror of Mike's death temporarily filed away we are understandably euphoric to find out that Wendy is again pregnant. Although a sibling for Oliver has always been on the cards, it wasn't planned this soon but when is there ever a convenient time to have a baby?

But caution once again prevents us from telling anyone until after our twelve week scan which isn't for another month. Nevertheless, we're like a couple of kids with a secret, bursting to tell but dissolving into fits of giggles instead. Mum is becoming irritated but chooses to say nothing. Like all mothers before and since I am fairly sure she knows exactly what is going on and it's that old gripe of feeling excluded that makes her tetchy.

Wendy first became pregnant on honeymoon in France. A fairytale, the overwhelming reason we had got married was to start a family.

We felt very lucky to have conceived so quickly. People said, 'aren't you clever!' So when Wendy had a show of blood, I went into instant denial. We both did.

This isn't part of the script, where does this fit into our happy ever after storyline?

Twenty four hours later it is obvious what is happening. Wendy is doubled up in pain, having regular contractions. And what imprints itself most vividly on my mind are her screams of agony, then deep sobs of despair as she sits hunched up on the lavatory seat and can only listen as our baby's life splashes into the water and my feeling of utter helplessness in the face of such terrible pain.

By the time we get to hospital there is blood everywhere.

Disorientated I head for the nearest door. It's the wrong one but I don't care and I stand in the middle of the ambulance forecourt and scream, 'We've lost our baby, someone help us, we've lost our baby.' I feel as small and as helpless as a baby myself.

Afterwards (and this only happens once you've experienced a miscarriage because the 'M' word is so totally taboo otherwise) you find out how common it is. Whether this is supposed to make us feel better I can't say but it doesn't help me. It just pisses me off and I think, 'I don't care about anybody else's miscarriages, I only care about ours'.

'And how are you feeling?' I haven't given any thought to that. Should I have since people keep asking? Wendy, is in hospital having given birth but we have nothing to show for it. All she can say is 'I flushed it away, did you see it? I flushed it away.'

I don't know what to feel. Because nobody talks about it, nothing has prepared me for the experience first time round.

Flowers and cards arrive in the days that follow. 'So sorry to hear of your loss' is the common theme. In hospital we are given leaflets with advice on how to grieve for our lost baby. Just words, I think and they're missing the point. I am grieving, but not for a baby. After all, I have heard no heartbeats, felt no kicks, seen no scans. I have lost something much deeper, much less tangible: Our newly wed innocence, our belief in the order of nature has been tarnished.

We lost another baby at six weeks just about three months after that. Being earlier it wasn't as traumatic (Mum rather tactlessly said at the time that if it weren't for modern pregnancy testing kits it would have just been dismissed as a heavy period – that's what happened in her day) but it was a loss nonetheless and adds to the pressure now.

Every twinge has become an anxious moment. I feel my heart race, stomach lurch, if I think she had spent too long in the lavatory. Routine hospital visits will be shadowed by the prospect of bad news. What all this is like for Wendy, I can only imagine. I'm too scared to ask and she's too frightened to even consider it, as if, somehow, talking about it will make it happen.

Of course, everyone says that now we've got Oliver there should be no reason to worry but that doesn't take away the fear.

It's been one hell of a year and we decide it is time for an impromptu autumn holiday. And where better than our old haunt, Roquebrun and Les Mimosas.

We are full of news of the castle and keen to share it with Sarah and Denis as well as to introduce Oliver to them. Even before we have parked the car Sarah is at the big red front door, thick enough to repel an army of tourists but always opened with such warmth. She scoops Oliver into her arms and we truly feel we have come home. It's our first visit back to the *chambre d'hôte* since we bought the castle and we are keen to tell our friends about how so much of what we do has been inspired by our visits to 'Les Mims' from the one table dining, to the honesty bar, to the lavender bags on the pillows and in the wardrobes. But most of all, about how we learnt that the business is about people first, place second although we have to admit it's difficult to get that across to the English.

Oliver is a hit and, as if sensing that this place has played such a pivotal role in our lives, it is while we are there that he takes his first steps.

We return home re-energised, full of new ideas and ready for all that another pregnancy and another round of repairs, decorating and spending money can throw at us.

When eventually it's time for the scan, we decide to make a day of it, have a good lunch in Kendal and then go on to the hospital.

The sun is shining and it's an all round perfect day. We've decided that Oliver will move into a room at the bottom of the tower which sounds desperately exciting for a little boy although he's still too young to appreciate it. So we get desperately excited on his behalf. The new baby will have the bedroom next to ours. Despite the obvious practical advantages of knowing the sex of the baby in advance, we agree not to ask, although if it is painfully obvious we'll not mind. How big does a three month old foetus's willie have to be to be that obvious? The question sends us into fits of giggles over lunch and we're probably making a spectacle of ourselves. But we don't care. It's a perfect day.

'I'm so sorry, I'm just not picking up a heartbeat.' The words sting like freezing rain.

'Perhaps it's just weak, isn't it sometimes difficult if the baby's turned round?' I am willing her to give us the answer we need. I look at Wendy but she has turned her face away, concentrating on the empty nothingness of the hospital-grey wall. She doesn't want eye contact. She doesn't want anything other than a heartbeat.

When Wendy lost our first baby, she lost a light in her eyes which I was powerless to bring back. Now we have lost three and it is as if we are locked in a windowless room with no key to get out. Even having Oliver doesn't take the anxiety and the pain away because we know we don't want to bring him up on his own, that he deserves a brother or sister.

But worse than all of this? We've got to go home and be strong and be happy: for Oliver.

Unlike our first miscarriage when Wendy gave birth to our baby in the bathroom, this is much more managed. It's less messy, but is it less traumatic? It's hard to say.

The nurse tells us Wendy can stay in hospital overnight for a D&C.

'It's quite painless,' she reassures us. Wendy screws up her eyes so tight I know she is fighting back the tears and I know that for her the pain is the least of her concerns. It sounds invasive, it sounds clinical, it sounds like the worst possible end of a human life and I dare not ask what it means because we both know it is necessary.

But later at home on my own, with Oliver happily gurgling in his sleep I look up what D&C means and this is what I read: The gynae-cologist opens (dilates) the cervix with instruments called dilators, and then inserts a hollow tube through the cervix. Suction is applied to remove the retained tissue.

And I cry. I cry until my face and my chest hurt. I cry because our baby is being sucked out through a tube. I cry because our baby is just retained tissue.

Next morning I tell Mum what has happened. She is, of course, stoic. Maddeningly stoic. But I'm grateful for it too when she says, 'take her away for a few days. I'll have Oliver. The castle's quiet. Take her away.'

For three days in Chester we surprise ourselves by laughing. We laugh a lot and we can see that we are stronger, we are more resilient. We are survivors and thankful for it.

For the rest of the year we throw ourselves into work at the castle, welcoming an ever more eclectic selection of guests as both our reputation and marketing budget grow.

Word of mouth is a big part of our sales strategy (since there's no budget for any advertising) and we work on any contact, however vague, to help spread the word.

Unfortunately our own families have never been terribly good at supporting the business. They are confused by the idea that we live and work in the same place, that it is a hotel and therefore if they invite themselves should they pay? If we invite them are we expecting them to pay? So on the whole they don't come that often. Nevertheless, on the odd occasion that friends and family do visit, a large house in the country is a blessing. Everyone can be accommodated in comfort which minimises the irritation of having one's privacy invaded for more than 24 hours, there are plenty of long walks for them to go on and there's no bathroom sharing.

But a large house in the country, hotel or not, also renders us fair game for a different breed of visitors: the friends of friends and invariably there is no confusion in their minds about payment. It simply isn't an issue.

'We're travelling up to Scotland and thought you'd be a perfect stopover,' chirps a voice on the telephone, ever so slightly too loud, perhaps because she thinks that the telephone may be less efficient this far north. There's a long pause while I attempt to gather my wits which is interrupted, 'we met at Jo and Sam's barbecue last summer and you did say...'

I want to reply, 'no, my wife said and in fact it was the sangria which was doing the talking,' but I don't. 'How lovely, which night were you thinking of?' I ask still scrabbling for a name.

'Oh well we thought maybe two nights as it's such a long way, you don't mind do you, we wouldn't want to put you out.'

'No, no, delighted.'

'Will it be alright to bring Max and Poppy?'

Now I am at a complete loss. I am old enough to remember a time when dogs had doggy names and children had, well, human names. We thought we were being terribly off the wall with Oliver until he got to school. Nowadays everything is thrown into the mix, so, who, or what, are Max and Poppy?'

'They'll share our room if that helps, they're no trouble.' This does-n't help since some people have a tendency to talk about children and dogs in the same terms (not without some justification in certain cases it has to be said).

I consider a further pause highly risky. Either the yet to be identi-fied potential visitor will jump in with further ambiguous demands, will elaborate and everything will become instantly clear or will con-sider me a curmudgeonly old sod and decide to cancel her plans.

I'm favouring the latter when she cheerfully suggests, 'they can sleep in the car as long as it's not too cold.'

I take a gamble that this has confirmed Max and Poppy's canine cre-dentials since these people are from somewhere in West London where over-nighting children in the back of the car is altogether less socially acceptable that up here in Cumbria.

We agree on a date and as my new friend rings off I am left hoping that Wendy will remember who they are and what they are called.

Three weeks later the doorbell rings. It's Max and Poppy. Apparently, Wendy ascertained from our real friends, they declared themselves not to be children types and plumped for dogs instead and wouldn't it be fun to name them after themselves?

This clearly is the sort of behaviour that is more socially acceptable in town than in the northern shires where taking your dog out for a bit of rough shooting and then calling for yourself to bring back the bird doesn't feel quite right.

Max and Poppy appear for dinner and Poppy seems slightly dis-gruntled that we are eating in the dining room and not the kitchen. It seems she has an idea that everyone in the country should live their life chained to the Aga. Or perhaps she is suddenly worried that she may be asked to pay something towards her stay if she is being enter-tained in the public domain. The truth is it has become far too hot to eat anywhere near the Aga since we insulated the roof space with some material apparently developed by NASA to protect the space shuttle from catching fire on re-entry.

Nevertheless, Max confides, Poppy feels the cold and she shifts uncomfortably in her chair throughout dinner, snatching wistful glances at the open fire at the opposite end of the room. We have little sympathy for her as it is the end of November and she is dressed in strappy sandals and a stringy top with more holes than material and no sleeves.

'Have you any more heating?' she eventually asks between pudding and cheese. Emboldened and feeling I have the moral high ground by entertaining this relative stranger at all, I reply, 'Have you any more clothes? Or perhaps a modest contribution?'

It's an ice breaker and we do all end up getting on. But Poppy, rather like Johnny Townmouse, leaves declaring that on balance she prefers life in London, although the doggies have had the most marvellous runs. If she is referring to their walks I am pleased for them, if she is referring to anything to do with their digestion, I am glad they stayed in the car. A few weeks later we hear from our mutual friends that while they had a 'lovely time' Max and Poppy wonder whether we have changed since we lived in London as 'life in the country seems to have got to them a bit.'

By December it's most definitely time for another holiday and we agree on a trip to visit Wendy's stepmother in Kenya in the New Year. There is no talk of laying ghosts to rest but it is going to be inevitable.

CHAPTER EIGHT

The trip to Kenya goes well. The few tears that there are, are well contained, and we spend two weeks visiting old haunts and on safari and a few days at the Mount Kenya Safari Club where we enjoy long sunny days followed by chilly nights wrapped up in sheep skins in front of a roaring fire in our lodge.

At one and a half Oliver is far too young to appreciate any of it so we hire the services of an *ayah* (a nanny) for about £4 per day and the heady mix of no toddler, crackling logs, sheepskins strewn in front of the hearth and big starry skies can result in only one thing: On our return we are plunged in to the bleakness of a northern winter but by spring are once again glowing with the news of another baby on the way. Despite the troubles we've encountered nothing can dampen the excitement. Rather as with the pain of childbirth itself, nature has a way of erasing negative memories, not of the lost babies themselves but of the trauma of the loss, so that we can go on and try again.

Winter has been mercifully short, the spring sunny and mild and before long the snowdrops make way for daffodils and they in turn bow their heads to the cherry blossom and the promise of our third summer.

At twelve weeks the scan looks healthy and all is set, we are told, for a trouble free pregnancy. The baby is due in November and Wendy promises to take it easier this time than she did with Oliver. It is, of course, an impossible promise to keep as we are busier than ever with six guest bedrooms now to fill and ever increasing debt to service. When we completed our first three rooms back in 1998 we neglected to budget for any furnishings or carpets. To be honest there was precious little left to budget for those things with anyway, so we slammed it all onto credit cards, the repayments of which on top of our mortgage are now starting to build up faster than our revenue.

We are both constantly worried about the castle finances and know that the easy fix of applying for yet another credit card is not sustainable. But it is just that, a quick, and easy fix and we have no other alternatives for raising capital since re-mortgage seems just a step too far but without working capital we can't develop the product.

I try to rationalise, 'you've got to speculate to accumulate.' In truth I can only speculate about how we are ever going to pay back our accumulated debt. Mum knows nothing of all this and tells anyone who'll listen how terribly clever we are at making our money go so far.

'I don't know where Simon gets such a level financial head from, certainly not from me,' she trumpets, almost proud of her own pecuniary shortcomings.

Still, one more mouth to feed will make no difference for at least a couple of months and the rest of us are doing very nicely off the guests' leftovers and we do, after all, live in a castle.

By September Wendy is seven months pregnant and the pressure of that and work is starting to take its toll on our relationship. We seem always to be at each other's throats and Mum's often ill-judged early morning comments to Wendy such as, 'Oh dear, you look awful. Not much sleep?' aren't helping.

Added to our workload is the fact that our own living quarters are barely more than a squat. Having spent every available penny of our own and anyone else's we can get our hands on growing the business, there has not been anything left over for us. But Wendy has made me promise that by the time the new baby arrives we can have a bathroom which isn't a health hazard and we can eradicate the last of the mushrooms from our bedroom wall.

And if that isn't enough pressure, we have also elected for a home birth. Why? Because something much more than just a new baby is at stake.

With what we hope and pray every day to be the imminent birth of our second child there is the prospect of a light returning to our lives. There is a glimmer of something in Wendy that I haven't seen since we were first married. I won't risk losing that, or another baby, again and we know that this will be our last attempt to complete our family.

And although it all seems so long ago now, like someone else's life, we know that what we have, and what we are about to have, is so special and always worth fighting that little bit harder to protect. Where better to complete the circle than at home?

Since the beginning of the year we have been constantly reassured that all is well and have even been supported in our plans for the home birth. So as we relax just a little, with the oxygen tanks and boxes of midwifery paraphernalia already sitting in the corner of the bedroom, other more mundane but equally pressing domestic concerns fill our heads such as having somewhere habitable to bring a new baby into the world. So, as the main summer season draws to a close we move out of our rooms into guest bedrooms and the builders move in. They have eight weeks to get the job done. New walls, new bathroom, new nursery and a complete re-wiring of the north wing.

The builders make a promising start but they soon slip into an all too familiar pattern. One day they're here, then they've gone, invariably without warning and never with explanation or apology. As the due date for our second baby's birth draws closer, there is so much still to do and, if it is going to happen at home, the last thing we need is a bevy of plasterers, electricians and joiners around as Wendy enters the throes of labour in the next room.

But through all the comings and goings, the emptiness interspersed with periods of mayhem when all the trades turn up at once, Oliver, now two and a bit, has been a constant on-site presence. Bob the Builder has a lot to answer for because he is mesmerised by the builders and sits for hours watching them work. He, at least, has an unshakable belief in them. 'Can Fix – builder can!'

'Ammers, schlewdribers, rrrmmms (that's drills to you and me) are all fair game and, even with the scarcity of actual manpower, are not in short supply.

With the baby due at the beginning of November, now just four weeks away, I decide to press home the gravity of the situation with a frantic telephone call as we still have no bathroom. We had promised ourselves at least a decent bathroom by the time Oliver was born but the credit card we applied for to pay for that got used for more pressing, revenue making needs.

But when the tiles started falling off the wall around the shower end of the bath and we were reduced to attaching a shower curtain to the wall with duct tape to prevent our showers being shared by whoever was in the kitchen at the time we resolved to have a new bathroom by the time we became a family of four no matter what.

It turns out to have been a timely decision. A week later the plumber arrives on site, typically unannounced and only alerting us to his presence by whistling through his teeth while we are still dozing next door.

I don't like the sound of it. I've heard that teeth whistling thing too many times and it's rarely good news. With as much nonchalance as I can muster, I wander into the bathroom to see how bad it is.

It's bad. It appears that the duct taped shower curtain arrangement that has served us so well for some twelve months was not as effective as we had thought. 'Smell that can you?' he says.

I can't smell anything today that I couldn't smell yesterday but the plumbers' highly tuned nostrils are clearly in a league of their own. Apparently a steady trickle of water onto the joists below has partially rotted them and, the plumber warns as he simultaneously draws a breath of doom across his teeth while inhaling more of the stench of despair, the bath could disappear through the floor into the kitchen at any moment. I'm taking this all with a pinch of salt but do concede that things don't look good.

But it's heartening what action a crisis can bring about. Within the hour a conclave of trades has gathered around the opening in the bathroom floor. From the general gesticulations I gather that there may be more than one solution to the problem. I retreat to the kitchen and wait for the white smoke to signify that an agreement has been reached. I can clearly hear a chorus of whistling air being sucked through teeth and some low rumblings which are either grave discussion or the floor beams giving way under the unprecedented weight of a full complement of workmen.

It doesn't help that we need this most fragile of floors to support a cast iron bath tub resting on four claw feet. But the joiner comes to our rescue. The rot, he has concluded, is skin deep and should not affect the integrity of the floor. Once it dries out, he assures us all will be well. However, just to be on the safe side he suggests that we alter the layout of the bathroom and install the bath on the opposite side of the room where the joists are sound.

This, we all agree, is a marvellously cost effective idea and everyone whose idea it wasn't says it is exactly what they were thinking. The floor is reinstated, the bath installed, and in true castle fashion, neither will get a second thought for another ten years at least.

A month later the bathroom is finished; our new bedroom is finished; Oliver has a new bedroom and between us is a newly decorated and furnished nursery. But there is no sign of a new baby.

Nobody is unduly concerned. After all, Oliver was two weeks late, even if there was nothing tardy about his eventual arrival, and I've been late all my life. But Angela, our long suffering midwife is starting to twitch more visibly at every visit. The longer we wait the more nervous she is obviously becoming about the whole home birth thing. In fact nobody else thinks it is now a great idea when we are 45 minutes from the nearest general hospital. It just seems like a wholesome thing to aspire to and the nice lady at the NCT meetings we attended during Wendy's pregnancy with Oliver said we should go for it. Mind you, we stopped taking her seriously following the *Hokey Cokey* incident. After that, Penrith was just too far to travel and there always seemed to be something more pressing than the meetings.

While we are waiting for nature to take its course, there are still guests to look after and they provide an effective, if not always pleasant, diversion. In this business dealing with tactlessness comes as part of the deal.

Not ours, you understand, but the guests'. And family. And friends. Whether it's the big house, the country lifestyle, or the luxury of being able to make up our own rules, ever since we have been at the castle people have, at regular intervals, said the most atrociously insensitive things. I'm sure they don't always mean to be rude but sometimes I have to wonder if it is the green-eyed monster rearing its ugly head.

With waters likely to break at any second we are blessed with a house full of American guests to occupy our thoughts. As dinner progresses they are clearly discussing us and the castle. Well, that's OK, it sort of goes with the territory. But as I come into the dining room to serve pudding, things take an unpleasant turn.

One of the guests, a gentleman from New York grabs at my wrist as I reach to place his pudding in front of him.

'We were just discussing that money is obviously no object for you guys.'

I'm momentarily stunned. 'I beg your pardon?' I reply.

'Money, it's obviously no object.' Far from reeling in embarrassment, the other half a dozen or so guests are looking at me in rapt anticipation of my reply.

'Sir, I'm speechless,' is my lame response but I am saved as, at that moment Wendy waddles through from the kitchen half balancing two plates on her swollen belly. I draw myself up to my full six feet. I am simply not going to put up with this.

'Do you really think, sir, that we would be cooking, serving and clearing up after dinner for you if money was no object? Do you really think,' and I gesture dramatically towards Wendy, who is now disappearing back into the kitchen, 'that my wife would be waiting on you in her condition if money were no object? Do you really think that our baby son would be sleeping upstairs at the end of a baby monitor instead of being cradled in his mother's arms if money was no object?'

The silence around the table is deafening. I am shaking as if a frost has filled the room but stand my ground.

'Do enjoy pudding, anyone for coffee afterwards?'

Back in the kitchen Wendy asks what that was all about and I fill her in. She, already being engorged with hormones, is enraged and is ready to tell the lot of them what she thinks.

I suggest this may not be good for business. When I return to the dining room the offending gentleman has finished his pudding and either been removed or has retreated of his own volition.

One of the other guests covers for him by saying, 'I don't think any offence was meant. It's just that you have such a beautiful place and you're both so young.'

'Thank you,' I reply, 'yes, we are so very, very young.' It's enough to put a grin back on my face.

With still no sign of baby progress, later that week fate takes over, dealing a scary and dramatic blow to all our plans.

I am in the kitchen making tea for Wendy who has grown so big she now has no option but to spend her afternoons watching daytime television. I turn towards the door and Wendy is half standing, half crouching, clutching the door frame. I ask what is wrong but she can't answer. She has lost the use of her mouth and then I realise, she can not stand or use her arm. Her entire left side seems paralysed. I am frozen to the spot and seconds divide into tenths of seconds and then, for a moment the world stands still.

This can't be happening, not after everything we've been through to get this far. Our fifth pregnancy, a near emergency when Oliver was born. And now what? A stroke? Has something terrible happened to the baby? Has it gone the way of the others? Am I going to lose my wife, our precious new baby? Both? What would the castle be without her but a rudderless ship? What would I do? How would we cope? I want to ask these questions but to who? Wendy's eyes are completely blank. No recognition or comprehension of what is happening. Bottomless, endless fear and a pleading that it can't all be going wrong again. Let this moment last forever if it delays the dawning of a truth too awful to face.

With a sudden jolt the world starts to turn again and I am telephoning the doctor. No sooner have we hauled ourselves to the surgery in Kirkby Stephen than he is summoning an ambulance.

'I don't like the look of this one bit,' is his sole diagnosis, me neither, and Wendy isn't looking thrilled.

Within the hour we are in hospital in Lancaster. Wendy is wired up to every available machine. For hours nobody tells us anything. There's just scuttling around, fiddling and monitoring.

And then, as fast as it started, she is better. Nobody can explain why. None of the tests have shown anything abnormal. The baby is fine. Wendy is fine and very cross. 'I've missed the end of a *Murder She Wrote* two-parter for this carry on.'

'Weren't you scared?'

'I can't really remember feeling anything.'

We are sent home on the strict understanding that if the baby hasn't come by the same time next week we must agree to have it induced and the next day Angela comes and takes away the oxygen, the medical supplies and all her other baby delivering box of tricks. We are in no position to argue.

A week later we arrive at hospital without having had to resort to inducement, Wendy's waters having broken just as the final credits roll on the final ever episode of *Inspector Morse*.

'Well at least I got to see the end of that one,' she says, 'come on, let's go.'

We have been asked to go straight to Lancaster in case there should be complications.

'Just a precaution, because of your history.'

'You don't say.'

As we pile into the car I ask Wendy if I can drive very very fast. I have always had a fantasy of driving as fast as I dare, being pulled over by the police and screaming 'my wife is having a baby, we need to get to the hospital,' and being escorted the rest of the way with blue lights flashing.

'Do whatever you want, Simon. It's your last chance, just get us there in one piece please.' I do.

The midwife asks us if we have a birth plan. Wendy tells her just to get the bloody thing out as quickly as possible. 'Get it out and seal me up! I never want to see this place or any of you ever again.'

This is going to be fun.

Once again there are complications, the baby's heartbeat fluctuating as wildly as Wendy's temper meaning that she is strapped to the bed to be monitored. This does nothing to lighten Wendy's mood and she periodically turns to me and tells me it's all my fucking fault. It's not unlike a re-make of *The Exorcist*. I decide to keep well out of things and sit in the corner eating fruit gums. I've brought lots.

After sixteen hours of labour a paediatrician is called and begins a conversation with the midwife over Wendy's head about the possibility of a C-section as 'this can't go on much longer.'

'Too sodding right it can't,' agrees Wendy.

'Please don't talk about Mrs Bennett as if she isn't here,' admonishes the midwife. I perk up. Suddenly things sound like they may be getting interesting. The doctor slinks off and the midwife turns to Wendy and I. 'We'll get baby out without his help.'

I just smile and offer everyone some fruit gums.

Sure enough, less than an hour later Emily is born, Wendy having succumbed to every pain relieving compound the hospital could muster. So much for Wendy's plan for a natural birth. Emily too has the umbilical cord wrapped around her neck but has the decency to stay on the table.

The midwife asks if this is definitely our last baby. I nod, a face full of sweets rendering me speechless and she invites me to inspect the afterbirth. 'It'll be your last chance,' she says.

What a horrific idea. 'I'll pass,' I manage to mumble through gummed up teeth. Whatever next, carpaccio of placenta? Sausages for breakfast made from the umbilical cord?

The following day Oliver comes to the hospital to meet his new sister. He, of course, has no comprehension of what a new baby is going to mean to his life and is more intent on making sure Mummy is alright. To that end he has brought with him a plastic hammer, a saw and some nuts and bolts. A week later, we are all back home and Angela comes round. 'I found these in amongst the home delivery equipment,' she says and produces another bright red and green plastic hammer, a monkey wrench and a clamp.

'Mummy needed fixing,' Oliver explains, 'all better now,' and he takes his tools off to find something new to mend.

Smugly, we think there's nothing to fix here.

It's job done. We have a healthy baby girl and a healthy little boy. In years to come we would talk to them both about how hard earned they were and about how Mummy had once dreamt of six babies.

Emily thinks hard about this and would tell us: 'But Mummy you have have had five babies, it's just that we're not all together. And,' in the matter of fact way that only children can get away with, 'you can always have another go for number six.'

> I: *Here was another grandchild without a grandad. 'The truth is Emily's arrival was overshadowed by so much stress, so much financial worry, it was that I needed to talk to someone about and there was literally no one. So I ended up internalising all the stress.'*
>
> He: *'I understand that.'*
>
> I: *'Do you?'*
>
> He: *'Oh yes, and here I won't let you rubbish me. I was shit scared most of my adult life.'*
>
> I: *'You had friends.'*
>
> He: *'I had drinking buddies. I had very few real friends. They all*

thought I was something bigger than I was. Stronger, more confident, wealthier, because that is the image I projected to protect myself, to hide my fear. What did you call it – a champagne lifestyle on a lemonade budget?

'I was never built for business, I wasn't a risk taker and every day I was expected to assess risk, make a judgement and run with it. I had a board of directors but 51 per cent of every risk we took belonged to me.

'The drink, Simon, was my escape route.'

I: 'I felt like that too. Sick, physically sick. Trapped. And then the added responsibility of two children. Children I knew I'd go to the ends of the World for, but the weight of responsibility was crushing.'

He: 'Drink more and it'll all seem easier until the morning. Drink's not a problem, is it?'

I: 'No.'

He: 'You've done what I didn't. You've turned to the one biggest tower of strength, your wife. I shut mine out.

'You didn't need anyone else to tell you what you already knew: It's a team effort and you get through it together.'

CHAPTER NINE

There's a crystal blue cloudless sky, not uncommon in early spring in Cumbria and then increasingly rare as summer sets in. The fells, so clear and sharp, with every contour, each fold in the landscape highlighted by the sun, still slung low in the sky, look as if they have been painted in as a backdrop to this unrealistically perfect morning.

It's February 2001. I am driving to Kirkby Stephen, three miles away, drinking in the landscape and remembering why it was we fell for this place. The trees, still bare and with no intention of giving up their promise of new life for at least another two months, stand in stark contrast to the gradually greening fields filled with sheep, expectant with lambs. Everything is sparkling.

But something is wrong. I can't say what. Do people look a little distracted perhaps? Is the traffic very slightly slower today? It's that feeling you get when you're on holiday, you haven't read the newspapers, seen the television or heard the radio for a week and yet you know something historic has happened in the world you left behind. Maybe it's a subconsciously overheard snippet of conversation, a glanced headline you didn't even know you'd seen, but somehow, wherever there are other people living other lives, great news, good or bad, has a way of finding you.

I meet our friend Molly in the supermarket and she looks troubled. She has just returned from London and tells me she doesn't think she'll be going back for a while. The concern in her voice and her expression don't register and I cheerfully tell her I'm writing freelance again and at last some decent commissions are coming through.

'Thank God for that Simon', she says, 'you're going to need something to fall back on once this thing gets out.'

Molly is in marketing or PR or something like that and she is tremendously well connected with all sorts of useful people in the know. She is one of those people who seem to get the whole story about things while the rest of us are still grappling with the sketchy outline. I am sure she is over-reacting. Only now she has mentioned it, I do recall hearing on the news as I woke up this morning that some sheep, or maybe it was pigs, in Northumberland had been tested positive for a virus called foot and mouth. Apparently it's not fatal and animals usually recover. 'There is no risk to human health,' the reporter said.

Foot and mouth. I look it up on the internet when I get back to the castle. It looks like just a few mouth ulcers and a bad cold to me. I tell Wendy what Molly has said and she is as baffled as I am. We enjoy a pot of tea outdoors in the February sunshine and our daily routine resumes. Emily is just being weaned and this is drawing most of our attention away from everything else around us.

But a week later, things are very different. While the sun is still shining, there's a shadow moving across the rural landscape. The telephone has stopped ringing. Guests are beginning to cancel bookings. Children at Oliver's nursery start disappearing, not allowed off their farms. The countryside is closing down.

Within weeks the sparkle of spring has gone, the skies have dimmed, the trees stand tall but everything else seems broken. Sheep are stranded in fields, unable to be moved and running out of fresh food to eat, cows are incarcerated in barns while their pastures lie empty outside. Farms become islands in a deserted sea, their animals and their people marooned waiting for rescue but from whom and from where they don't understand.

'THE COUNTRYSIDE CLOSED FOR BUSINESS' and 'NO GO BRITAIN' scream the newspaper headlines.

Quite suddenly, and for the worst of all reasons, we are no longer outsiders, no longer the southern upstarts at the castle, we are united with our friends and neighbours in the hell that is unfolding around us as Cumbria's image around the world shifts from lakes, mountains and Peter Rabbit, to pyres of smouldering carcasses billowing plumes of acrid smoke into the still blue but lifeless sky.

Ironically it is one of the best springs we have had since we moved here, day after day of cloudless sky, crisp mornings and warm afternoons but there is nobody here to enjoy it, no visitors to whom we can sell a slice of our dream.

We have no livestock to lose and although our fledgling business teeters on the brink, we manage to limp on as the crisis deepens. I continue to build up my feature writing which gets me out and away from Cumbria. But it's not a guilt-free relief because every unnecessary car journey is frowned upon and we know that there are whole families, even small communities who are stranded. Every day we hear stories of farmers losing a lifetime's work, or even several generations of breeding as government vets condemn their stock to death. Not always because they have been infected, invariably they're not. It's cull first and test later. And then it's too late.

Farmers, and even vets, who cannot endure the waste and the madness become victims, taking their own lives having been party to the destruction of a lifetime's work. In everyone's ears ring the radio reporter's words, parroting the ministry's reassurances, 'there is no risk to human health.'

There is no death here. The culling is all in the north of the county, some thirty or so miles away. Information is conflicting, tempers run high and accusations fly. Urban myth overtakes the truth and nobody believes anything they are told anymore. Tales abound of stock intentionally infected, haulage companies cashing in and contractors profiting from the government's panic and ineptitude.

Farms become death camps as animals remain stranded and waste away and it is easy to see how farmers could wish for a quick fix, a chance to clean up and start again rather then watch helplessly as their animals suffer. In it's own cack-handed way the government is helping, even if it is just throwing cash, completely unchecked, at the problem.

There is no such help for the county's biggest industry – tourism – like the livestock, it is dying. The government stresses that the countryside is open for business but all the footpaths remain closed.

We carry on with what business we have left and over the weeks up to Easter manage to salvage something from the real truth: our countryside is not littered with burning bodies. The footpaths remain closed, but everything else is open.

Across the road, what started as bewilderment in our farming neighbours' faces gradually turns to a steely determination. They keep their heads down and their farm gates securely closed. That determination is to keep the disease out at whatever cost. As spring turns to summer their resolve strengthens. The disease moves gradually further south but the frequency of confirmed cases is decreasing.

Tentatively, hope creeps in. Tourists begin to tire of being told where they can and cannot go and begin to return. It turns out that Americans have been peddled a confused message and many of them can't distinguish between the facts of foot and mouth and mad cow disease. They come confused, to find the countryside is not as it has been portrayed on their television news programmes back home.

By early September it seems that things might eventually be under control and then we hear that the ministry vets have been seen at our neighbour's farm. Having held out for six months their herd has been culled as a dangerous contact because there's a farm nearby with a confirmed case. It's September 9th. They won't talk about it but I suspect there is a mixture of relief as well as despair in the final act, although the pill is that much more bitter as just a few days later the country's final case is confirmed and then, as quickly as it started, it's all over.

Two days after our neighbour's life's work is destroyed the world is reeling from the news of the terrorist attacks on the World Trade Centre in New York. There is no arguing that the political and social landscape of the entire world changes instantly as a result but in Cumbria we are still numb from the effects of the previous six months and, in some perverse way, insulated from the full horror of 9/11. Someone else's Armageddon takes the focus off our own and we watch events unfold more with detached fascination than a sense of real shock.

But there's no doubt that the twin horrors of foot and mouth and 9/11 are going to change our lives.

As the barbarity of foot and mouth becomes a recent memory and the outrage over both that and 9/11 is a little less raw, the Blanchard-Caffertys come to call.

'What a lovely surprise,' Wendy lies as she answers the door. 'Simon, do look who's popped in.'

'Wendy!' exclaims Martin who lurches towards her ready for an embrace. Unfortunately, being a man of diminutive stature, an embrace would find his face planted squarely between Wendy's breasts – while there is little doubt that this would please Martin Blanchard-Cafferty no end, Wendy is less than keen and effects a skilful side-step to avoid the encounter.

The B-Cs have come to talk about a charity ball.

'After all the ghastliness of F&M,' I don't think Clarissa is referring to Fortnum & Mason from where she has Italian biscotti ('I simply can't drink coffee without them') and petit fours (which are trundled out after dinner parties but which guests are discouraged from touching) delivered twice monthly, 'we thought it'd be a wheeze to have a big bash, raise some cash for the farmer's benevolent fund.'

'Benevolent fund?' I want to ask, 'what you mean for the poor sods who didn't cash in quick enough when the government was dishing out the cash?' but think better of it.

'Lovely', squeals Wendy, reading my thoughts, 'when were you thinking?' She has developed a good nose for cash.

'Well in about six weeks before the weather closes in because we're thinking of a marquee. About 200 peeps. Invitation only. Can you do it? Oh dooo say you can. Ever since you came up we've said it's the perfect place for a bash.'

It's all quite civilised and we begin to think we may have wrongly judged the B-Cs. But as soon as we start to talk about the cost the mood changes.

'It's for charity, for the farmers who were left with their lives in tatters,' Martin says, clearly irritated that there should be any question of payment. I want to scream at him that we're about the only buggers in the valley, and obviously very stupid ones at that, who made no money out of the whole fiasco.

'But a marquee alone, just a basic one, is a couple of thousand pounds,' explains Wendy with more pleading in her voice than she'll be happy with.

'We thought you might put it on and then we'll invite the guests and pay your costs out of the proceeds.'

'I'm very sorry guys,' I've had enough, 'we simply can't underwrite the whole thing. It's too much of a risk, it'd cripple us.' I'm keeping my cool while all the time thinking they could probably just sell off half a fell and give the cash away.

'We'll do the best we can but we can't take a loss on it.'

Martin and Clarissa get up and thank us adding that they'll be in touch with possible dates. 'We'll have to do some sums, what a disappointment, I thought it was all going to be so easy,' comments Clarissa.

As they walk back to their car I hear her mutter to Martin, 'they can't be doing as well as we thought. What a shame, still perhaps they'll sell up and someone a little more suitable will take over.'

To our surprise the B-Cs are back in touch within a week and the ball is on. We are, apparently to do nothing. It is all going to be organised by a committee and all we need do is donate the space for the marquee. We agree to sell rooms in the castle for a knock-down price for anyone unable to stagger back to their Range Rovers.

It seems that anyone who is anyone is being invited and we wait with rapt anticipation for our own invitation. But a week after everyone else has received theirs there is no sign of one for us.

'What should we do?' asks Wendy. 'Surely they have invited us. It must have got lost.'

'But if they haven't and we ask where our invitation is...' the mere thought of such a potential social gaffe sends shivers down my spine.

'Surely they'll be in touch when they haven't received a reply' reasons Wendy.

Clarissa and various members of the organising committee are indeed in touch on several occasions to talk about arrangements, to ask for advice, to fuss about inconsequential detail.

'These women couldn't organise an artificial insemination in a piggery. God knows where they'd be without me,' Wendy tries very hard to disguise the fact that she is hurt about not being invited onto the committee, let alone not getting an invitation. 'I shall have done all the planning and those bitches will take all the credit.'

Martin is in charge of the manly pursuits. 'We're having a Bucking Bronco, where do you suppose it could go?' he enquires. 'A lot of the chaps are looking forward to a jolly good hump on the back of that,' he snorts, 'How about it Wendo? Fancy a bit of bareback?'

'Oh piss off,' Wendy says entirely without words.

And so it is that by the day of the ball Wendy has organised the flowers, table decorations, chosen the wines and found a band ('nothing too pricey dear, but no trash').

As the guests begin to arrive we simply do not know what to do with ourselves. The catering and service has all been taken on by an outside catering firm, it was always going to be far too big for us, so we are redundant in that respect. The guests who have plumped to stay at the castle breeze past us without the slightest acknowledgement and as the evening closes in and the guests all take their seats in the candlelit marquee we are left on the lawn feeling like Buttons and Cinderella. We're at our own castle but we've not been invited to the Ball. 'Unlike that ugly cow and her cronies,' Wendy chunters.

Even now I'm half expecting Martin to come running out of the tent to beckon us to our seats. But no. What I do see is he and Clarissa glance in our direction and then lean in to whisper to their guests.

'Ghastly people. Upstarts. How they'd ever think we would be interested in consorting with trade.'

'But jolly nice of them to allow you to use the castle.'

'Oh yes, we saw they'd be useful for something the first time we met. So eager to please. Sign of low breeding if you ask me.'

Although I'll never know for sure, that's how I imagine the conversation goes and their behaviour towards us in the future will do little to allay my suspicions.

In the weeks that follow there is the odd casual enquiry about why we weren't at the event but most people assume we were organising things behind the scenes and congratulate us on a first class do.

Wendy happily takes the praise especially as she can envisage Clarissa Blanchard-Cafferty choking on her coffee and biscotti at the very thought of it.

CHAPTER TEN

There can surely be nobody in Cumbria who isn't glad to see the back end of 2001. Six months of foot and mouth disease were followed, within days, by the horrors of 9/11 and overnight what had been a buoyant American market dissolved and it would be several years until its return.

For us, the stresses of raising two young children against a backdrop of all this turmoil are further compounded by Mum's increasingly erratic behaviour. Her relationship with Wendy has hit an all time low which we can only suppose is due to her lingering resentment at not being allowed to take on the mantle of substitute mother. Her regular Saturday mornings with Oliver which have been a life-saver to us for two years are suddenly and inexplicably cancelled and she refuses to help with anything of a domestic nature at the castle.

Half way through the foot and mouth crisis we quietly put the castle on the market and planned a move back south where we have more family and friends for support.

Mum, who had bought one of the cottages in the grounds that weren't part of our original purchase, is overly enthusiastic about the plan. She agrees to market her cottage jointly with the castle but leaves nobody in any doubt that if we have trouble selling the business she'll go it alone and move regardless. This reaction is, ironically, symptomatic of the reason why we feel we can't continue. There is no other support network and since she is all we have, we feel utterly isolated.

We are advised to put an advertisement in *Country Life* like the sort of drool-inducing ads for properties you wonder if anyone can afford which always look so manicured, inside and out, that they can surely not be inhabited.

Our agent tells us that it is customary to have houses made over for such celebrity exposure. Since we can barely afford to run the advertisement this is not an option and we plump for a quarter page (rather than the full page the agent would prefer) working on the logic that a smaller photo might disguise the shortcomings of the exterior (slipped tiles, missing lumps of masonry and the odd infestation of bind weed) and the interior (more than the odd chair fished from a skip, some ill-matched armchairs and some pretty ropey inherited curtains).

Small though it is, the ad does the trick and the agent manages to shift all of the 250 glossy brochures we have also had printed, at further extortionate cost, within a couple of weeks and there are a good half a dozen viewings in the diary.

When we first approached the estate agent, one of those upmarket international outfits which sell luxury yachts and waterfront developments in Key Largo and Marbella alongside The Old Rectory in Little Snobbing, Hampshire, he cautioned us about being too hasty.

'You'd be surprised at the number of people who start this process and then pull out.'

'No, no, we've thought about this long and hard. We're ready to move. This was never going to be forever, someone else with more cash can take it on and finish the job.'

And then, in the end, we decide to stay and we eat our words. Having seen some truly awful places in the south west of England we realise just how little we can get for our money compared with the castle. And, anyway, is it really the south of England we have our heart set on? Are we really yearning for more family support or is that just another word for interfering relatives? Don't we really want to be somewhere far further south that seems so utterly out of reach?

But it is the prospective purchasers who come to view who really put us off selling.

'Why isn't it finished?' asks a Chinese woman.

'Because we haven't got the money,' we reply.

'Obviously,' she says as she looks us both up and down and adjusts her jacket.

'Why are there so many flies?' asks another, 'is there something wrong with the place?'

'It's the country, you get flies.'

'Well, I've never seen flies like this in Kensington Gardens and I ride out there every day.'

But the real clincher comes towards the end of August. Having been sent on a very wild goose chase down to Devon to see what the agent has described as 'a hotel with the very best owners' accommodation he has ever seen,' we arrive back at the castle despondent. The owners' accommodation comprises a bedroom accessed from behind the kitchen and a basement living room which was once the disco. Even the mirror ball in the centre of the ceiling remains. So we are less than well disposed for a castle viewing scheduled for nine-thirty.

'Having difficulties making it pay?' asks Gerald who hails from somewhere in the Midlands.

'No, it's just with a young family...' but he's not listening.

As we walk into the music room he stops dead.

Wendy grew up in Africa so there is quite a bit of African art and other paraphernalia about the place which we can understand is not to everyone's taste.

'What yer got a bunch of bloody kaffers on the wall for?'

'I beg your pardon?' asks Wendy, astounded.

'Janey, come and look at this, it's like the League of Nations,' he calls to his wife who is bringing up the rear. 'Fucking blacks all over the walls.'

Wendy is having none of it. 'Do you mind, these are Joy Adamson's Kenyan tribal portraits and my father gave them to me.'

'Well I'd burn 'em, bloody savages. I hope you're not still speaking to him after a gift like this.'

'He's dead,' Wendy looks Gerald straight in the eye, 'now get out of my house and off my fucking land you bigoted bastard.'

The following day the agent rings to tell us he has a complaint.

Wendy doesn't even wait to hear the details. 'Who gives a fuck?' she says flatly, 'the castle's off the market.'

'Well, that's that then,' I remark, mostly to myself.

The process of marketing the castle shows us the potential we have in the place that is never going to be realised by moving elsewhere and focuses our minds on the job still to be done and our reaction to Gerald's invasion shows the place has a much greater hold over us than we would like to admit.

The agent is not surprised when we tell him we're staying although the manner in which Wendy delivers the message is, perhaps, a tad unconventional. 'Thought as much, I can usually tell.'

'Bet he can,' Wendy muses, 'but not before he's extracted as much cash out of us as possible in the process.'

The whole thing costs us the best part of £5,000 which we don't have. Luckily, offers of credit cards are dropping on to the doormat almost daily so we stave off the prospect of insolvency once again, this time courtesy of Citibank and face up to the pressing necessity to remortgage. If we're staying we're going to have to invest and do up the rest of the castle properly and we can't keep doing it on credit cards.

On reflection it's all a bit of a mess. We are still in love with the dream of another life which selling the castle may have allowed us to follow but we didn't even consider it at the time because of a loyalty to my mother. When we started the process we imagined we were all moving together and whilst we knew we wouldn't end up in the same place there was an assumption we'd be in the same region of the country, relations would be less strained and we would once again be able to play 'Happy Families'.

Now Mum decides to continue on her own course and we feel we have little choice but to buy her cottage. Having maxed every credit card, taken advantage of every cheap, no strings, no credit checks personal loan, spent all the child benefit, we have no option but to remortgage. Fortunately for us the value of the castle has increased significantly since we bought it, probably thanks in part to the eradication of the fungal growths.

When we moved in we bought just the main part of the castle, the Coach House and various cottages converted from the stables having been sold off separately before our tenure began. Mum had managed to buy one of the cottages when its occupant moved on and we had thought it the perfect solution. Space of her own, on site but not in our pockets.

But it wasn't to be and in many respects forced our hand in what would happen next.

So by early 2002 Mum has gone and we are truly on our own, more isolated now than if we had seized the opportunity to flee to France and that life we had always promised ourselves. And so, while we are resolved to stay and make the castle work, we are also resentful of having been corralled into a corner and maybe missing our best chance to go where we really wanted to.

I: 'I still don't get why she did that. She said it was too crowded with her and me and Wendy. We pleaded with her to stay and then told her if she wanted to sell the cottage, she could go and rent somewhere locally until she was sure she wanted to move away.

'She basically turned her back on the children and everything. What grandparent does that? Maybe she wasn't thinking about the consequences. She told others that she felt used and taken for granted.'

He: 'Have you ever stopped to think that perhaps you empowered her for the first time in her life to be able to do something for herself and not for anyone else?'

I: 'So she went to the other end of the country. Left us on our own. Selfish.'

He: 'Oh come now, she uprooted herself for you to buy the castle. That's not selfish.'

I: 'But we paid her back. She didn't have to just abandon her only real family. It was selfish.'

He: 'She spent her life not being selfish. She was a single mother after the war, gave her little girl up for adoption when the selfish thing would have been to keep her, nursed my father, she was practically a single parent to you and your brother and she nursed me. What was left for her, of her, out of all that? You picked her up, made her a part of something incredible but then she realised you didn't need her as much as she wanted you to so maybe that's when she decided it was her time.

'Clumsy, perhaps, ill thought out, probably.'

I: 'Don't you think she ever thought she'd made a mistake, when she saw the children becoming more distant, when she realised she was never going to have a proper relationship with Emily, that what she'd already built up with Oliver would crumble?

'Christ, Emily was scared of her when we went to visit. She would have loved Emily, the art, the painting, the sewing. They would have been like peas in a pod.'

He: 'Yes.'

I: 'She must have understood she'd thrown that all away.'

He: 'Yes, but she was never going to admit that to you, now was she? You who is so intolerant of other people's weaknesses and failings.'

I: 'And why am I so intolerant?'

He: 'Oh I expect you'll tell me it is because you haven't learnt to tolerate your own shortcomings. You're angry with yourself for not being perfect and that's all as a result of me being such a lousy father, expecting too much of you, making you feel like a disappointment to me and not reassuring you that it's OK to be a fallible human being.'

I: 'Something like that.'

Business bounces back, due in large part to a sizeable chunk of public money which lands in the lap of the Cumbria Tourist Board to help rehabilitate the county's tourism industry, rather belatedly acknowledged by the government (and perhaps grudgingly, by the farming community) as the biggest victim of the foot & mouth debacle.

To help us with the increased business we find ourselves becoming employers. To be fair, we wouldn't have got this far in one piece without Faye, our trusty Girl Friday who has been with us for a couple of years now and who so effortlessly fits in to every one of our family dramas that she hardly warrants a label, but our increased family demands mean we need further help.

As luck would have it a solution lies not very many yards away. Our neighbours, Bill and Esther are the farmers whose cows were culled at the very end of foot and mouth. Bill, who I have yet to see without his woolly hat, no matter what the weather, rather like Reg, catches up with me one day on the drive. I am filling potholes, sweating buckets and the sight of that woolly hat makes me wetter still. I have a whimsical notion that it may be knitted into his hair and only comes off once a year, maybe on Christmas Day when Esther presents him with a brand new one.

'I know it's a long shot but have you anything Esther could do for you?'

Esther has been a good neighbour to us, often riding shotgun on the tractor when we've needed some mechanical muscle to move fallen trees, dig ditches or bury... no, that's another story. But we haven't got to know her, she's always stayed in the shadows, out of the spotlight. So when Bill explains that since the cows have gone Esther has become more and more withdrawn I can see that he is really concerned.

'We can always keep ourselves busy,' he says, 'but Esther doesn't know what to do with herself without the routine of the farm. She's lost.'

Esther would later tell us that she found herself one morning lying in bed, something she had never done in her life, thinking 'there's nothing to get up for' as she listened to the unfamiliar silence of the farm yard outside her bedroom window.

It's no exaggeration to say that when she starts work with us the following week Esther wouldn't come out from behind the kitchen door. But, within months she is a different woman: talking with passion to guests about the countryside she has lived in all her life, joking with us and volunteering to do whatever is necessary. In fact, we can hardly keep her away. The children love her too and are always keen to hear about life on the farm.

Later that spring Bill finds me again. 'You've made a different woman out of our Esther. It's incredible. She has a whole new lease of life.'

'I'm glad Bill, really pleased, she enjoys it here.'

'Enjoys it? She loves it!' he grins.

Then the smile drops and, in an altogether more serious tone he says, 'But I need to ask you something. Esther really, really does love working at the castle but, and of course say no if you want, is it alright if she has some time for a holiday?'

I resist a wry smile as I know that matters such as holiday entitlement, sick pay and maternity leave will never have featured on Bill and Esther's radar.

'Yes, Bill of course and she'll get paid for it.'

Another victim of foot and mouth were the county and village agricultural shows so this year there is renewed enthusiasm for making them bigger and better than ever. There are the big shows such as the Westmorland Show, the Cumberland Show, the smaller shows like Penrith and Appleby, but some really serious business goes on at the individual village shows such as ours.

Our own Brough Show takes place on the third Thursday in August and we feel honour-bound to enter a few classes. The format is identical every year. And while sheep showing is the real reason for the event's existence, the goings on in the craft and industry tent are no less fiercely contested.

In future years we will find ourselves under pressure to enter various classes in the names of the children and then spend several frantic evenings during what is already our busiest month of the year creating edible monsters, a scale model of the entire Eden Project on a nine inch biscuit tin lid, a novelty knitted egg cosy (theme: *Doctor Who*) and a flower arrangement of two lilies and a daisy in half a grapefruit.

We will happily do this for the chance to see the children's delighted faces at being presented with a certificate and a little brown envelope containing up to 30 pence which, of course goes towards defraying expenses.

But for now the children are too young. So this year we are showing Holly, now four. She's not old enough to be in the 'vintage bitch' class which is a shame as we are breathless with anticipation at who might be showing in that one. Mentally I make a list of likely contenders which is inevitably headed up by Clarissa Blanchard-Cafferty but sadly it turns out to be just a lot of other dogs.

Emily is showing our cockerel, Keith, in as much as he arrives in a box secured to the back of her pushchair. We have to forfeit our place for Orville the duck because after 48 hours of trying, we give up on catching her. And for good measure we've entered a wild card in the 'random bantam' or some similarly named category.

Having surveyed the amount of work clearly involved in entering classes in the craft and industry tent we feel relieved that we are not making and doing in the names of the children, although Wendy has decided to try her hand at some adult classes and has entered a Victoria sponge, a photograph entitled 'a study of childhood', a flower arrangement of 'assorted colours of sweet peas in a Wellington boot' and a loaf of bread.

All entries are to be in the relevant tents by 8:30am and Wendy's hopes are pinned on the Victoria sponge. Working on the premise that it's all in the presentation she has gone to town with whipped cream, lashings of raspberry jam, icing sugar and a fancy glass cake stand. There is even a tiny posy of wild flowers on top. As she enters the cake tent and sees the other entries she is further buoyed and feels sure of a prize as every other cake is lying forlorn and forgotten on paper plates with no more than the merest scraping of jam between two halves.

The rest of our entries are duly positioned. Due to a lack of time we have delegated the bread to Faye, who confesses to be not very good at baking but is game to have a go. The animals deposited, we plan to return at lunch time, once the judging is complete, with Holly prepped for the afternoon dog show.

At one o'clock we're back. Wendy is in high spirits, sure she has triumphed with her Victoria sponge. We make first for the animals to find Keith has a third prize, and the random bantam has got a first prize rosette. Reg later tells us that Keith would have done better had we familiarised ourselves with the accepted protocol that fowl in shows are washed and blow dried the day before. I fix him with a sceptical gaze, unsure whether this is another slice of Westmorland blarney. We had just about managed to wash the mud off his feet and I can imagine taking his advice and turning up next year with a just-out-of-the-salon cockerel to howls of derision. No, Reg, we will not be washing and setting the chickens.

The random bantam must have had a lucky break because to our untrained eyes she is far from the most splendid specimen but we are happy to pocket 50 pence prize money.

Our modest triumph is somewhat overshadowed by a commotion on the other side of the tent. A guinea pig which was awarded a rosette has since expired and there is heated debate about whether the prize should be forfeited. The rodent's owner, a boy of around ten, is in tears. Whether it is because of the animal's demise or his impending loss of honours is unclear.

There's an announcement over the tannoy: 'Please can the secretary, please, attend the feather and fur tent. Please.' It's obviously a desperate plea. Several officials are already leafing through the rule book in vain as this is clearly a scenario which has no precedent. I decide to leave before things get even more heated.

Wendy has already gone ahead to check her entries, choosing not to linger in a tent filled with caged birds, rabbits and various domesticated rodents. We're a rosette, a certificate and 80 pence up on the day so far as we head for the produce tent. But as I catch her up, dark clouds are gathering inside.

Wendy's Victoria sponge has won nothing and she is spitting feathers. Apparently she overheard two of the judges reviewing their decision and one said to the other, 'Well it's not so much a cake as a gateau.' The winning cake is indistinguishable from the other entries and all are an unappetising shadow of Wendy's entry. I say that lessons may be learnt for next year but it's not a suggestion met with approval.

She is further enraged to discover that Faye's bread has won first prize. To add insult to injury, the judges have clearly missed the telltale hole in the bottom of the loaf made by the bread maker paddle. The winning photo in the 'study of childhood' class is a snap of a singularly un-photogenic child on the beach who is mercifully blurred whilst the comely blonde lying some ten feet behind is in pin sharp focus. Below the faces of our angelic duo is some 'positive criticism for next year' which we choose not to take on board.

And to top it all, Wendy's flower arrangement has been disqualified as she used a ceramic Wellington boot shaped vase whilst the unwritten entry criteria had called for a real boot. Other entries have arranged flowers in holes cut in to the boot which we feel is a terrible waste of a perfectly good pair of wellies when the prize money won't go anywhere near the cost of a replacement pair.

I suggest we go next door where tea is being served. There I ask if anyone would like cake with their tea.

'Cake!' exclaims Wendy, 'I wouldn't eat their cakes if I was starving.'

'Flapjack then?' My alternative suggestion fails to lighten the mood. Our one hope of family salvation is going to be Holly in the show ring as the tannoy announces: 'Would all vintage bitches please proceed to the centre of the field to be put through their paces.' Oh, if only I muse, spotting Clarissa Blanchard-Cafferty on the other side of the field. And then I wonder if perhaps it was she who was judging the Victoria sponges.

Holly disgraces herself in the gun dog retrieving class by running out of the ring and consuming a discarded burger by the refreshment van rather than retrieving the luridly coloured bean bag. Later we are so ashamed we try to switch dogs but are unsuccessful. Wendy is leaving and I too decide enough is enough, there being little point hanging on for the dog show prize giving.

But we'll be back next year on safer ground as I spy the entries in the classic vehicle rally which comprise a 40 year old tractor and a Morris Minor. Surely our splendid bright red 1967 MGB Roadster (bought on yet another credit card as part of our accumulate-debt-and-disguise-it-as-an-investment plan) is in with a chance, especially if Wendy agrees to take the wheel scoffing slices of her own sponge cake.

CHAPTER ELEVEN

Just as we are about to sign on the dotted line to buy Mum's cottage and effectively buy her out of the castle partnership, having already had to consign the possibility of another life in another country to the archives of our dreams, the Coach House, a substantial family home behind the castle, comes on the market. We're torn. Do we buy Mum's cottage which is effectively an integral part of the castle, will make good additional guest accommodation and is probably the better investment, or do we let that go to someone else and buy ourselves a stand alone family home?

It's an agonising decision made worse by the dalliance of other potential purchasers of the Coach House. One day it's on, then it's off. It is as if the house itself is tormenting us. Added to that you could hardly slip a fiver between the prices of each property; one a two bed-roomed holiday cottage, but part of a listed castle, the other a five bedroomed family house behind a listed castle. Clearly they are each worth much more to us than to anyone else but we can't have them both. The Coach House is separate in every way and although it is just twenty yards from the castle back door we convince ourselves that it makes more sense to let that go to strangers than the cottage. So the chance to have a home allowing us to have our own kitchen, own front door and some privacy slips through our fingers. And it would be a long time before the opportunity came up again. It's a major opportunity to materially change our lives. We have missed it and I blame my mother.

I: 'Did she realise that? Realise the consequences?'
He: 'I like to think she can't have but in reality I think she didn't care.'

I: 'She thought we were so loved up that it didn't matter where we lived.'

He: 'You're sounding bitter.'

I: 'Well I was at the time. We were living in two rooms above the kitchen. All we had to call our private living room was also the office. We had to share the kitchen so even when there weren't any guests we couldn't come downstairs for a cup of tea starkers because of the staff.

'We couldn't have a row without being overheard. We were bringing up our children in a goldfish bowl. Every bit of bad behaviour, every tantrum was on show and we had pretty much nowhere to drag them to for a good beating.

'Even upstairs staff could hear us through the ceiling. We even had a guest call the children brats who didn't know how to behave in public and that we made no effort to control them. It wasn't in public for them, it was the only place they could call home. But it was public for us, so what were we supposed to do? Public lashings every evening at six?

'The irony is that if we'd bought the Coach House, she'd have seen what a difference it would have made to our life, how the privacy would have relaxed us, and she would have felt much more a part of it, I'm sure of it. She'd have been part of something completely different.'

He: 'And you told her this?'

I: 'No, of course not, I told myself "she's being so stubborn just let her go!"'

He: 'Who was being stubborn? Perhaps you cut off your nose to spite...'

I: 'No! Well... it just wasn't that simple, that's all.'

A huge chunk of the capital we raise through the remortgage of the castle goes on buying Mum out so she can flee south. 'It's just so bleak up here,' is one of her parting shots as she practically throws her keys at us. It's not a personal criticism but it cuts deep into all our choices and all that we've worked towards and it hurts.

'Will you come back for Christmas?'

'I doubt it, I'll be busy unpacking.' There is no outpouring of emotion on the day she leaves. Kisses are cold and perfunctory. It's as if she is just going home around the corner. Ironic, as that is exactly what we tried to persuade her to do, move around the corner, up the road, to the next village but never to the other end of the country.

After she has left Wendy turns to me. There are tears in her eyes but I can also see her determination not to allow them to spill on to her cheeks.

'What did we do? She'll regret this for the rest of her life.'

'Probably but she got one thing right,' I reply.

'What's that?' Wendy asks almost pleadingly, unsure what could possibly be right about such an absurd situation.

'When she said during that row we had that first new year that we were so together we didn't need anyone else. She was right. We don't. She's just proved it by walking out of that door.'

'Maybe, but I'd really like to have someone else to choose not to need. We've got no choice now, we're on our own sink or swim.'

'Better start paddling then,' I'm putting a brave face on things but secretly I'm feeling bloody lonely and very, very isolated.

The rest of the capital we raise we use to renovate parts of the castle that are still barely habitable, strip out the school-style toilets and install some fabulous reproductions of Victorian thunder boxes which are utterly impractical but a great talking point, replace the rotten casement windows at the back of the castle with new sash windows to match the originals and refurbish our newly acquired cottage. We try pathetically hard to rename it to expunge the bitterness it represents but for several years it will remain 'Mum's Cottage' although to our guests it becomes Stableyard Cottage and later Stable House.

The completed project will result in an en-suite ground floor wheel-chair friendly bedroom, a bedroom suite with private conservatory, a brand new bathroom with vaulted ceiling, to complement Pendragon, our biggest bedroom with the back of the castle looking as good as the front and lavvies to be proud of. And then there is the cottage. We toy briefly with the idea of moving into it ourselves but it seems just not big enough and, while OK for a week's stay is not great for a permanent house with just two bedrooms and precious little storage or room to create it. But we don't have the cash to gut it so it will remain a throwback to the 1980s when it was first converted and, for a few years yet, will be the weak link in the expanding Augill estate.

As there is a fair bit of restoration involved as part of our new scheme we engage our good friend Elaine Blackett-Ord, the conservation architect, and our project seems right up her street. She has, in the past, been scathing about some of the things that Roddy, our previous architect, got away with but we remind her repeatedly that we did everything in the beginning on a shoestring.

Elaine jokes that it looks in places like he did his measurements with a shoestring but she does appreciate the relative luxury of now being able to help us with a project on which we have two shoestrings to spend. And she admirably counters any reticence on our part to spend. Elaine's husband Charles is a structural engineer, so together they're jolly useful.

When we were first introduced Wendy's reaction could not have been more unexpected. 'The Blackett whatnots?'

'Blackett-Ords.'

'Why does everyone around here seem to have double barrelled names?'

'Something to do with in-breeding probably,' I speculate, 'or because they're all prodigies of marriage out of wedlock.'

'A bunch of bastards then,' she concludes and we fall about laughing not least because, while we go by the name of Bennett my family name is Temple-Bennett and our family tree includes plenty of evidence of some serious action on the wrong side of the sheets.

Like the Blanchard-Caffertys, the Blackett-Ords are a family with much land and many houses. Unlike the Blanchard-Caffertys they are fairly modest. They own two of the largest houses in the vicinity (other than ours, of course) and like ours they are both fairly crumbly. But while our castle comes with 20 acres, their estate comprises 6,000 acres of land, most of which to me seems pretty much useless for anything other than shooting birds which is, of course, exactly what they use it for. Much like us they are not universally understood by the locals, so we've plenty in common (including, it must be said, a lot of the muddling through).

Elaine and Charles live in neither of the big houses but rather in another house on part of the estate. Just as our living quarters are always the last to be done up, so they live in a permanent state of unfinishedness, always, presumably putting their own plans on hold in favour of another job for clients.

The first of the family's homes is an imposing Georgian mansion, Helbeck Hall, on the other side of the village with impressive views of both Brough Castle, originally a Roman fort, then a Norman castle re-built in the reign of Elizabeth I, and now an English Heritage cared for ruin. The second is an equally gorgeous manor house dating from the 16th century at Warcop, the next village towards Appleby. It backs onto the army training camp which goes to show nothing's perfect.

We have, on occasion, been asked to cater for shooting parties in the the billiard room of Helbeck Hall, while we have been at pains to point out the advantages of our own establishment as a superior shooting lunch stop, an added attraction of the billiard room, which we simply can't match, is that there are separate tables for the guns and the beaters. It's all rather feudal and egalitarian at the same time. An unusual family, but in a comfortable sort of way. Many, it's easy to reflect, say the same of us.

The project is due to be finished by Easter in time for our 2003 summer season.

To say that things go smoothly would be an exaggeration but our friendship with our architect does ease the pain and eventually our expansion project is complete and we are ready for the summer with a total of eight letting bedrooms.

Reg comes and paints the new windows which takes three times as long as it should because he keeps sharing his pearls of wisdom on the state of the world.

'Tha's just got t'internet,' he tells us proudly and clearly it has broadened his horizons allowing him to travel the world in the darkened safety of his front room whilst still having never actually crossed the Westmorland county boundary. Clearly an early adopter in these parts, he is now an expert, or at least has expert opinions, on Gaza and the Palestinian issue, the war on terror, various 9/11 conspiracy theories, Iraq and George Bush. He talks almost intimately about Tony Blair and not in a complimentary way and idolises anything Tory as do most people in these parts much to the annoyance of Elaine who I regard as a Socialist leaning Liberal (her's is *The Guardian* that is kept hidden under the counter at the Post Office).

This, of course, is a red rag to a bull as far as Reg is concerned.

'Tha'd have ta give sheep a voting card and then a lobotomy ta geet enough votes for Labour in these parts.'

'Don't worry,' I reassure him, from my own very right of centre perspective, 'she takes her Socialism with a good glug (or should that be Krug) of champagne.'

And so the windows get painted by degrees. Slowly.

As we come to terms with our new situation and our increased financial burden we try to settle ourselves in to a mindset that this is where we have made our life now. The remortgage has allowed us to further develop parts of the business but also further binds us and the castle together in a shared destiny.

It's a tough pill to swallow as, in our hearts neither of us feels truly settled in this northern outpost. For several years my grandmother has allegedly been telling her bridge friends that 'she hardly sees her family anymore since they buried themselves alive in Cumbria.' Despite her very skewed view of the world, she can be remarkably perceptive. Then fate, that fickle friend, deals us a wild card. We get news that Sarah and Denis are quitting the south of France and moving back to New Zealand. Les Mimosas is for sale. It's as far south as this is north, as far towards our dream as this is away from it.

The weeks that follow are filled with soul searching. Are the cards stacking up in our favour? We've already lost out on the chance of a proper family home in the guise of the Coach House. Mum has abandoned us. The children aren't yet of school age. We've spent money on doing up the grotty bits that had put people off buying last year. Will this be our best chance to cash it all in and follow our hearts? What would the agent say whilst rubbing his hands gleefully if we went back to him now?

But foot and mouth, 9/11 and one expensive shot at selling the place have made us nervous. We ask ourselves if marketing the castle has made us see it's better to stick with what we've got than plunge into something new. But why? We've proved ourselves to be risk takers. We did it before, what has changed?

The answer: We have. Our circumstances have changed. Everything has. With a regret that we will never quite rid ourselves of, we turn our backs on the opportunity.

'We'll never be able to go back there with other people living our dream,' Wendy says.

'Perhaps not, but time will tell,' I reply gazing out of the window, south. Again I need someone to blame, and again it's my mother.

Over Easter we are persuaded to host a wedding later in the year for a local couple who have fallen in love with Augill having got engaged in the gardens on a visit the previous summer.

'We looked everywhere for a venue but nowhere has the same magic as Augill,' they swoon.

We have never done anything bigger than a dinner party for 24 and when they tell us they'd like to invite 120 guests we feel ourselves swooning.

We'll need a marquee, staff and a whole lot of thinking on our feet but we agree and the date is set for the beginning of September. Only once we have said we'll do the wedding does what we've taken on hit home. As we face up to this reality I am once again lost for appropriate words.

'Fuck.'

'Simon, will you stop saying that,' Wendy implores.

She's right. Oliver, now four was in the garden with his plastic tool kit just the other day and was heard quite clearly swearing to himself. His Mum told him that was bad and he replied, 'Daddy says that sort of thing about the guests all the time Mummy.'

'Sorry.

'But listen we have one domestic cooker, one domestic dishwasher, one kitchen table that can hold a dozen plates at a time and two members of staff. See my point?'

'Fuck,' Wendy replies.

Notwithstanding our verbal paralysis, we don't give in to defeatism and resolve to give the thing our best shot.

We find a reasonably priced marquee much closer to home than we had anticipated – two fields away. One of the tents from Brough Show is not booked out for a couple of weeks so we agree to take it early in return for a hefty discount.

It is not uncommon for people here to have several jobs and sometimes the size of their vans seems determined by the space required on the side to advertise the number of different jobs offered.

'S&M Services. The very highest levels of personal service assured. Large or small, we tackle it all' or 'Decorators, joiners, plumbers. Plus all electrical and computer servicing work undertaken. No job too big or small,' are not uncommon sorts of slogan on the side of a local tradesman's van.

The marquee people are also the local undertakers and joiners. It is obvious how the undertaking and joinery dovetail. The marquee business apparently supplements the undertaking in the summer months as there are less funerals. People, it seems, really do die of the cold which is perhaps why they don't advertise themselves as heating engineers. A clear conflict of interest. Another local marquee outfit also deals in tropical fish and aquariums and the link there is a little less obvious.

It's not the most salubrious tentage. Unlike the Blanchard-Cafferty's fully lined affair a couple of years ago with chandeliers dripping with foliage and scantily clad nymphs dancing around the central pole (actually that's what Martin might have wished for but he got his Bucking Bronco to ride instead), it is unlined, there is no hard standing floor and no lighting. Just as well they're having a barn dance.

The day before the wedding we manage to get a carpet and by the time Wendy has worked her magic with flowers and ribbons everyone is able to ignore the fact that, entirely lit by candles, the tent is actually a potential death trap. The marquee looks just as it should for a late summer country wedding.

We draft in family, neighbours, their children and friends to help. Clive and Jo, our slaves from Bath, both of whom we have seen a lot since Mike's car crash and have made much of what we have been through easier and much more fun than it would otherwise have been, help us to run the show. They are as clueless as we are about catering for such big numbers but that somehow makes the whole thing more manageable and definitely much more entertaining.

We balance a couple of four foot by eight foot plywood sheets on two sofas to make a serving table big enough for 120 plated starters and then it's heads down for three courses of hard graft. Once the food is over, we are invited to join the celebrations and it's three o'clock in the morning before anyone even begins to think about bed.

The weather has been fantastic and the day goes without a hitch prompting some serious outpourings of emotion from the bride the next morning.

'You were fabulous, both of you. You should do this again, it'll be a real hit.'

We mull this over and over and having experienced the fickle nature of tourists during foot and mouth and after 9/11 agree to apply for a civil marriage license for the castle. People will always, we reason, get married whatever else is happening in the world.

'Perhaps we'll get invited to join in with every wedding. It'll be like being paid to party every weekend.' We laugh at the thought as we nurse our aching feet and throbbing heads in the morning.

And with that another chapter opens and a whole world of experiences we could never have dreamt of are going to make our lives, if not a whole lot easier, then certainly a lot more fascinating.

Chapter Twelve

As the castle becomes ever more popular I grow more and more irascible. Whether it's the pressure of being constantly on show, the sheer absurdity of some people's behaviour or the burden of responsibility for such a great hulk of crumbling history, I am unsure.

Of one thing, though I have no doubt. Some of the situations in which I find myself would make the mildest mannered individual seethe.

It must be every householder's worst nightmare, but in a 200-year-old castle water dripping from the ceiling is more than just a bad dream.

It's howling a gale outside, the rain is coming at us horizontally and the roof is clearly not keeping it out. I'm walking up the main staircase when I feel a sudden cold clammy something on my head. I look up and another spot of water falls directly into my eye. As I squint to see where it is coming from I can make out with horror a dribble of water trickling down one of the ribs in the vaulted ceiling and it's running ever faster.

The last time I checked there was no vaulted ceiling section in B&Q. No easy three step click together panels for repairing curved plaster cornicing and gilded bosses. So there is nothing for it but to drop everything and investigate before the whole thing ends up on the floor.

First stop is the loft. The main access hatch is some 30 feet away from the staircase ceiling and there is no direct access above it so it's a case of shimmying along some beams and rafters and sticking my head, one arm, a shoulder and the torch sideways through a small access hole to see what's going on.

What I can clearly see (and it is rarely the case that anything is this immediately apparent) is that water is being blown into the roof space under some dodgy lead flashings. This means I am going to have to get out on to the roof and do some emergency repairs.

Time is of the essence, it will be dark in an hour and a half, the wind is blowing ever harder and I don't like heights unless I'm inside a pressurised cabin at 33,000 feet. As I tog up, Wendy tells me to be careful. I say that I will bear that in mind and thank her for the advice.

The roof is only really accessible in two ways: Either a) by abseiling down on to it from the top of the tower or b) squeezing through a tiny window half way up the tower and landing in a mucky puddle in a rain soaked gutter – rather like re-enacting Oliver's traumatic pub car park birth. It is, however, my preferred option of the two.

Once on the roof I fancy I'm quite dextrous and am soon in the required location straddling a ridge and ready to slide down the tiles to the valley gutter twelve feet below.

I've come armed with some sheet lead in one pocket of my Drizabone which has done nothing towards keeping me dry as a bone since I snagged it on the TV aerial on another heroic rooftop escapade when I was almost left dangling over the battlements by my sleeve.

I did manage to rescue myself on that occasion but my tales of near death and heroic self-rescue were eclipsed by the family's indignant howls that I'd completely messed up the television signal. I was hurt at the time that being left fatherless seemed less catastrophic than being left without TV. Fortunately we've now got a satellite dish instead (delivering more or less exactly the same programmes we all watched through the aerial) and I'm nowhere near it.

In my other pocket I've got some duct tape, some sticky gooey roofing tape and my super tool (a sort of Swiss army knife on speed, particularly as it's got a jolly good corkscrew on it). Wendy believes every man should take care of his super tool as she says you'll never know when it will come in useful. Along with 'do be careful on our storm lashed roof' it's invaluable advice I couldn't do without.

I'm soon done and sure that the problem will be at least temporarily fixed – which in castle speak means it should hold for a good ten years. But a far bigger problem now presents itself. As I turn to retrace my steps I'm faced with twelve feet of very slippery black slate roof tiles at about 45 degrees, the wind blowing straight at me and no resources other than my super tool and half a roll of duct tape.

The only way down is going to be to scale the battlements and get a long ladder brought round to the front of the castle. I ring down – never, never go onto the roof without a mobile phone – but it's engaged. I ring again and again – still engaged. Surely, I kid myself, someone must be concerned for my safety up here.

It's not long before I begin to wonder how long it will be before I am reported missing, will my swollen and bloated body be discovered next summer by a chance passing microlight fly past? After what seems like hours but is, in fact, probably about 60 seconds, the phone rings. I think, 'they've remembered me and while I'm up here they just need the television re-tuning.'

But no.

I answer, 'Hello, thank God, I'm stuck.'

'I'm trying to find reception.'

'What?'

'I'm looking for reception.'

'Never mind the bloody TV, I can't do anything about the reception, I'm nowhere near the satellite dish, who is this anyway?'

As I peer over the battlements at the front I see a very angry red-faced man jabbing his finger at the doorbell with a phone pressed to one ear and I realise that the castle phone must be diverted to me. I've been trying to ring myself and now this irate man is ringing me. I don't much care for the look of him but it's clearly unreasonable to blame him for my current predicament.

'Oh yes, sorry, reception speaking, how may I help?'

'I'm at the front door, it's raining and there is no answer to the door-bell.'

'I'm terribly sorry, I'm in a similar, perhaps slightly more precarious situation. I'm on the roof, it's lashing it down up here and nobody's answering the phone, I don't suppose you'd be able to nip around the back and fetch a ladder would you?'

'What?!' he bellows.

'No, OK, bad idea, just bear with me a moment.' He looks up and I duck out of sight behind a turret.

Just then I spot a cable to my left running vertically up and over the roof ridge and decide without any real thought for the possible consequences that this may be just the extra support I need to get over the top. It is indeed just enough to allow me the support I need to plant my feet in the right spots but as I reach the top the cable comes loose and although I am saved from dying a cold and lonely death, I can't help wondering if that might not have been a better end, for as my eyes follow the cable in my hand I realise it leads back to the satellite dish, or did.

I'm now faced with a choice: squeezing back through the tiny window or abseiling down the castle wall on the now disconnected satellite cable. I opt for the squeeze.

When I get downstairs (happily the repairs have been successful and the leak has stopped) I find Wendy placating the gentleman who says he has been insulted by a raving lunatic who claimed he was on the roof and demanded that he should fetch him a ladder. 'What sort of place do you think you are running?' he booms.

At the same time Wendy is trying to calm the children who are equally irate about the snowy screen on the television and the horrific prospect of an evening having to converse with each other. I back out stealthily and wonder about ending it all honourably and quickly by throwing myself on the pointy end of my super tool.

The roof incident highlights the twin demands of maintaining some family order whilst trying to preserve a level of decorum in front of guests and drives home to us the desperate need for a review of our living arrangements.

Elaine and Charles come to the rescue with a small farmhouse they are renovating for rental.

'We need to move, can we be your tenants?' is the simple plea over lunch one Sunday. They are somewhat non-plussed having not really witnessed the full scale of the turmoil that we have been going through since both children grew out of being happy with being clamped to the end of the kitchen table. But they are agreeable even though we all know, but are too wary of admitting, that the idea of mixing friendship with a landlord/tenant relationship is fraught with danger. Having survived the client/architect relationship, there is hope.

A few weeks later we are loading various choice pieces of furniture on to a trailer and trundling them a mile up the road to Lane Head Farm, our new address.

Strangely I have been drawn to this house for several years and even before knowing who owned it I once said, 'one day I will live there.'

The move confuses several people who cannot grasp the notion that a family who live in a castle need to move into a small farmhouse and rumours regarding our motives abound.

A few weeks after the move Wendy is shopping in the supermarket in Penrith when a tannoy announcement asks if Wendy Bennett could please go to customer services. Surprised that anyone should know she's in the shop she nevertheless does as she's told.

'Hello, you asked me to come. I'm Wendy Bennett.'

'No you're not,' the customer relations executive answers back, tersely.

'Yes I am.'

'No, Wendy Bennett works here. How weird,' the executive laughs. 'Would you like to meet her?'

'Not bloody likely,' says Wendy, horrified and she flees.

A couple of weeks later a mum at school says to Wendy, 'how's the new job going?'

'What new job?'

'In the supermarket... I heard your name called, asking you to go to the fruit and veg section. I was so glad that you'd got a job so quickly after having to sell the castle.'

Wendy is speechless and not because of the misunderstanding over the castle.

'Can you imagine,' she says to me later, 'me wearing a green and white striped tabard? Ugh.'

I laugh, 'and a white polyester trilby if you're turning the spit roast at the back of the shop.'

Despite the local confusion, the move gives us some long overdue privacy. There are, of course, guests who don't like the fact that we are off the premises. We have to drill Leighton, our latest Australian live-in help in how to be circumspect in sharing details of our exact living arrangements after we lose a wedding booking because he tells the bride that we are at home and just on our way to meet her to discuss details. She is horrified, not because we live elsewhere but because it means we may not be personally immediately at hand for the whole 48 hours of her wedding. It's one of the many examples of the unrealistic guest expectations that we have become accustomed to, and I tell Wendy that's one we probably can afford to lose.

As autumn turns to winter we revel in our new found independence. There are tearful farewells as Leighton, who has become almost a son to us, possibly because he has crashed the Land Rover so often that it is practically a new car and yet still managed to charm his way out of trouble each time, leaves for the next part of his world adventure.

Kerry, a vivacious Canadian steps into his shoes. She is the latest in a mini tradition of itinerant colonials who have kept Augill going, and us sane.

Matthew and Rebecca were our first live-ins when it was just us and Faye running the show. With children not much older than ours, Faye's hours were restricted and we desperately needed someone to cover overnight, house sit for holidays and babysit for the odd escape. We advertised in London with the offer of living in a castle as part of a young family. We were inundated with applications and when we went to London to interview everyone – in a corner of a coffee shop – Matt and Becca stood out a mile.

They came for six months in late 2001 and stayed for a year. They allowed us to take a holiday while keeping the castle open – a first – and they gave us a first taste of what it would be like to have grown up children.

Leighton followed in their wake and proved himself more than capable of filling their shoes. Many a late night he spent trying to convert us to a life of Christian purity. Unfortunately his own purity didn't extend to his year-long attempt to master the guitar. The awfulness with which he tortured the instrument only eclipsed by his enthusiastic but tuneless singing. Thankfully many a guest arriving at the castle forgave being serenaded in to the strains – a word used advisedly – of *He's Got The Whole World In His Hands.*

Whether because, or in spite of, Leighton's musical efforts we decide it is time to give something back and plan a charity Christmas concert for the second Sunday in December. Secretly, Wendy is thinking that if the Blanchard-Caffertys can put on a charity bash so can we and do it better.

Wendy spends much of the rest of the autumn cajoling local talent to give us their time and by the date of the concert she has assembled a line up of varied local musical talent who do, indeed, have varying degrees of talent.

We have sent out invitations, pointedly including one to the Blanchard-Caffertys who decline citing the fact that they have their own charitable causes. We hear later that they also have a grumble about the price being a bit steep if there's no dinner included.

'It's £25 including champagne and canapés. What do they want, blood?' Wendy is much more irritated than she'd like to be.

'Probably. They won't do anything unless they've had a good feed with their snouts in the trough.' I am of the view that it's another lucky escape.

As everyone gathers for the evening of choral delights, I'm struck at how familiar a scene it all is. It's like an episode of *Midsomer Murders*. One verse in to the first song, I'm fully expecting a discordant twang from the piano and the discovery of the body of a church warden, with a hitherto unsuspected shady past, stuffed inside.

Wendy, of course, is Joyce Barnaby, and I fancy that I, with the inevitable migration of my waistline towards all southerly points of the compass, make a passable Inspector Barnaby.

Sadly, though this is not to detract from the quality of the singing, there turns out to be no body and by the interval, having gasped several times at the talent of our local ladies, we are all now gasping for a drink. The children have been told that they must attend to listen to Mummy's singing whether they like it or not and the first half has not been without its trials. Half way into the first number, Oliver has counted up how many songs there are until the end and is happy to share this information with anyone who'll listen.

Having all downed a hearty supper of chilli and rice before commencement of the proceedings, Oliver is the first to announce in a stage whisper that he has let one off. This, of course, sets Emily giggling in the sort of uncontrolled way of a four-year-old that invites attention. I am no more grown up about the whole thing and before long all three of us have shoulders heaving up and down and we are farting in time to the music. I can only guess how Wendy is coping in the choir as she had second helpings. Fortunately, we are hidden from Wendy's view by the conductor so she doesn't see us misbehaving and our gas releases seem to have been absorbed into the soft furnishings. Nevertheless, it's a relief to eventually get to the bar where it's bliss-fully quiet because most of the rest of the audience have gone in the opposite direction for tea, coffee and the champagne and canapés they have paid good money and skipped supper for and are not going to be done out of.

Shortly before the second half, Oliver and I disgrace ourselves again. Oliver is standing in Wendy's place imitating her singing facial expressions and I am waving the conductor's stick around in the style of *Monty Python* when the pianist comes in behind us to check her music. I resist the temptation to lighten the moment by reassuring her that I have checked the piano for bodies and it's all clear, replace the baton gently on the music stand and back away quietly. Oliver just legs it.

There's a sudden shriek from the dining room. A murder perhaps! I hurry to investigate and yes, a crime has definitely been committed but the blacksmith's wife doesn't get out much so she can't be held guilty of wearing pink, orange, and green together. It's clearly her late sum-mer herbaceous border look and we can only be thankful that she did-n't plump for her spring look as daffodil yellow, pink and green would surely have warranted an arrest. The shriek was, in fact, in response to Sooty, our very old but still agile jet black cat who has sneaked up onto the table and is making light work of the spicy lamb koftas. The inevitable after effects of those mean he's definitely being shut out tonight.

It's time to resume our seats for the second half not a moment too soon. Emily, Oliver and I decide to take up seats on the back row on a squishy low sofa where nobody can see us. Holly, our omnipresent black Labrador, joins us so we all squeeze up and try to behave our-selves. Holly hasn't had any chilli for supper but this seems to make no difference to the workings of her insides and she has soon disgraced herself as well so we shoo her away to join Sooty outside.

It's a lovely evening. People from all walks of local life have come together to enjoy some pleasant music and Wendy loves being involved in it all.

Once the entertainment is over, there's a marked segregation of the crowd. With the champagne exhausted, the 'I need to park so I can get away' two thirds of the audience have their coats on and are effecting a speedy escape.

'Lovely evening dears but I can't help feeling it's a bit late,' confides one elderly lady as I help her on with her coat. It's 11pm and looking around the hall I can't see many people who will have to worry about getting up for work in the morning.

The rest of us, most of whom do need to get up in the morning but have still got some *joie de vivre* left in our lives, head for the bar and against everyone's better judgement Wendy breaks out the homemade limoncello.

Chapter Thirteen

Now that we are feeling more settled as a family and have a routine independent of the castle our attention turns to the children's schooling. Oliver is not thriving at school and we can see that his progress since reception, when he made such a good start, has faltered and now, in year two, has stalled.

The headmaster, who had originally encouraged us to start Oliver at school aged four and one week rather than to hold him back until after his fifth birthday, completely against our own instincts, now says his lack of progress is just due to his immaturity.

'You mean he's in the wrong class?' We counter.

'He is very young for his age,' he says flatly.

'This is only a small school, surely he should be able to get some specialist help?'

'He's too young to identify any specific problems, he's just immature.'

'He's six – of course he's immature.'

I am exasperated, being chair of governors I am at once dissatisfied with how the school is failing to address my concerns as a parent but loyal to the school as an institution.

But we are increasingly worried. Emily is due to start school in September and we are not confident that Oliver's needs are being addressed.

So it is that after Easter Oliver begins a new school. It's a big wrench for him as he has made good friends and the new school is twenty miles away. It's a culture shock for us too as we have taken the big step of going private and we are far from sure we can really afford it. The decision has been made easier by the death of my grandmother who left a modest legacy with instructions, albeit informal, that we should use it to 'launch the grandchildren' and we consider school fees to be a worthy embodiment of that sentiment, although I suspect her motives may be driven by her belief that they are already at a distinct disadvantage being brought up in the north of England.

The new school suits Oliver in many respects, not least because it provides ample outlet for his sport for which he shows, if not yet an extraordinary aptitude, certainly a healthy appetite. In any event, it is certainly the release he needs from his frustrations in the classroom and we see him slowly begin to blossom. Our minds are then made up that Emily will join him in September.

The decision to educate both the children privately is not, of course, met with a great wave of approval at their former village school.

'CHAIR OF GOVERNORS OF CHURCH SCHOOL EDUCATES HIS CHILDREN PRIVATELY' is not the sort of headline any school seeks. The diocesan director of education makes it clear that my position as chair is now untenable as if paying fees for one's child's education is like cavorting naked with Lucifer himself. Other governors are unsure about their position and are split between their loyalty to the school and their personal relationship with Wendy and I.

Surprisingly we receive most gestures and comments of support from the teachers. Oliver's reception teacher, a formidable character, sums it all up. 'You have to do what you think is right for your children, not the school. Only you can make that decision. Only you know what's best for Oliver and don't let anyone tell you otherwise.'

In a rather over dramatic manner, rather akin to a Secretary of State's resignation speech to the House of Commons and wholly unnecessary for a village school I deliver a statement to the governors at our next meeting. Outlining our decision and affirming my continued support for the school, I invite them to decide whether they wish me to continue as chair. I leave the room while they discuss the matter but it is little surprise that I am soon called back in to be told that I am welcome to continue in the post.

My suspicion is that nobody else wants the poison chalice of being the chair and, if I'm fool enough to carry on, they're happy to have me.

Our move to Lane Head, the continued growth of the business and change of school coincides with a marked improvement in our local relationships. Whilst we have always had our staunch supporters and only a relatively small number of detractors, the majority of the local populous have viewed us from afar with suspicion and a great deal of caution.

Like Reg they see us as exotic imports. But unlike Reg they translate this as 'handle with care'. There are times when we feel like our menacingly overgrown London shrub: Gorgeous to look at but from the safety of the other side of the road.

Consequently I am delighted to receive a phone call from Richard Gilbert-Standish inviting me to a meeting of the Upper Eden Rotary Club. He makes no bones about his motivation. 'We're all getting on and we desperately need some young blood.'

I am particularly delighted because he obviously isn't holding a grudge over my nearly killing his wife. I want to assure him that I have not since picked up a shotgun but his manner is such that I feel further discussion of that incident totally unnecessary.

It's six and a half years since we moved to Augill and the place is unrecognisable. We now have ten letting bedrooms (having converted the rooms we used to live in in the north wing) and two self catering cottages, having said goodbye to another set of neighbours.

But if the castle itself is unrecognisable, so is the business we're in. Since we moved to Cumbria we have seen the birth of the technological revolution. Websites are now a must, most people have mobile phones and email has become the primary method of communication. We are feeling terribly grown up with a computerised reservation system and we are on to the second version of our website. And with all this technology comes a new breed of guest.

Whilst a few years ago we had a guest who remarked, on seeing one of our bedrooms, 'I suppose super kingsize beds haven't got this far north yet,' we are now more used to comments regarding communications. 'No need to ask if there's any mobile reception all the way out here,' and they are pleasantly surprised to find there is. And in just a couple of years' time it would be an insatiable need to stay connected that would drive guests to demand wi-fi in every corner of the castle (a question to which we would proudly be able to say, 'yes, throughout the castle there is a great wi-fi signal, even on the lavatories).

Would the simple life we'd once hankered after in rural France have brought the same kind of demands? The simplicity of everything that is so readily accepted in a culture that seems to attach far less importance to material surroundings just wouldn't make the grade here. Perhaps that's because in southern Europe, where a bedroom is just a place to sleep because the rest of life happens outside, hospitality is about the people not the place. It's what Sarah and Denis told us years ago at Les Mimosas. That is what we have tried to create here and while we are pretty good at focussing on people, too many people still put place and surroundings first.

In France, Italy or Spain a lack of rural mobile reception is charming. In Britain it is taken as nothing short of a personal affront. Inevitably such attitudes tend to be attached to urbanites, especially those who have deigned to leave London to visit us. And they often bring a lot of other baggage which is quite alien to our conservative northern cultural landscape. Perhaps it's the same with Parisians who travel south but I prefer to think not.

A friend has called to warn us of some guests she is sending our way. It seems an odd thing to do and she is reticent to give me any details but I detect a hint of mischief in her tone. My suspicions are confirmed later that evening when Saffron and Basil arrive at the castle. They are typical London types. Saffron has that sort of north London respectability with a slight edge which suggests she was brought up in Hampstead but has reinvented herself to originate from down-market Camden down the hill or at the very least Belsize Park. Basil, on the other hand is one hundred per cent Notting Hill (or North Kensington if you prefer).

They clearly work in media as neither of them can be parted from their mobile phones and as soon as they have crossed the threshold are stressing about the best reception hotspot and whether they can get a full signal on their phones. When I tell them that we have reception for all known networks as long as they don't stand too close to the leaded windows they survey me with utter incredulity.

'It's true,' I grin. But they don't believe me and Saffron is already walking through the castle sweeping her device from left to right at arms length in front of her for the best signal. 'I don't think it makes any difference how far...' I begin but think better of it. 'Basil, let me show you around and then we'll go upstairs to your room.'

'Ooh Basil,' trills Saffron, 'that's the best offer you've had for weeks.' It's hard to say, given Basil's Notting Hill skin tone, but I'm pretty sure he's blushing. I, on the other hand, am just covered in confusion.

When we eventually reach the bedroom I am wondering whether we have made a terrible gaffe with the booking and that perhaps Basil and Saffron are not, shall we say, compatible bedfellows.

No need to worry however, since Saffron, who clearly has no secrets from anyone and doesn't respect anyone else's either, proceeds to tell me that Basil has just broken up with his partner Horatio, whom she apparently never much cared for, to the extent that she even tried to sabotage a trip Basil had planned to introduce Horatio to his grandparents in St Lucia, and she has taken it upon herself to 'reorientate him sexually and spiritually'.

'OK...' I am feeling increasingly uncomfortable, 'so this is your room key, please keep it with you and ensure your bedroom door is locked at all times,' and I'm out of there, making a mental note to lock my bedroom door tonight as well.

By breakfast the next day we have named Saffron and Basil the herbivores. They are clearly late sprouting herbivores at that, eventually surfacing at noon. We ask them if they would like a late breakfast and Saffron shoots us another one of her looks of incomprehension. It seems she has no idea what breakfast is or what it looks like and even if she did she'd have no time for it as she is already giving her right arm another workout waving her phone high above her head searching for that elusive fourth pip of reception whilst simultaneously texting.

Basil, who I'm sure is now glowing rather than blushing, perhaps due to a hot bath, perhaps not, says they would like to walk to the nearest lake. It is now my turn for incredulity. Firstly, I tell them that the nearest lake is half an hour away by car and secondly I point to the weather. But Saffron looks positively hurt.

'I've bought all this outdoor gear specially,' she wails. Saffron is wearing a pair of silk pink camouflage cargo pants, a pair of knee high black leather boots and a bat wing cardigan over a flimsy shirt. Catching my reaction she continues moodily, 'I've brought a coat and a hat too.'

I don't venture to ask what camo-colour they are and opt instead to show them where we are on a map although this may be of limited usefulness since we are well beyond even the northernmost end of the Metropolitan line.

While Basil and Saffron are out I ring our friend to thank her for the recommendation. She roars with laughter and asks if they have had dinner yet. I tell her that they haven't but that they are booked in later and the peals of laughter die away as she has obviously fallen to the floor in the throes of a mirth induced orgasm. And so it is with some trepidation that we await the herbivores' return.

I happen to be in the hall when Saffron tumbles through the front door and so have little choice but to enquire after their day although I know I'll regret asking.

She excitedly tells me that they have been to the highest pub in England, the Tan Hill Inn which is about nine miles away.

But she's not happy. 'There was a sheep.'

'Just the one?' I manage to sound surprised, if not interested.

'In the pub. There was sheep in the pub!'

'Oh yes, that's quite normal,' which is no lie.

'But look,' she is becoming hysterical as she shows me her trousers. She has got sheep poo on her combats which she is concerned isn't going to come out. I suggest that in my experience all poo of whatever origin comes out after a good boil wash.

'Boil!' she shrieks. 'One, these are DKNY, two, they are organic silk and three, washing anything above thirty degrees is going to destroy the planet.'

I then learn that this is not the worst of the afternoon's events as she continues her tirade. 'And when we got to the pub we couldn't get anything, nothing at all.'

'That's odd', I say, 'they usually serve food all day and I've never been up there and not been able to get a pint at the very least.'

By this time Saffron has reached the pinnacle of her hysteria. 'I'm not talking about the food or the drink, I mean we couldn't get any signal,' and she's jabbing at her phone to reinforce her point. When Basil walks in, in an altogether better frame of mind, I suggest he takes Saffron upstairs and draws her a long hot relaxing bath with, perhaps, a bottle of champagne. Surely things can only get better from here. How wrong I am.

Unfortunately Basil doesn't drink and by the time they reappear for dinner, Saffron has drained the whole bottle of champagne by herself, plus the decanter of sherry in the bedroom, and all this on top of two pints of Dirty Ewe Ale she had at lunch, presumably to try to get over the dirty ewe whose poo is now on her trousers.

By the time the three of them (that's Basil, Saffron and Saffron's phone) join the table for dinner she is incoherent and quite unable to coordinate eating and texting simultaneously). Basil asks if it may be possible for Saffron to retire to her room with perhaps just a starter. That's no problem and I suggest that we can take the rest of her meal up to her.

'No need, she may just manage the starter and then she'll be out cold.'

Unencumbered, Basil is a delight and thoroughly enjoys his evening. We don't see Saffron again and after breakfast as Basil is paying his bill he tells me that he fully intends to give things another go with Horatio.

Add to this sort of encounter an ever more bizarre array of dietary requirements, the need for non-allergenic pillows, allergies to anything that can be eaten, allergies to anything which moves or even which doesn't, and it is no wonder perfectly good men and women lose their minds at the hands of the public.

Day to day we just don't know what is going to happen next or who is going to step through the door and yet the 'Ten Steps to a Successful Career in Customer Service' manual (or should that be Manuel) by B Fawlty will tell you that we should anticipate the customer's needs before they even know what it is they need themselves. Trouble is, customers are much more *au fait* with their own requirements than ever and while they may not always be good at communicating them in advance, they are usually very vocal when we haven't anticipated them. But there are always those who, not only keen to share the information, as a bonus also have an intimate knowledge of everyone else's needs and know exactly what we need to be doing to run a better business.

We call them our SNC (special needs customers).

Luckily our anticipation antennae can usually spot them at the initial telephone enquiry stage at which point any one, or a combination of a battery of tactical avoidance measures can be deployed such as, 'I'm sor...{crkhrkrkck}...ry the line is ver...{crhckhk}...y bad, I'm los...{crkhcrkhcrh}...ing you... beeeeeeep' or 'can you please hold I have another call' and then 'sorry about that... hello, hello, hello.'

Occasionally, very occasionally, the antennae breaks down and then the fun really begins.

It is a Friday like any other. We are prepped and ready for a full weekend and you can cut the anticipation laden atmosphere with a knife.

The doorbell rings. I have had a troubled week and Wendy reminds me that we must not let the guests know that we have a real life too, complete with real issues, where everything doesn't always go swimmingly and so I should always smile and be enthusiastic.

'We are selling a fantasy. Remember to smile and be enthusiastic.'

I don't know why she tells me this but I sense that she feels these are qualities which don't come naturally. Nevertheless, I bound towards the door with such exuberance wearing the ridiculous countenance of the Cheshire Cat that I must look as if I have recently mistaken a slab of chocolate brownie for either a hash cake or a bar of ex-lax. Or maybe it is just a sugar rush.

'Hello I'm anaphylactic.' I'm taken aback. Usually I find myself introducing myself first and then looking enquiringly for a response. More often than you'd think, I have to actually say 'And you are...? But not so today. I'm only left to wonder whether I should address our newest guest as Ana or Miss Phylactic.'

I'm tempted to say, 'Well, welcome to Augill, I'm Heinrich Manoeuvre, do come in,' but resist. I don't get a chance to enquire as to her real name as she has so much to tell me. As I am showing Ana and her partner (who has yet to utter a word, and it's not difficult to see why) around she is telling me that she has sent emails and discussed her requirements with reception on the telephone. I assure her that, although we don't have a reception, it's all been noted, making a mental note that the antennae must be rigorously tested as it's obviously developed a fault.

As we walk through the dining room she's clearly not one to mince her words and asks, 'Are there any nuts for dinner?' Again I think, but don't say, 'Only you love'.

In the bedroom I am quizzed about the bedding which we have already anticipated, the toilet paper which we haven't but it's alright because she's brought her own, the toiletries which she can only be satisfied are organic if I produce a hazard analysis sheet and finally there's a request for the coffee to be removed from the tea tray (she doesn't explain why). She is happy that there is a fridge to store her soya milk in but only if we remove the real milk first. Fortunately we have two guest fridges and a dairy free exclusion zone is soon in place.

By the time I get back downstairs I'm exhausted. I feel the need of a mug of caffeine with lashings of lactose and a slab of gluten.

I recall a recent guest who commented that we'd made so little fuss about her very serious dietary requirements by incorporating them into the menu that she could almost forget them, which for a terminal cancer patient is a pretty big deal. But the truth was, it was her own lack of unnecessary fuss that made the whole situation so easy to handle. With the right information up front, nothing more need be said.

Just then the telephone rings. It's the Phylactics from upstairs. I hope that the window hasn't swung open and she's had an adverse reaction to the fresh air but happily it's nothing quite so serious. She just wants to check that the flapjack in the bedroom is safe to eat.

'In what way safe?' I ask.

'Brian is gluten intolerant so wants to know if it contains flour and I'm unsure about whether there are nuts in it.' I explain that we started baking flapjack instead of shortbread for the rooms so that coeliacs could enjoy a little something with their tea too and no, there are no nuts in the flapjack, just lots of sugar. I sense a sharp intake at the mention of sugar but she seems impressed that I know what a coeliac is and leaves it at that.

As well as the challenges presented by the ever increasing expectations of our regular guests, we have now to contend with a steady stream of brides as we are now hosting the equivalent of one wedding every other weekend. This is, of course, terribly good for business and the accountant nearly wets himself when he sees the effect this has on our profit and loss account which until recently was just a loss account. But he is not having to deal with the reality.

Neither of us could have anticipated what sheer hard work running a wedding really is, regardless of whether the bride (for it is always the bride who is the pivotal character) is stressed or not stressed, likeable or detestable.

It's an eighteen hour day for us from the early breakfasts for the bridesmaids prior to their three hour makeovers (more in some unfortunate cases) to the chucking out of the last, often flirtatious, always drunk and sometimes violent stragglers. And one or both of us is expected to be there every step of the way. Luckily a good seven out of ten brides are delightful and in fact, several become personal friends and their weddings are, inevitably, the easiest gigs.

Another one out of ten are so stressed that they just aren't really with it and miss the entire thing, not relaxing until after breakfast on Sunday morning when it's all too late. One such bride, realising this is what had happened, insisted that everyone should get dressed up again for another round of photos on Sunday morning which was a good decision since she was so stressed out in the original photos that her face resembled that of a Gloucester Old Spot. Unfortunately her de-stressed unmade-up face wasn't a great improvement but she was, at least, smiling.

A further one out of ten are so unstressed that they are incapable of making a decision. This becomes very stressful for us as we don't really know what is going on and usually have to take matters into our own hands which, of course, suits the bride who can then remain metaphorically, and sometimes physically, horizontal for the remainder of the weekend.

And then there are the Bridezillas, a term I always thought ridiculous – until we started doing weddings.

Bridezilla refers to, of course, not the bride's physical size (a larger than life bride would surely be called a Bride Kong – more of her later) but to her angry and aggressive manner or just to her distinctly outlandish ideas.

One bride is determined to have her two cats as bridesmaids but the registrar tells her that it will demean the solemnity of the occasion so two life-size feline cardboard cut-outs survey the ceremony from either side of the registrar's table instead. They had been kitted out with white taffeta dresses for the photo shoot.

Another chooses to hold a seance before she gets married in order to bring her late mother into the proceedings. We are then asked to lay a place for her at the wedding breakfast and serve a full meal at the empty seat.

One demands that Wendy should be on site and available for the entire day to the extent that when she is not at the bottom of the stairs before the ceremony she refuses to go any further. And another is so big that her dress is actually two stitched together (although you can't see the join). She is our Bride Kong whose over-bearing personality actually frightens us into submission and we are obliged to spend the entire evening with her and her family singing songs.

But if weddings can be bizarre we can console ourselves that we have a house to go home to where there is nobody lying across the herbaceous border, no vomit in the toilet and no drunken sing-songs keeping us awake until God knows when o'clock.

And yet we are strangely unsettled.

Our neighbours may have a point. Why are we living in a rented farmhouse when we have a whole castle at our disposal?

Chapter Fourteen

Our second Christmas at Lane Head is approaching and we are feeling more unsettled than ever. We have found ourselves spending more and more time at the castle, returning to the farmhouse later until it is almost no more than a dormitory. The children find it difficult.

'I don't know where home is anymore,' complains Emily.

Sometimes the smallest things can trigger the biggest changes. During the second week in December our usual batch of Christmas trees arrives at the castle and we spend a day feverishly decorating them before the children return from school because of Wendy's insistence on symmetry of colour and design.

That evening we erect a smaller tree at Lane Head and unpack a motley selection of leftover decorations and in stark contrast to the nine feet high blue and silver, red and gold and pink and white tress we have at the castle we have a three feet wide, two feet tall shrub covered in every colour of the rainbow plus the children's school-made offerings.

Wendy stands back and surveys the thing with disdain. 'It's crap,' she spits.

'Mummy!' exclaims Oliver indignantly.

'Well it is. The tree, this house. We're like refugees. We own a castle, we market it as a family home and we're not there. It's not working. Children where do you want to live?'

'The castle,' they both chime.

'Daddy, where do you want to live?'

'The castle. But where? We've turned our old rooms into guest bedrooms.' I'm trying to sound a note of reason even though I can see Wendy getting excited already.

'Mum's old cottage, the Stable House. It's not really working as a holiday house, it's letting us down. It's grubby, it's damp. We can gut it, re-model it and it'll be fine. There's room for three bedrooms, just. We don't need a laundry or a big kitchen. It'll be the best of both worlds. Our own house next to the castle, I don't know why we didn't think of it before.'

And while we all know that it is small and it will take some adjustment – the children will have no space for toys in their bedrooms so will have to have a playroom somewhere else in the castle, there'll be no room for a study or office and our dirty smalls will have to be mixed in with the castle's laundry again – nobody can think of a strong enough argument against doing it.

There are decisions in life that, only once they are made, do you realise that everyone else was just waiting for you to do so. This was one of those decisions.

'Oh at last,' 'Thank goodness, you didn't seem settled' and 'you'll be so much happier back at the castle' are just some of the comments from the staff, our friends and family that follow a common theme.

We engage the services of a local builder to do the renovations, but it quickly becomes obvious that the job is way beyond him and as the project drags on for month after month we become increasingly frustrated. It doesn't help that when we tell him we need to be in by Easter or we'll be homeless he tells us he has a two week holiday to Florida planned.

'Cancel it,' I tell him and I'm not really joking.

'I'll do as much as I can before I go,' he promises and we hardly see him again.

Eventually we decide the best thing to do is to give up Lane Head and move temporarily into our other holiday cottage, which is also not up to the same standard as the rest of the castle's accommodation. It is an even smaller version of our intended new home and, stuffed with our favourite pieces of furniture that we're loath to give back to the castle, we face the prospect of an indeterminate stay having to edge round the corner of a sideboard to get to the bathroom and peering over the top of a chest of drawers to watch the television. But at least it's a base from which we can exert daily pressure on our errant builder.

It's all far from ideal but we're back on our patch and feel happy for that. The children settle straight back into castle living and we realise what it was they missed. Freedom to roam and limitless outdoor space.

And it's not long before Oliver is making plans. He has decided now we are once again surrounded by our own fields we should start farming. God knows why. Up at the crack of dawn, toiling for eighteen hours a day feeding and watering ungrateful beasts – sounds too much like running a hotel to me.

'Well, we've got chickens,' I say encouragingly, 'and we grow a lot of vegetables'.

'No, Daddy, properly. Sheep, cows, pigs.'

He is a canny lad and has noticed that it is farmers, particularly some of the parents at his new school, who are running around in shiny black hearse-like pick-ups (apparently there are tax advantages even with turbo charged four litre engines) and new Range Rover Vogues (invariably driven by mums who look as much like farmer's wives as Victoria Beckham) with ultra low profile tyres that probably couldn't even cope with your average B road. But that is North Yorkshire. On this side of the Pennines things are a little more grounded – the Range Rovers have proper chunky tyres and some pick-ups have even been spotted with sheep in the back (although I am sure that the tax advantages still trump the sheep in most cases). He is an entrepreneur and has heard there is money to be made from selling lambs, producing bacon and even milking cows (although of the latter I am not so sure).

To this end, he has already eyed up a corner of the workshop for a chest freezer for the bacon and other prime cuts from two fattened pigs and last year at summer camp proudly came home with a present he had made especially for his mum: a three legged milking stool. Needless to say Wendy is under-impressed when she produces it from the back of a cupboard, even more so when I suggest that someone might knit her a Heidi-style woolly milk maid's hat with dangley bits on it. To make matters worse, she sits on the stool and it collapses under her. This is, of course, greeted with peals of laughter from the rest of us and I, rather tactlessly, comment that it was just as well that didn't happen when she had a couple of teats in hand, a pail of milk between her legs and a bovine tonne or so bearing down on her.

Emily is totally behind the farming scheme but with very different objectives. She does not approve of killing anything, although this has yet to come between her and a good fillet steak (or *foie gras* for which she developed a particular taste on a recent trip to France) so sees the future of a farm at Augill as offering animals longevity and a full-rites funeral when they eventually pass away of old age.

So, it is down to me to introduce some common sense to the debate. We have often talked of keeping pigs. Chickens we already have and since we are permanently surrounded by other people's sheep, it seems a natural progression to have a few of our own. But cows? None of us would know where to start with a cow other than that grass goes in one end and either milk or pats come out the other. It seems most likely we would end up with grassless fields, lots of manure and not much milk (perhaps just as well given the current state of Wendy's milking equipment).

'We'll look into it,' I say, to which there are harrumphs all round as this is, apparently, what I say to every idea that I have no intention of taking further. 'No, honestly, we'll go and talk to Bill and Esther.'

When I mention the idea that the children want to start a farm, Bill roars with laughter and Esther rolls her eyes. They put me right on the bureaucracy of keeping livestock, something I hadn't even considered, and start talking to me about holding numbers and transfer licenses.

I report back to the children. 'Darlings, it's not as easy as it sounds,' which is greeted with more harrumphing and wails of what a useless parent I am which is no more than I was expecting. 'Just because it's more complicated doesn't mean we can't look into it further...' but nobody is listening anymore.

In truth, our oft discussed piggery has moved a step closer since we were offered a couple of pigs which are part of a breeding programme to reintroduce the Cumberland pig (of sausage fame). Apparently some DNA has been extracted from a Penrith peasant's purse made out of an old Cumberland sow's ear and this has been analysed to find the best genetic match in modern cross-bred varieties.

It sounds exciting but given that humans, pigs and cabbages all share enormous quantities of the same DNA it could all be nothing more than bubble and squeak. And still, just like Beatrix Potter's *Pigling Bland*, there's the matter of the pig license. Not to be deterred by the bureaucratic delays, a few days later Emily finds an alternative fluffy distraction.

Charlie and Lola have beautiful soft silky black coats, little pink snouts and big paws not unlike a Hobbit's feet. They are quite endearing up close and belie the devastation they wreak in the wild. Emily has stumbled upon them in the hedgerow – it's quite an achievement.

They are not demanding but Emily decides she should make them a couple of cotton bonnets as she feels they need warming up which is hardly surprising as Charlie and Lola are moles and are stone cold dead. Emily has found them in the hedgerow between one of our fields and Bill's; Bill being a first class mole catcher much in demand.

Em is old enough to know that dead moles can't come back to life – they are much happier to be digging up the big green lawn in the sky and so am I – but if there were marks for wishful thinking she'd be top of the class.

But Charlie and Lola have given Oliver another idea and he's off on his bike in the direction of Bill and Esther's farm whilst I resign myself to the inevitable need to arrange a funeral in the garden, a ritual I would become all too accustomed to.

A couple of hours later we are laying Charlie and Lola to rest. 'Ashes to ashes, dust to d...'

'The going rate is £2 per mole,' Oliver shouts across the front lawn cutting through the solemnity of the proceedings. He has returned with half a dozen mole traps jangling from his handlebars.

Emily is, of course, horrified and so am I, although for entirely different reasons. 'It's murderous,' she wails and runs off to tell mummy what atrocities the boys are now planning.

'Fifty pence,' I shout back, knowing full well that it'll be me that has to bury the traps, check them and empty them.

'A pound,' a wry smile flickers across his face, 'and Emily won't find out what we're up to.'

'You mean she'll never know where those new moleskin Barbie doll trousers will have come from?'

'Never.'

'It's a deal.' And with that Oliver's first commercial agricultural activity is born.

With Easter a distant memory and still the house not finished Emily, too, has designs on how to populate our lives with animals but of a very different variety. To date our only pets have been Holly who is now a middle aged lady and probably the most relieved out of all of us to be back at the castle and Sooty who is an elderly gentleman of a cat and now couldn't care less where the family lives because he never left the castle in the first place.

Emily's plan is to create a menagerie of rabbits, guinea pigs, hamsters and when the time comes, and she is pragmatic enough to know, even at four that it will, a new cat.

'White next time, Daddy, because we wouldn't want Sooty to think we were replacing him – he's too special for that.'

Eventually the end of yet another renovation seems to be in sight and I ask Reg to help me begin decorating the upstairs of the cottage while the builder carries on plastering downstairs at a pace that wouldn't leave a snail breathless.

Not that Reg's decorating is likely to leave the plasterer standing. After his painfully slow progress on the windows a few years back I fully intend to supervise him and not leave him alone for long periods with the builder, as they are both far too easily distracted, so that we may have some chance of getting the job done by Christmas. I tell him this, tongue in cheek, but he doesn't seem to get the joke.

'Tha'll never get this dun ba Yuletide lad,' he says woefully.

'It's only a small cottage Reg, come on.'

'Me an' tha'll can mek a start but we'll need professionals ta finish th' job if tha wants te be in by th' back end.'

Roughly translated, this means 'I don't do fast.'

Three weeks later I concede. It might be a small cottage but, having been gutted, every single surface needs painting and we have fitted oak doors, skirtings, mouldings and staircase which all need oiling. I call the decorators.

'I can't afford this,' I confide in Reg, there's no money left in the pot.

'Agin?' he asks wryly, 'tha'll find a way lad, thou allas do.'

He's been listening to Wendy. But he's right, they both are, we'll find a way.

And despite all the delays and frustrations of another project way off course and woefully over budget life is good and we feel safe and happy in the knowledge that everything we've achieved we've done for ourselves and that we are in charge of our own destiny now.

Chapter Fifteen

Having camped out in our holiday cottage for many more months than we ever intended Stable House feels almost palatial although, in fact, it is just eighteen inches wider all round. It doesn't take us long to put our stamp on the place and it's soon looking like we have lived there for years.

The spring and summer pass in a frenzy of activity. We host more weddings than ever before but manage to fit in a ten day holiday between them and Emily gets her first guinea pig, Molly, as company for Moonie, a rabbit she got for Christmas who has grown into the most sour tempered creature.

Unfortunately, Moonie's foul temperament doesn't dispose him to sharing his quarters and poor Molly soon has a back covered in scabs.

'It's quite normal,' an assistant at the local pet shop tells us, 'just keep an eye on them, the rabbit is probably just asserting himself.'

I'll say he is but if she expects that any of us is going to mount an all night vigil in order to catch the rabbit mounting the guinea pig she's got us all wrong.

Moonie's behaviour doesn't improve. A few days later Emily goes to feed the animals and there's a howl from the garden. Molly is as stiff as a board. Either Moonie has tried to have his wicked way with Molly and the guinea pig has died of shock (particularly understandable since Molly was actually a boy but because Emily insisted on a girl guinea pig... familiar story) or has just got fed up of sharing and kicked the poor rodent to death.

I have little time for either animal. There are far too many rabbits digging up the garden already and frankly, what is a guinea pig any-way? Apparently they're a delicacy in Peru but when I shared this with Emily she found that piece of knowledge too much to swallow. So my inclination is to dismiss the death and get on. It's sod's law that we have a lunch invitation and are already on our way out when Molly's demise is discovered.

We are keen not to be late for one of Miss Worth's pre-luncheon sherry receptions at The Dower House in the next village. Happily Emily is a very stoic nearly-six-year-old and after she has recovered from her initial indignation that a guinea pig should have the audacity to die so soon after paying good money for it, announces that there must be a funeral. Immediately.

I explain that we really don't have time before lunch and that Miss Worth wouldn't understand if we are late. She seems to take this all surprisingly well and agrees that Molly will come to no harm lying in a shoe box until teatime.

Miss Worth is an elderly spinster of the old school. She wears hats: a church hat, a hat for the shops and one for the WI. They are not interchangeable. She issues written invitations to luncheon and afternoon tea (she frowns on any other daytime treats and wouldn't entertain popping in for a coffee) and expects the same courtesy of a hand written reply in return. Any modern form of communication would be unacceptable. The telephone, she says is for emergencies only and not for idle correspondence. But while she may seem formidable, children always seem strangely drawn to her.

We arrive a few minutes late but decide it easier to weather the look of disapproval than to explain the reason for our delay. I had suggested to Wendy we might text ahead with an outline of the incident. But we thought better of declaring in text shorthand, Guinea Pig croaked (GP X), keep sherry (SHEZ) on ice. CU L8R.

Of course not a word is said on our arrival, sherry is served (warm) and once we have knocked it back with unseemly haste we are soon being seated. There are thirteen of us for lunch and, being a superstitious old sort, Miss W has laid a fourteenth place at which she has placed a rather moth eaten old teddy bear.

Emily makes a bee line for the teddy and sitting in the place next to it, starts to engage it in conversation. Suddenly, and from where I cannot say, she produces the corpse of Molly the guinea pig which she lays beside the teddy at the table.

Richard, a decidedly rotund country solicitor who is sitting next to me and, having arrived in good time, has tanked up on the sherry, simply exclaims across the table, 'By God there's a stiff on the table.'

I freeze with my fork midway between my plate and my mouth, transfixed by the corpse at the end of the table.

But Miss Worth ignores the whole episode and it is clear we are to carry on as normal. Emily, whom I am ready to disown, is also oblivious to the effect of her unannounced introduction to the table and continues a three way conversation with Teddy and Molly. The rest of the afternoon passes in a haze and it is with relief that we return home. I dig a shallow grave which I fleetingly fancy might suit either myself or my daughter.

Emily is happy to lay Molly to rest and to say a few words of farewell and produces the body wrapped in a handkerchief monogrammed with the initials HW.

'Miss Worth gave this to me before we left,' she says, 'she said it would keep Molly comfortable and help her sleep better underground.'

On the face of it things are going swimmingly but the truth is we are paddling furiously below the water to keep the elegant swan afloat. There is constant angst about money, cash flow in particular, we are almost crippled with short term debt over and above our mortgage and the wage bill has ballooned.

Added to all that the children are demanding more of our time and becoming more challenging. And neither of us was ever any good at juggling.

> I: 'This is where it started to get really difficult. The sheer weight of responsibility. The castle, the cost of it, putting off essential maintenance and then lying awake worrying about it. Being responsible for other people's livelihoods, their families. The children looking to us for everything, material and emotional. Knowing that we couldn't shake off any of these responsibilities. Not like a job you can just walk out of when you've had enough. And nobody to turn to for advice or support. Fuck all support.'
>
> He: 'But your mother was only at the end of the telephone.'
>
> I: 'Dad, she'd given up by then. Since she left she'd nursed your mother

until she died, had major abdominal surgery and gone into denial.'

He: 'Denial about what?'

I: 'Well denial that she was a grandmother frankly, except at Christmas when she showered the kids with ridiculous amounts of stuff.'

He: 'This is sounding like old ground, son.'

I: 'Yes, I know but it hurts. It's like an ache that never goes away except when I talk about it and it becomes a stabbing pain. Anyway, I was saying that she was also in denial about us as kids. Even if I asked her what we were like, did we argue, how did it make her feel, what did she do to cope, she just said we were perfect children and she enjoyed every single moment of us growing up.

'I know it's bullshit. We all know we weren't perfect. Of course Wendy thought she was just saying it to get at her. As if to say, well I don't know why you can't cope, I never had any trouble.'

A week or so after the children go back for the new school year Mum rings. She has, she says, got some news. A couple of years ago doctors discovered she had an abdominal aneurysm growing at an alarming rate. A sort of ballooning of the wall of the aorta, unless discovered, in her case by accident during a chest x-ray for something else, it often goes undetected until it bursts and then is invariably fatal.

She was operated on pretty swiftly and things seemed to go OK in as much as she got out of hospital alive. But her mobility was compromised.

'I'm selling the house and moving,' she tells us. 'I'm starting to find the stairs difficult so I want to move before it's too much of a problem.'

'Nanny can come back and live with us,' chime the children. Despite my own bitter disappointment, they have remained loyal to their nanny. I pick up the baton, 'seriously, come back up here, we'll find you somewhere suitable and you won't have to worry about being on your own. A nice little cottage.' I hope this will resonate with her motives as I can understand why a three storey Victorian terraced house no longer fits the bill, gorgeous as it is and I know that this will have been a tough decision because she loves old houses and will miss its quirkiness.

She surprises me with an irritable snap, 'I'm not on my own, Simon,

I have Sally,' and right on cue Sally, her detestable terrier, starts yapping uncontrollably. The conversation stops while the dog is being calmed down (a wholly unsatisfactory alternative to being put down). 'I have friends,' she continues.

'Mum, Sally is a dog, your friends either can't drive, are missing a full complement of limbs or are tied up with their own families. You've got no life down there,' and even before I form the words I know it's the wrong thing to say.

'Look, I didn't phone for an argument. I've sold the house and I've made an offer on another place.'

'What?' I'm trying very hard to keep calm, 'what's it like?'

'I'll send you the details,' and with that I know that she knows that I'm not going to like what she's done.

And she's damn right. She has bought a one bedroom apartment in a sheltered housing complex.

'It's a furnished coffin,' Wendy exclaims. 'She's given up. She's waiting to die.'

I decide to go down and try to intervene, to inject some reason, because I am sure there is a back story that we're not getting.

'I've got to have another operation,' Mum confides in me a few days later as we sit surrounded by half packed boxes. As soon as I'd arrived I could see there was no point dissuading her from the move.

'Two more aneurysms near my heart, they're going to try to fix them both. It's a bit experimental.' While she's trying to sound matter of fact about it I can see she's terrified.

I, on the other hand, am incandescent. 'What! Have you not asked anyone to see the doctors with you? Do you understand the full implications of what they're saying?'

'Not really,' she replies sheepishly, 'I don't like to make a fuss.'

'Oh, for fuck's sake! Well too bad, you're going to have to get used to being a nuisance. The NHS works best if you keep reminding them you're there and that you're a human being. Otherwise you just become a patient file that gets wheeled between departments on a trolley and a slab of meat on a table.'

As I come to the end of my rant I realise that she is quietly, without wanting to make a fuss, sobbing. Her face, so familiar and constant, tear-streaked and snotty like a child.

I put my arm around her and am transported back to our moment on that New Year's Day at Augill and then back again to her moment on the edge of that bed with the crumpled bloody sheets on the night she became a widow.

'I'm so scared, I wish I'd never found out about these things. I could have just keeled over in the street but now I wake up every day and wonder, will it be today?

'I don't understand what they're all saying most of the time, the doctors I mean. They say I'll die if I don't have the operation but it's big and risky and there's a forty per cent chance I'll be paralysed.'

'Jesus, Mum,' and I squeeze her harder towards me. 'So this is why you want to move somewhere else. Why haven't you told us?'

'You're so busy and you've got the children, I didn't want to worry you.'

That makes me really angry. And she know it. But I say nothing.

Later, over tea I make her promise never to keep anything from us. She agrees and doesn't argue when I say I will go with her to every consultant's appointment, every hospital visit and be her ears. 'We won't leave any appointment without having all our questions answered, OK?'

It's not the right time to start asking why she left, why she cast aside her relationship with the children. After this next operation, when she's well enough is when we can have that conversation.

Four weeks... after just four weeks and innumerable consultant's appointments (all of which I travel almost the entire length of the M6 and M5 to attend) Mum is in hospital in Bristol being prepped for the operation. The NHS can move surprisingly quickly at times.

'My big day,' she has been calling it and we have been joking about all the things she is going to do when she's recovered.

'The crazy thing is, I don't feel ill. My legs are a bit stiff, but I'm having this huge op for something that isn't even making me feel ill.'

And we both know that, if she didn't know she had an aneurysm, she'd be going about her ordinary life now none the wiser, happy in herself, just accepting the usual aches and pains of advancing years without a second thought.

I had cautioned her about being sure this operation was the right choice.

'You feel well now, you could go on feeling well for some time yet. Or you could drop down dead. If the operation goes wrong you'll be paralysed, need 24 hour care.' It's something even I can hardly bear to countenance but I know for her it must be so much worse. She's always said she never wanted to end up a vegetable, dependent on others.

But the consultant has been optimistic, saying that there's every chance she'll make a full recovery and live longer as a result, although he stopped short of saying a ripe old age. It's all surgeon bullshit. I know it and she knows it too.

As she is wheeled away towards the operating theatre or wherever it is people get taken to when they're wheeled away in hospital still breathing, she says simply, 'You know I love you? But I'm not afraid, not anymore.' And then she continues, 'And the children, tell them that I love them. Wendy too. I'm fonder of her than she thinks. I see her as my daughter, I do.'

'I know Mum, it's difficult for her but she loves you in her own way. We all do.'

'I know. It's going to be different afterwards. I think there are mistakes to put right. Things to say.'

She's right. It's going to be very different afterwards. But as for things to say? Only if we get the chance.

Twelve hours later I am sitting in my hotel room (I was never going to sit around waiting for news in that depressing and frankly filthy hospital filled with surly staff) but I haven't had much sleep. I am surveying myself in the mirror, my eyes staring back at me, dark and sunken, like a couple of brooding teenagers glaring moodily from beneath their hoodies, the rest of me looking as far removed from a teenager as it's possible to be, when the telephone rings.

It's the consultant to tell me that the operation didn't go quite according to plan.

I don't register the detail of the conversation, how long we are on the telephone or how I get from the hotel to the hospital. But the next thing I remember I am standing at the nurses' station on the cardiothoracic ward, the last place I left Mum, asking for her.

'Mr Bennett, she's not here anymore.'

'Your mother is in intensive care on the ninth floor.'

I ask for the consultant when I arrive and he wastes no time in coming down to see me.

He invites me to sit down and sits next to me. As he begins to talk all I can think is how immaculately he is turned out in a clean suit, freshly laundered shirt and highly polished shoes. 'You didn't do it, did you? There's no blood on your hands, you didn't do it. Or you've washed away the evidence of a botched job.'

And then I snap back into reality and everything is in such pin sharp focus all of a sudden I feel momentarily dizzy before steadying myself and saying, quite without thinking, 'OK, I'm listening now, what's happened?'

'Your mother's aneurysms were much closer to her heart than we had thought. There were complications.'

Over the next twenty minutes or so the consultant paints a graphic picture of how my mother has an incision that extends two thirds of the way around her torso, how her internal organs were clamped outside her chest cavity for much of the operation, how dangerously close to the heart the repair in her aorta is and how they found additional smaller aneurysms that they have also operated on "for good measure".

'She is very weak but she's a fighter.'

'But can she walk?' I ask. 'Is she paralysed?'

'She's only just coming round and she's very confused but early indications suggest her mobility has not been compromised.'

'Can I see her?'

'Of course, but be prepared for a shock, she won't look herself until she's fully come round.'

At the door of the ICU I steal myself for what I am going to find. There are three beds down each side of the room, each one plumbed and wired in to so much gadgetry it's difficult to see the person in the middle of it all. I walk the length of the room, peering at each bed.

She's not here. She's dead, they've taken her away, she's not here.

'Excuse me,' I say to a nurse as she checks the chart of one of the patients, 'Mary Bennett, I'm looking for her but she's not here.

The nurse replaces the chart on the end of the bed and nods towards it's occupant.

'She's doing fine, she's a real fighter. Is she your Mum?'

I stare at her and then at the patient. Is she my Mum? I can't tell.

'I'll leave you alone. You should be very proud of her, a lot of people wouldn't have made it.'

Gingerly I creep towards the bed head treading as softly as I can as if the sound of my foot steps are likely to cut through the thick blanket of morphine she is sleeping under.

But as I draw closer she opens her eyes.

'John, is that you?' she whispers. 'Are the boys OK?'

He: 'She asked for me?'
I: 'Yes, she asked for you!'

'No Mum, it's me, Simon.'

'Mmm...' and she holds out her hand, I take it gently in mine, she closes her eyes and sleeps.

Incredibly, ten days after the surgery she is sent home wrapped up like an Egyptian mummy. She is in a lot of pain but in good spirits too. We joke that the bandages are either to hold everything in or to hold the two halves of her together. A nurse is to come and see her every other day and her sister is coming down to stay.

I feel guilty about returning to Cumbria but there's nothing more I can do and I have to trust that she is in safe hands. I know I have nothing to reproach myself about but it doesn't help. I feel even more guilty about the wave of relief that breaks over me when I am at last in the car and heading for home.

He: 'Guilt, Simon, comes from within.'
I: 'I know. I regretted those years when we could have made more of an effort to see her more. We could have wasted less energy on the resentment and channelled it into making what we had work instead of wishing for something else. Wishing she was someone else.

'I wanted more than anything to wind back the clock to just before the operation when she said there were things to say. We should have said them

then because I was now itching to get the air cleared and she wasn't fit.'

He: 'But you knew you had time, time to wait until she was fit enough.'

I: 'I thought we had time left.'

He: 'We didn't have time, your mother and me. We never made time until the end when we knew it was all over.

'That night when she nursed me we talked for hours. Well, she talked mostly, I listened and squeezed and smiled. I couldn't talk, obviously.

'We laid our ghosts to rest in a way that's only easy to do when you know for certain that the sand in the timer is about to run out.

'I like to think she knew I loved her, that I was sorry for the things I'd done, the wasted life I'd led.

'But she was the one who needed to offload, so that she could move on. She needed to find her own peace with me and with herself. And I think she did.'

Chapter Sixteen

As if our being settled has a positive effect on everything, the castle goes from strength to strength. Our children are becoming much more of a tangible presence around the guests, no longer happy to be fobbed off with a babysitter or chained up in a distant turret while we work. Attempts to bribe them with sweets and chocolate to stay out of the way have had limited success ostensibly because they scoff the sweets in one go and then demand more to do what they were meant to do in the first place.

And so it is that the business makes a fundamental shift to becoming actively family friendly. The rationale is simple: if we can't stop our children causing mild chaos about the place we might as well welcome other children who can then take their share of the blame.

In reality, we don't set out to do anything differently from what we have already been doing. We have always been welcoming and understanding of the needs of young families. It's a simple matter of empathy but we also know how to balance their needs with those guests who do not have, or do not enjoy, the company of children.

With this new strategy in mind we seek out new family orientated websites on which to advertise, re-write our own website and brand ourselves 'the famously family friendly castle.'

It's a winning formula. A family run hotel which treats children as part of the family, doesn't tolerate hushed voices and false formality and allows everyone, children and adults alike, to relax knowing they are all equally welcome. All in a castle – and we find that we're actually rather good at it. Perhaps this is because neither of us has a close-knit family; no parents of our own nearby, no grandparents for the children on hand, and distant siblings, so we are happy to surround ourselves with other families.

By February half term families are arriving in their droves. The drive is positively clogged with people carriers, four wheel drives and estate cars all disgorging their contents onto the gravel forecourt with a palpable sense of relief from parents and shrieks of delight from the children. When our well oiled machine occasionally gets stuck we don't even have to explain because everyone is so laid back they don't want to make a big deal of it. A smattering of childless couples take offence at being corralled into a castle with, God forbid, children, and take it upon themselves to air their grievances.

'Everything's lovely, but we didn't realise it was a family 'otel,' off-loads one guest with an ill-disguised snear on her face who turns out to be a teacher with a self confessed dislike of children (clearly the public sector pension scheme trumps any thoughts of job satisfaction).

'Can't imagine why,' Wendy replies, 'half the website is about families.'

'Oh we don't read websites – you can't trust what hotels say about themselves. We go by the pictures.'

'Well, do come back, perhaps out of school holiday time and you'll be able to enjoy the castle in peace,' Wendy tries her best to be encouraging.

'Oh we wouldn't want to come when it's too quiet, there'd be no atmosphere.'

Some people just aren't to be pleased, although not being pleased is often what pleases them most. But other than that, we love it and the children love it and so do the guests. Occasionally welcoming families as part of our own does mean that we do have to accept a few idiosyncrasies.

At spring half term we are especially busy with families who have obviously decided that a stay in a castle is more prudent than skiing. Take note, please, the guest who complained publicly about our gin and tonics costing £3 each (and, horror of horrors, they had to serve themselves). It's a lot cheaper than a *vin chaud* in Val Thorens.

With families comes a mini Augill industry which has grown up around them. There are children's welcome snacks on the bed. These have also been complained about because, 'Quavers just aren't what little Francis is used to in the afternoons and wouldn't an apple have been more appropriate?' (Francis didn't seem to agree and having stuffed the empty wrapper down the side of a sofa asked for more). Then there are nappy disposal units, play boxes, baby listeners, travel cots, children's high tea, DVDs and popcorn... even the children's cookery school.

But it's still never quite enough for some people. Lilly is twelve. She doesn't want high tea with the other children because it's pizza and mummy says pizza is evil and anyway, she doesn't like cheese. Well, unless this is pizza mafioso and is packing a machine gun under the mozzarella, it's probably safe enough this once, but Lilly's mum asks if she can join the table for dinner later.

'Yes, of course, what would Lilly like instead of the goats cheese first course?'

Lilly decides on the crostini without the goats cheese... or the salad... or the roasted red onions... or the dressing. That'll be toast then.

Main course is pushed around the plate and afterwards, mummy confides that lamb may not have been Lilly's first choice as she is considering vegetarianism. Hmm, more toast perhaps?

As dessert is served Lilly is in tears. The pudding, apparently is too rich for her constitution. Mummy asks if there is any ice cream. Moments later there is a wail from the dining room and Lilly is seen fleeing to her room. The ice cream, it seems, is too cold.

'Oh for God's sake,' exclaims Faye in the kitchen, 'the clue's in the name: ICE cream.' Thankfully Lilly is the exception and kids at Augill are invariably our unpaid sales force, badgering their parents to return for another castle adventure. And sometimes, it is tempting to encourage them back without their parents in tow.

Amelia and Adam have booked for a week and have been here for three days already. So loved up with Augill are they that they have forgotten that their children are actually still their responsibility. Not only have they become oblivious to the antics of their offspring but also to the effect they are having on everyone else. Luckily Wendy is never backwards in coming forwards when it comes to acting in *loco parentis* and has ensured that Marcus and William didn't bleed to death at the cookery school, having already tried to see what effect a chilli up each other's nostril would have, didn't get mauled and disfigured while playing real life Bucking Bronco with Holly, and weren't permanently brain damaged after discovering what would happen by bouncing on the trampoline with half the springs disengaged.

At breakfast on day four Marcus and William have wolfed down cereal and scrambled eggs and are off in search of further danger in the company of Oliver (he's still our responsibility) who has promised to show them the most 'mintage' tree for climbing leaving Amelia and and Adam to enjoy a leisurely breakfast with Chloe, their nine-month-old.

The trouble is, Chloe had her breakfast some time earlier and as the dining room fills up with other guests there is a distinct atmosphere... a whiff of something not on the menu. Chloe has digested her breakfast and filled her nappy with what's left.

'There's a changing mat and nappies in the downstairs loos,' Adam is heard to say to Amelia.

'Oh she's alright, she doesn't seem bothered,' Amelia replies.

'But the rest of us do,' the other guests and all the staff scream silently.

By the time they have finished their cereal the pong is becoming invasive. In the kitchen I hatch a plan to accidentally stab Chloe with a fork in passing making her scream which will prompt A and A to assume that Chloe has now not only filled her pants but also her trousers but Wendy thinks that a little too extreme.

As I formulate another idea, fate plays a cunning hand. Marcus comes screaming into the hall with news that William is stuck in a tree, hanging upside down from one ankle. Adam and Amelia, momentarily fail to register, then remember that William is their son (and therefore still their responsibility) and dash to assist leaving Chloe parping and pooping contentedly by herself. Quick as a flash, Wendy takes the initiative and with one hand delivers a full English to one guest while scooping Chloe up under her arm with the other.

By the time A and A return relieved to report that all's well and that William is already eyeing up another tree, Chloe is back in her high chair, changed, happy and surrounded by lots of smiling appreciative faces.

That evening, Adam and Amelia reveal that as well as Chloe, seven-year-old Marcus and ten-year-old William, they have teenaged twin boys at home and that they can't remember ever having felt so relaxed as they do at Augill. This, of course, prompts an outpouring of sympathy from everyone until William puts a bag of un-popped microwave popcorn on the open fire to see what happens.

Next morning as we are still finding blackened nodules of corn embedded in the furniture up to six feet away from the fire A and A tell us that they hope to bring the whole family back very soon. No wonder then, that in mid-February, late-May and late-October, when we get enquiries from people without children we always ask, 'you do realise it's half term that week, don't you?'

Not that that's a guarantee of avoiding chaos because Adam and Amelia aren't tied to school holidays as they are home schooling their children. 'It's so liberating for them not to have to conform to the same boundaries as everyone else.'

Our attention to families attracts the attention of the press and we enjoy some excellent coverage topped off, later in the year with news of an award from a respectable marketing organisation.

Augill Castle is now officially (at least according to this particular organisation) Bed & Breakfast of the Year, Great Britain and Ireland. It's a bit of a mouthful and even more of a misnomer. We are clearly so much more than a bed & breakfast but there is nothing else in the English language to succinctly describe what we do. The French have chambre d'hôtes which is closer to the mark. But Wendy wouldn't hear of us mixing English and French. 'Very *gauche*,' she says. Hmm, but to be honest I agree. I wince whenever people ask if our facilities are en-suite. 'Yes, our rooms do have their own bathrooms.'

So, it is that we are Britain's best B&B (with bells, whistles and knobs on). Reg is one of the first to congratulate us. 'Ah saw thee on Border crack an deekaboot.' I know that he is congratulating me because he is shaking my hand and grinning, two things Reg does not exert energy doing without good reason. I have no idea what he is

---

* I discover later that Border Crack is the local colloquialism for the regional ITV Border News, and Deekaboot is what they call the TV news magazine programme *Lookaround*. Personally I rather like the mental image of a Border crack between here and Scotland.

talking about, wondering if the Border Crack is a reference to some symbolic geographical line between Scotland and England akin to that drawn by southerners just beyond Watford Gap to keep the northerners at bay. Anyway, for now, I take the congratulations and smile appreciatively making a mental note to make enquiries about what on earth he has said to me.*

Awards are, of course, a great pat on the back and I defy anyone not to be seduced by them, particularly if they are yours. A regular guest who happened to be up for her own tourism award last year didn't attend the ceremony. She stayed with us a few weeks later and said she'd spent so many nights at awards she couldn't face it. Can success really become that tedious? I hope not. But while what we do at the castle may be award winning, we don't do it to win awards, unlike one particular place we stayed at a couple of years ago which was so intent on cramming judge-wowing gimmicks into the rooms that the poor old guest who had to try to navigate through it all got forgotten. Is it really necessary to have remote controlled curtains? And does anyone really need a television in the bathroom? I certainly don't relish the idea of sharing my ablutions with Jeremy Clarkson.

We are not yet jaded by the whole self-congratulatory jamboree of award giving and receiving. After all, having sweated blood and tears to get the castle to where it is and balanced all that with the needs of the children, we haven't got out much, so a free feed is not to be sniffed at. The ceremony is in one of London's Grande Dame hotels on Park Lane which is unfortunately far beyond our budget for the night so we end up staying at a less illustrious address south of the river.

We are both pretty lousy at networking so as soon as we arrive at the hotel we grab drinks and hide behind a large arrangement of exotic foliage. From here we can see all the goings on through a gap in the leaves, through which Wendy is also able to extend an arm to grab champagne glasses at regular intervals from passing waiters with such lightning speed and dexterity they hardly notice us. She's like a venus fly trap in a posh frock.

We are feeling terribly out of our depth, having never been to anything like this before and we are considerably younger than most of the other guests. But there are a few familiar faces – celebrities of the hospitality world – so we content ourselves with a bit of star spotting.

Eventually, after what seems hours, we are called to dinner. Wendy's dexterity didn't extend to replacing the empties back on the passing trays and we're genuinely taken aback to notice a dozen glasses scattered around the base of the plant display.

'Shmall glasshes,' whispers Wendy who is leading us into the dining room. This is a mistake as she has no idea where she is going on account of the fact that she couldn't focus on the table plan. Having successfully hidden ourselves throughout the drinks reception, we're now stuck in the middle of the room surrounded by 200 people all taking their seats. It's like an Alice in Wonderland version of musical chairs. Eventually, we are the only couple left standing and the occupants of a table right at the front near the stage are gesturing wildly to us that we must be with them.

We find ourselves seated between a journalist from the BBC and Ruth Watson, later to become television's *The Hotel Inspector*, but for now grasping at the first rung of the ladder of fame having just published a cookery book. Ruth and her husband David are delightful company and we share more than a decent portion of cynicism together as the meal wears on. The journalist proves to be positively repulsive.

Unfortunately, Wendy, fuelled by an ever flowing supply of red wine, tells him that the BBC is a broken and irrelevant organisation and that most of its employees wouldn't last five minutes in the real world. While he is still reeling (deservedly) she turns her attentions to a chap opposite who introduces himself as the chief executive of the whole organisation of whom we are guests.

This is the point at which we should realise that we are here as more than just award nominees. But we don't. Wendy takes it upon herself to tell our host that she doesn't much like the design of his guidebook and that our entry is peppered with typos. She goes on to say she is less than impressed that it is far too big to fit in her handbag. Surprisingly, he takes this all with very good grace, agrees that there have been some design problems with what is, after all, the first relaunched edition and by the end of dessert has steered Wendy into conversation about what she's been doing in London all day.

This is a mistake. In a single movement Wendy pushes back her chair and plants her foot in his lap, exclaiming, 'Shoes! Look at my fabulous shoes, a girl can't come to London without buying shoes,' and the whole table has little option but to admire Wendy's new red snake-skin stilettos. I can't bear it but I can hardly blame Wendy. The waiters haven't left us alone and their eagerness to refill our wine glasses every time we drain them borders on harassment. I have partaken of my fair share but have also managed to keep my shoes firmly on the ground which is just as well as the room is starting to spin in a very unpleasant manner.

Salvation comes swiftly in the form of the compere for the ceremony, one of those annoyingly familiar minor celebrities who recognises himself much better than the rest of us do. Thankfully, as the room settles down to attend to the business of the evening (although the spinning doesn't come to a complete stop for some time), the waiters stop bringing more wine and Wendy has started gulping down water as nerves take over. 'I think we might be up for a prize,' she whispers.

'You think? What category?' I ask barely disguising my irritation because I am horribly intolerant of anyone more drunk than me.

'Lush of the year for me and stuffed shirt of the year for you,' and it's as much as we can do to stifle the giggles and maintain what little composure we have left. Ruth Watson tells us we should be quiet, although I think she is secretly enjoying our irreverence and is clearly delighted that we are annoying the repulsive journalist.

There are regional and national awards in each category and we end up walking, well barely staggering actually, away with both for B&B of the year. Thankfully there's no acceptance speech required.

Chapter Seventeen

Buoyed by our recent marketing and award success I am bitten by the PR bug and enthusiastically come up with ideas to raise our profile. The children's cookery school, Augill Little Cooks has proved an instant success and has the dual effect of bringing in more families during the school holidays and, in particular the half terms, guaranteeing a full house.

However another of my PR schemes proves decidedly less wholesome. Being a castle we are inevitably asked if there are ghosts and the answer is that there have been ghostly goings on.

We've all scared ourselves half silly with the news that Lorenzo, a frankly terrible but nevertheless popular and therefore semi-regular wedding singer has seen a ghost. It's all ridiculous but we're nevertheless half aghast and half willing it to be true!

When he tells me the full story of how he encountered the unannounced visitor after returning from a smoke I ask him what exactly he was smoking. He looks decidedly shifty and I sense a slight whiff of something mildly hallucinogenic in the air.

To be truthful, I have never seen a ghost, but, not very long after we moved into Augill, we did have a once and once only (thank goodness) ghostly experience.

We are well into our routine of leaving the restaurant in London late on a Friday night and driving up to Cumbria in time to start on a weekend's renovations on Saturday morning. We crash into bed at about 3am and, having piled every piece of clothing and bedding on top of ourselves to keep warm (we have no spare cash for frivolities such as heating) fall into a fitful slumber.

Our room is at the far end of the main first floor corridor and the farthest door bangs. It is loud enough to wake me but could easily be the wind or mum, who is still living with us. Then the second door on the corridor bangs shut. It couldn't be the wind as the two doors open in opposite directions.

It seems odd for mum to be coming in our direction and I wait to see if it is her. The third door and fourth doors bang, I call out to see who is there. It's a sort of loud stage whisper as I want to know if there is anyone there, but I'm so spooked I don't really want an answer. There's no answer.

If it is someone, they are now right outside the bedroom door. I want to wake Wendy and tell her what's happening but I'm too frightened to move.

After what seems minutes but is likely just seconds, a strong aroma of fresh cigarette smoke mingled with Yves St Laurent Rive Gauche perfume fills the room. I know who it is because Wendy has told me many times about her mum who smoked continuously and wore far too much Rive Gauche. She's been gone now for some fourteen years.

I am frozen stiff with fear, and spend the rest of the night lying rigid and motionless. In the morning I turn to Wendy and begin to tell her about the experience but she's beaten me to it as she was also awake, paralysed with fright and we had both experienced the same thing, not wanting to disturb each other, although what we really both wanted to do was jump into each other's arms like Scooby Doo and Shaggy (make up your own mind who is who). Yikes!

We check with mum over breakfast that she was not wandering about in the middle of the night having a sneaky puff but she only wants to know who on earth was slamming doors at 4am!

Since then, we have not had another supernatural experience and are happy for that. So imagine our reaction when we are contacted by a group of ghost hunters who want to conduct a 'Most Haunted' style overnight vigil at the castle. I am clearly overcome by some dark force which has manipulated my mind because before I know what I'm saying, I have agreed. Surely, I think to myself, there has to be some PR mileage in this. A date is set and the ghostbusters are on their way.

As the day of the ghost hunt draws nearer most of the staff are adamant that they don't want anything to do with it. Our housekeeping is now under the regimented control of Val. Nothing but perfection is good enough for her and she is concerned about the state of the bedding if we all scare ourselves stupid in the night. Mum is convinced that we are going to summon up the devil himself. She is actually very agitated about the whole idea and I think she has visions of the castle being engulfed by a fiery hole, consumed by the very flames of hell itself and is relieved that she no longer lives with us. I'm trying to take a more pragmatic line, thinking up likely PR angles and possible photo opportunities. But the ideas aren't coming thick and fast.

It is a Friday afternoon in early November when the ghost hunters arrive. The clocks have just gone back giving us long dark nights and the remnants of carved pumpkin lanterns still sit menacingly in the porch. It is all very fitting and I am beginning to feel more positive.

But I'm soon let down. In fact I'm very disappointed. The ghost hunters arrive in a Ford Focus and a Vauxhall Astra estate. Where's the Scooby Doo mystery machine? A simple VW camper van would have done. As the two cars disgorge their passengers I can also see that useable photo opportunities are going to be pretty thin on the ground, at least until it gets dark.

Ralph (I doubt this is his real name and guess he looks much more like a Bernard) is wearing a spotty red cravat, has long grey hair tied back in a pony tail and a salt and pepper beard which I fancy might be as dishevelled as it is, in order to conceal a secret beard-cam. He is about 50, has the air of someone who has seen a lot of life and is now pretty weary of the whole thing. He bears himself with a stiffness that marks out older men whose walk was once the arrogant swagger of youth but has deteriorated into a slightly awkward gait verging on a mince. He is clearly in charge.

With him are Graham, a graduate in something way outside my sphere of understanding and the sort of person who wears hiking boots and a fishing jacket (which in this case smells as if it still has last week's catch in the pocket), and Serena, who, in green pockety combats, a baggy sweatshirt, hobnail boots and with no make up what-soever to disguise her rather unfortunate complexion, looks nothing like her name might suggest.

Wendy has told me I must keep further thoughts about Serena and her obviously lesbian leanings to myself since last time I was caught thinking out loud I almost enraged an entire half-term household of newly checked-in mummies by exclaiming too loudly from the kitchen about what a quality delivery of breasts we had received that afternoon. I was referring, of course, to the pigeon we were serving for dinner but apparently others thought differently.

Finally, there is Art who is the most presentable of the four but is let down by the most hideous set of teeth which make him look like he bottled it half way through filming an edition of *Extreme Makeover* at the point where his old teeth had been chiselled out ready for the new ones to go in. Surely any half decent ghost isn't going to come out for this bunch of misfits.

Wendy merely turns to me and says in a very mouthy half whisper, 'What the hell have you got us into?'

It takes about an hour to haul all the equipment into the castle and while we are helping with this, Ralph is surveying the castle for possible spectral hotspots or some such thing. I mention light heartedly that we have a WiFi hotspot since we went wireless in the office earlier in the year (something of which I am justifiably proud as it's pretty cutting edge for a business of our size) but he is less than amused. I decide to go and make supper which, in deference to the company should probably involve mung beans, something made of tofu and goji berry tart but is going to be far more elaborate and eminently more palatable since we do also have some regular guests staying. They have been forewarned and are very excited about the prospect of contact with the other side.

Equipment assembled, it's decided that the vigil should begin at around 11.30pm. We are all told we should go about the business of the castle as if everything is normal. This is, of course, a ridiculous suggestion, not least because we are completely entangled in cables at every turn and are all agog to know whether we have been sharing the castle with The Others.

The rest of our guests do take Ralph's advice to behave normally and are getting happily plastered on their own spirit quest in the bar, working their way along the top shelf of malt whiskies. Wendy, on the other hand, has been agitated all evening and has taken some of the malt medicinally to settle her stomach and gone to bed. I finish off what little she's left in the bottle to calm my own nerves.

A couple of hours later, there has still been no spectral activity, our guests have either retired or passed out and a bottle of wine has done wonders for my nerves but not much for my head. I bid the ghost hunters good night, remind them where they can find the coffee and go to bed.

It must be about three in the morning when there is a sudden commotion and a scream. Either Ralph has made an ill-advised early morning move on Serena or somebody has spotted a ghost. It's a difficult call as to which is the more unlikely scenario.

Of course, everyone wants to know what is happening and the whole household is soon assembled at the top of the stairs in various states of dishevelment and undress. (It is interesting that, on the rare occasions the fire alarm sounds in the night it doesn't command the same response.)

Was it a child searching for answers about the unexplained death of its mother, a servant doomed to eternal exploration of the back passage after being ill-treated by her master or a poltergeist angry at being disturbed?

No.

It seems Serena dozed off and was woken with a start by Sooty our very aged cat who jumped (just about) into her lap. Ralph got over excited, and in trying to switch on the spectral mass illuminator thingy pulled the whole thing over, frightening Sooty who dug his claws into Serena's breast.

Wendy looks at me and turns to go back to bed, muttering, 'bloody idiots.' I ask if she'd like a little something to help her get back to sleep but she doesn't look as if she's going to have any trouble on that score.

At breakfast Ralph, whom I am now convinced is really Bernard, tells us that the vigil wound up after the Sooty incident as any spirits would have been disturbed.

'Bullshit,' mutters one of the paying guests.

I get a strong sense that everyone around the table is thinking it's not the spirits who are disturbed. I refrain from offering Ralph and the gang Scooby snacks for the journey and thank them for not finding any ghosts. I politely enquire after Serena's left breast but she is too busy packing up the Astra to acknowledge me.

All the time we have been courting the press and winning awards Mum has not been well. There have been complications following her operation ranging from, in no particular order of severity, a hospital acquired infection, a bone infection leading to a further operation to remove the infected bone which led to a further infection. It seems that not being paralysed has turned out to be a small consolation for what she has subsequently had to endure.

Her first re-admittance came just five days after she was discharged. She had an unspecified bacterial infection. Consequently she stayed in hospital receiving the post operative care she was denied first time round. Since then she has spent as much time in hospital than she has out of it. We have been keeping a vigil and I have spent more time than I care to recount on the M6 and M5 between Cumbria and Bristol.

And yet, despite spells in hospital lasting up to twelve weeks, she remains remarkably calm. Almost, dare I say, content. The nurses love her. And she seems to love them.

I: 'Well, no surprises there. She was thriving on the attention. It was her way of finally admitting, without actually saying it, that she wanted to be looked after, taken care of.

'I didn't see that at the time though. I only realised it afterwards. If I'd been a bit more perceptive perhaps we wouldn't have made such a hash of things later on.'

He: 'Maybe you would have done things differently, but then other things would have turned out differently as a result and who knows what would have happened.

'I don't think she was asking you to change, she was admitting to herself that it was alright to be a little self-indulgent and let others do the looking after, that's all.'

I: 'But what if we'd said to her then, come back and live with us? Things could have been different.'

He: 'But not necessarily for the better. In making that choice you'd have had to make other different choices. It's the same as how you feel about me. You may think you wanted me there for you and yes, perhaps we'd have forged a better relationship if I'd been around longer. But what else would have changed as a result? What wouldn't you have achieved if I was still alive?

'How would your lives have changed if you had brought your mother up to live with you? It would have affected your relationships, your business, your finances...'

I: 'It might have been for the better.'

He: 'More likely for the worse. For everyone.'

Whatever Mum is going through, physically, mentally, in the private confines of her own mind in her own hospital room, our relationship, albeit at opposite ends of a motorway, has not been this easy for many years. There is a new freedom, a new openness that we haven't enjoyed since she was widowed. There are still many things to be said, on both our parts. But I'm not asking, she's not offering.

'When I'm better we'll talk and put things right,' is always the unspoken message running through our time together.

But the sadness is that it is a relationship between two people. The children aren't part of it and neither is Wendy. It's almost as if she's decided there simply isn't room in her weak and damaged heart for everyone so she's closed it off for fear that too many people might try to need her at once and it will finally stop beating.

I: 'But can she really have thought that or was she just shutting them out because, really, she didn't know how to let them back in?'

He: 'I think you already know the answer to that one.'

Right now, at this moment, I wish it could be different. But it isn't and I'm past resenting her for it, although not over blaming myself.

Chapter Eighteen

If one thing in life is predictable, it's unpredictability.

We are undoubtedly squeezed into the Stable House and Oliver's bedroom is no wider than a corridor with a bed suspended from the ceiling. But it is our own house and when we are there we know there is almost no chance of running into guests or staff. We are also happy to know that the monumental debt we ran up in the early years to get the castle going is slowly but steadily being eroded without the pressure of an extra mortgage which moving to a bigger house would entail.

So it is with a mixture of excitement and a heavy heart that we are presented with an opportunity. One of the portions of the estate that was not included in the initial sale back in 1997 is the Orangery, a single storey wing to the west of the main castle with floor to ceiling gothic arched windows and a south facing secluded terrace overlooking the croquet lawn. If it sounds idyllic, that's because it is. If it sounds like the most pivotal piece of the jigsaw that is putting Augill back together, it's that too.

For ten years it has been the home of a couple who have latterly worked for us and become friends. Never an easy mix, it's a relationship that has worked well, founded on a mutual need for what each other can offer. They had always acknowledged that when they were ready to move we would have first refusal on their home and there was an unspoken promise that they would not spring the news upon us.

So, to say it is something of a shock to be presented with a *fait accompli* on the final day of the summer term, just as we are readying ourselves to go to school speech day, and departing on our summer holiday the next day, is an understatement.

We are sitting in the conservatory which, with a small bedroom extension attached to the back, over ten years has morphed from a leaky waste of space, to Mum's initial leaky living quarters, to a leaky bedroom suite to a leaky playroom and children's activity space. It has frankly proved unsuitable in all its roles to date and quite why we are sitting in there at the moment we hear the news I am unsure.

'We have found a place nearer to the family and it's time for us to go,' George tells me without so much as a hint of regret.

'Oh, right,' I'm stuck for anything else to say, but feeling I should add something, continue, 'we're going on holiday tomorrow.'

'So we're looking for a move as quickly as possible,' he adds, oblivious to what I've just said. 'Obviously if you can't raise the money we'll have to put it on the open market.'

'We have no choice,' Wendy says.

'I know we have no choice but how the hell are we going to raise the money?'

'We'll have to remortgage. Again. And use some of your grandmother's money for the deposit.'

'But that money is supposed to be paying the sodding school fees. She said she wanted the money to give the children a better start.'

'Well giving them a bigger home and Oliver a bedroom rather than a corridor is a pretty good start, don't you agree?' I can't argue and don't try to.

'We'll have to find the school fees from elsewhere as and when we can.' Wendy has always been the optimist in this partnership but that has sometimes rendered her judgement less than realistic. Where precisely she thinks we can conjure up several thousand pounds plus every year is beyond me. And that's just prep school. She is, however, right. It's our only option.

We are able to raise a commercial mortgage which requires us to put up at least 30 per cent of the purchase price. It's a big ask but somehow we manage to pull it together and, in line with George's ultimatum, are ready to exchange contracts by the beginning of September.

And then we wait.

George goes quiet and our solicitor, who is poised and ready with our contracts can only tell us to be patient but as weeks drag on, that patience begins to wear very thin.

While this is going on Mum's health deteriorates further and I decide it is time to put aside the niceties that inevitably infuse my occasional, albeit, regular visits and adopt a frankness that is usually reserved only for family or friends you see on a daily basis, when all the niceties have run out.

When I arrive at her apartment there is no answer to the doorbell. Since she is practically housebound I know she's at home so let myself in with the spare key which is cunningly hidden under a flower pot. Is it a particular idiosyncrasy of an older generation that as long as it can't be seen, a key giving access to your entire world is perfectly safe under a plant pot by the front door? The only thing that might make a burglar's life easier would be a note on the front door saying, 'key under flower pot with pansies in it (not to be confused with the begonias on the other side under which I keep my pension book and passport). Please don't make too much mess and/or too much noise while ransacking the house as the cleaner isn't due until Wednesday and I'm trying to sleep.'

I call out as I enter, not wanting to startle her and find her slumped in a chair in front of the fully raging gas fire. It's early September, all the windows are closed and by the look and smell of her she's been there some 24 hours or more.

'Mum, Mum,' I'm shaking her shoulder, first gently and then with increasing urgency.

'Mum, wake up.' She stirs. Sweat is pouring off my brow, it is so hot, and I fling open all the windows and switch off the fire. After a few minutes she is awake enough to realise she's not alone. I let her come to her senses before speaking but it is she who breaks the silence.

Very groggily she whispers, 'I must have dropped off, any chance of a cup of tea.'

I put the kettle on and then begin the interrogation.

'What time is it?' I ask, perhaps a little too harshly. It is all I can do to stop myself grabbing her shoulders and shaking her furiously. She looks at me blankly.

'What day of the week is it? How long have you been asleep? Why aren't you in bed?' She has no answers and I can see she is getting distressed not just because she is confused but because she realises she has wet herself and she can smell it. Without another word I help her to the bathroom and while she cleans herself up I make tea and toast. Twenty minutes later someone much more like my mother returns.

We sit for a long time, eating, drinking and saying nothing. And then I can't continue to say nothing any longer.

'This can't go on.' I am looking away, not wanting to make eye contact. 'It's just ridiculous.' And she remains silent which I choose to take as a tacit agreement.

'You're not happy, are you?' But she doesn't reply, choosing instead to stare into her empty mug.

'Mum, tell me, are you happy, can you honestly say this is how you wanted to end up?' I know I am starting to sound as if I am bullying her for an answer.

'No,' and her face crumples, her body slackens and half a decade of regret finally comes tumbling out. From both of us.

I tell her about the Orangery and how she could live there and maintain some independence but have the support she needs and how she can be part of a family again. But she doesn't want it. So we compromise, as we so often do with those we love, not because it is the best solution but because it is the easiest.

Mum agrees to sell her apartment and I agree to find her a cottage in Barnard Castle.

'You've always loved it there, the children are at school nearby so we're there every day and only twenty minutes away if you need us at any other time.'

We convince each other that it is a perfect compromise and I embark on a mission to relocate Mum to somewhere we can better care for her.

And significantly, she doesn't argue.

Before I leave I arrange for my brother to come and stay with Mum for a few days. A community nurse has been coming every other day to change the dressings on her operation wounds which remain infected and aren't healing but she tells us it is not her responsibility to keep an eye on Mum's general welfare, 'It's not my job.' And she maintains she hasn't noticed any deterioration in Mum's ability to take care of herself.

'It's crap,' I say to my brother.

'Bollocks, more like,' he replies. 'Bloody job's worth.'

But Mum has been having a home help, Christine, who rises to the challenge when we explain what has been going on and is sympathetic to the situation.

'I know she struggles to eat and I know she's spent nights in the chair because she says it's more comfortable than lying down, but she's always perked up when I've been there. She's a fighter your Mum, no mistake,' Christine says and she is clearly fond of her charge.

'Well maybe it's time she stopped fighting and gave in to the inevitable,' I say and Christine doesn't disagree.

Two days later my brother phones. He was awoken in the early hours by moans from Mum's bedroom and found her on the floor in a pool of blood with blood soaked sheets tumbling from the bed. Her infected wound had burst open and she was losing blood fast. He'd called an ambulance.

'I thought she wasn't right yesterday afternoon,' he says, 'I called the GP and he told me to make an appointment the next day. I said it was serious but he told me to make her comfortable and call in the morning if there was no change. He sounded as if he'd had enough of hearing about her.'

She was unconscious by the time the paramedics arrived.

The Orangery eventually becomes ours at the beginning of October and, having dallied with the idea of converting it, first into a granny flat for Mum and then guest bedrooms, we decide that space is now at such a premium in our own house, which adjoins it, that we should knock through and connect the two.

But plans are not easily made when there are so many other matters to think about. Finance, for one thing rears its ugly head again. We have no spare cash to pay someone to knock a hole through the dividing wall, although Wendy once again says, 'we'll find a way.' And for another, I am practically living on the motorway between here and the West Country.

Following a barrage of tests which have spanned several weeks the doctors have discovered that a one inch long portion of loose bone has been rattling around in Mum's chest cavity following her previous operation to sort out an infected rib.

Of course there is no hint of an apology, other than a private room. They give a blanket, 'well these things do happen' response – astonishing coming from the very doctors responsible for the whole mess in the first place. There is a general agreement that a further operation is required but not until Mum is fit enough because the bone shrapnel has made her very ill and very weak.

'Yes, we know that,' is my weary response.

A lesser person would surely have given up the will to live by now but, ten days after being admitted Mum is on top form. She's thrilled with her hospital room with views over the whole of Bristol, has had time to catch up with all her old nurse friends and is on a special diet of build up milk shakes which she proclaims to be far superior to the usual muck they serve up. She is, in short, feeling thoroughly well looked after and feels that at last the cause for her years of pain and illness has been identified.

'At least they didn't find a set of surgical instruments in there as well,' she jokes but I'm not sure I see the funny side. Particularly when, in response to my query about how this large piece of bone hasn't been detected during numerous previous scans I am told, 'It may have been hidden behind something else.'

But there is no point any of us dwelling on past mistakes because Mum isn't, so we look now to the future.

'I've found you a lovely little cottage in the middle of Barney and we can get a stair lift put in. And we've found a buyer for your place,' I tell her, and she is excited.

'We can put all this behind us. We can make up for lost time I hope,' she says.

'Yes, the children are looking forward to having you just around the corner from school.'

'When they're a bit older they'll be able to come round for tea and I can pick them up from school, they can even sleep over.' The words are tumbling out with the enthusiasm of a young child who wants to tell you everything on their Christmas wish list all at once for fear that if they don't say it out loud, it won't all come true. And all I can really says is, 'yes, Mum,' and smile.

On my return home Wendy is excitable. She has good news and

wants to show me something. She leads me into Oliver's bedroom and says, 'look!'

'Look at what?' I'm genuinely mystified.

'There, in the end wall.' I look closer and there is a one inch diameter hole in the wall.

'Go and look through,' she urges me.

I do and what I see is the Orangery on the other side.

We both jump about like idiots, laughing until we cry because of an inch wide hole in the wall. For so many reasons it seems that little hole represents light at the end of a tunnel.

CHAPTER NINETEEN

The castle's reputation continues to grow and we decide to enter the Cumbria Tourism awards. Regardless of whether it's because we enjoy the accolade or whether it is just the promise of a good night out and an excuse for Wendy to buy more new shoes, we are excited. And there's always the prospect of another gong to display on the hall table.

Awards do have their downside, however, as sometimes guests don't see past them and find themselves in a place they neither expect or desire. This is never truer than with visitors from abroad.

'The Russians are coming,' this was the shout going through the castle. Well, in fact they've been and gone but they leave quite an impression.

'Vee are vanting your best rooms for tomorrow.' The dialogue starts on a Tuesday afternoon.

'Well, all our rooms are the same price and quality.'

'Zay must be interconnecting and have a view of ze lake.'

'Ve're not near any lakes, ve've got a wildlife pond though.' Oh dear, I'm slipping into Russian. I check myself.

'You are not in ze lakes district? How fars is ze lakes avay?'

'Forty minutes.'

'Ve can vawk zere in forty minutes?'

'No, forty minutes by car.' At this point, Anastasia, turns to her partner and says 'zey are in ze middle of nowhere.' I'm outraged as this is an observation often made of us that simply is not true. While Siberia might be in the middle of nowhere we are in fact very well connected to everywhere.

'Um excuse me, we're not in the middle of nowhere, we're just not in a town or village and people find that very charming.'

'So you're in ze middle of a field?'

'We're surrounded by lots of fields.'

'Well zis is a very special birthday so ve vant ze best interconnecting rooms you have, and a table in ze restaurant for ze dinner.'

'We don't have a restaurant, everyone eats together. It's very egalitarian.' (I'm hoping this may appeal to any communist leanings she may have but suspect she is more of the new monied type of Russian).

'Look, I hope you don't mind, and I'm not in the habit of turning away business, but I don't think this is going to be the right place for you.'

'You don't vant us?'

'I think it's more a case of you'll not want us,' I reply. Anastasia can't quite take in what I'm telling her as I explain that I'd rather help her find a hotel that better fits her expectations than for her to stay with us and be disappointed by her expectations not being met.

I suggest she tries Gilpin Lodge, The Samling and Holbeck Ghyll, some of the finest hotels right in the middle of the Lake District. She thanks me for my honesty and help and as she rings off I breathe a sigh of relief. But it is short lived.

At 11.30pm she calls back (I am always inclined to answer calls at this time of night because they are usually pressing emergencies from guests who somehow have actually got past my stringent vetting procedures such as, 'we forgot to tell you that we are allergic to feathers and will die in the night unless the bed is changed' or 'please can you remove the canopy from my four poster bed because I'm arachnophobic and am afraid a spider will fall on me in the night and I will die'). She tells me that she has looked at all the other places and ours is still the one they prefer.

'You are holding of so many avards already, so ve are still cummink, how far outside London are you?'

In a last ditch attempt to put them off I am tempted to tell them we are twelve hours from London, a trip which will include two river crossings by manually propelled ferry and a traverse of the Pennines on foot or by pack horse if they can find a willing local guide. Then I think that if they have already escaped across the Ural Mountains to get this far with all their cash in suitcases being pursued by angry

Soviet secret policemen, even that is not going to put them off.

'Six hours, maybe seven,' well, I'm allowed a little manipulation of the facts at this time of night. She tells me they will be leaving London at nine so we should expect to see them around teatime.

'Lovely.'

The next day four Russians arrive at around teatime and are delighted that the journey was less onerous than they had imagined and they have been able to take in Chester on the way - quite a feat given that they apparently left London via the M1. They seem to be genuinely delighted to be at Augill and there are many compliments about the magnificence of our 'charmink baronial styling guesthouses.'

I take them upstairs and explain that I have managed to give them rooms at the front of the castle which, while not affording them a view of the lakes, they do have a view of the gardens (including our wildlife pond) and the Yorkshire and Lakeland fells and that just behind those fells are some lakes which they can visualise with a little imagination.

However, this, rather inexplicably, does not go down quite as well as I anticipate.

'And also ze Scotch Highlands ve can see zem from here?' asks Anastasia's friend, Natalya, who is dressed in a complete designer running outfit that probably cost more than a small mountain in Scotland. I swear there are diamonds on her trainers that match the ones in her teeth (definitely not a communist).

'No, you can't see Scotland from here,' but they don't seem to be listening.

'I vant to taste all zat is best of Scotland's food and drink tonight,' she exclaims airily, waving her hand at what I take to be an imaginary flunky but which is actually aimed at me.

'You do realise we're not in Scotland don't you?' thinking as I say it that the only typical Scottish food I could rustle up would be leftover haggis from New Year followed by some more modern deep fried Mars bars and perhaps a dash to the local chippy may yield some chips with gravy.

'Zis is not Scotland? Ve are not in Scotland? Ver is Scotland? Ver is zis place?' Her pitch and tone rising hysterically with each question.

'This is England,' I want to add a lyrical but melancholy eulogy to our great seafaring, industrial world conquering past but decide against it, 'Scotland's about fifty miles up the road.

'You could get there and back by dinner time if you hurry,' I add helpfully.

She's clearly not amused and I decide to skirt around the geographical confusion by launching enthusiastically, as I back away towards the door, into what there is to do in this majestic corner of England. All that's missing is Elgar on a backing track. A little later, Anastasia's partner, Igor, finds us in the kitchen.

'I sink zer has been a terrible mistake. We are tellink all our friends already ve are celebrating tonight in Scotland and zis is not ze case. I sink ve vill haff to leaf in ze morninks and not stay ze second night.'

We offer, perhaps a little too readily, to help with recommendations in Edinburgh, suggesting the city is a part of Scotland not to be missed (the only part in Wendy's book but let's not stimulate a cross border feud here).

'Sankyou but zat vill not be necessary, ve are vanting a country place with lots of character in ze countryside surrounded by hills and scenery.'

'But...' If I'd kept my mouth shut they'd never have known the difference between lakes and lochs, dales and glens. They're only lucky they didn't get all the way to Scotland and mistake it for England. Goodness only knows what would have happened to them then.

A further dividend of our higher profile is that local shoots which have never given us a second look in the past are now beginning to recommend us to their clients. Shooters, rather like the Russians, are a strange bunch and there are always some that really ought to have stayed elsewhere.

One particular couple haven't been recommended but found us some time ago when we were much smaller and cheaper. And they seem surprised that anything has changed. The shooting party is going on up the valley and we've picked up the overspill who presumably aren't quite good enough to stay with, you've guessed, it, the beastly Blanchard-Caffertys. Apparently our guests came to the charity ball we were duped into hosting from outside the tent a few years ago.

There's something about shooters and shooting parties that I just don't get. Maybe you've got to be part of the set which, since my antics with a shotgun a couple of years ago, I am definitely not (I suspect word has got round).

For one thing, in these days of modern, high tech outdoor clothing, Goretex and the like, to which a whole industry is devoted, what on earth is anyone doing tramping across wet, windswept moors in heavy cotton drill plus-fours tucked into woollen socks above a pair of polished brogues wearing a tweed jacket and flat cap?

Not only do they look ridiculous but it is totally impractical. If it's raining they must come back at the end of the day weighing twice what they did at the start. In the village is a tailor's shop dedicated to kitting out shooters and gamekeepers in just this sort of attire and incredibly people come back year after year for a re-fit. Champions of the sport will argue that it's all in the name of tradition but tradition can move with the times and adapting one's attire doesn't mean the demise of the shoot.

More people climb Mount Everest every year but they sure as hell aren't wearing the same garb and using the same equipment as Edmund Hillary and Sherpa Tensing did in 1952.

But if the uniform of shooting gets me riled it is nothing compared to the attitude and pomposity that can go with it. As a black Mercedes pulls up outside one murky early autumn afternoon I'm quickly at the door as it's pouring with rain. Out get two decidedly tweedy types and the car really doesn't fit the image.

'We've hired the car,' I'm quickly told by way of an apology, 'one simply doesn't need one full time in Kensington.'

'Right-ho! I'm Simon,' and being September I proffer a well worn, season-weary hand and smile.

'Quentin Farquhar-Smythe, delighted,' and I get the impression he thinks it's me who should be delighted. 'And this is Chla...'

The lady is of some central European extraction and I just don't catch her name. It sounds like Chlamydia but surely it isn't. Unfortunately I am not given a chance for a second enquiry.

'Do come in out of the rain,' and I gesture them into the hall.

Chlamydia is wearing a fitted tweed jacket, white jeans, high-heeled and highly polished shoes and is sporting a small Harrods carrier bag on her wrist by way of a handbag. She spies me eyeing up the bag.

'It's my Bag for Life,' she snorts, 'do you approve?'

A Louis Vuitton bag would have been classier, I think.

'Do call us Quen and Clam,' I am invited. Oh must I? And I resist making an offer for them to call me Si. 'Let me show you round.'

'We've been before, to the B-C ball,' Quentin tells me. I expect you do jolly well from Martin and Clarissa's overflow?'

A mental image forming of Martin and Clarissa's overflow I quickly put out of my head. 'Um, well I don't think we're top of their list of recommendations,' I counter.

'Oh yes, they say they're terribly good friends of yours.'

'Really?'

'You've done it up in here,' he says, as we enter the music room, unintentionally changing the subject which is a shame as I am keen to know more about our apparently inseparable friendship with the B-Cs.

'Yes, and we've had some new sofas.'

'Well done,' he says, stroking the sofas appreciatively, 'I seem to remember it was all looking a bit shabbers before.'

Quentin is carrying a shotgun over his shoulder and I offer to lock it away in the safe.

'Going to shoot the guts out of a few dozen baarrds,' he exclaims in a sort of gutteral, rather overfed, over-stuffed with self-importance sort of way.

'Excuse me?' I didn't quite catch that.

'Baarrds - grouse.'

'Oh, birds.' I feel like shooting the bollocks off a guest or two right now but I think better of telling him so. With the gun safely stowed I take Q & C to their room, a garden suite.

'Bit inconvenient having the door from outside opening into the bedroom,' he observes.

'Is it? Where would you have us put the door?' I ask politely through gritted teeth.

He doesn't answer but shouts at nobody in particular 'Lights?'

'Um yes, on the ceiling,' I am perplexed by both the question and why he should be shouting.

'How d'you switch em on?'

'With the switches, usual sort of arrangement,' but he's not listening and is rattling a door in the bathroom.

'Lavvy in here is it?'

'No, that's a store cupboard the lavatory is behind you.'

'Jolly good. Need a good turnout after all that driving.' Oh for goodness sake. Even Chlamydia winces.

'See you for drinkies then, got the Blanchard-Caffertys coming at about seven fifteen.'

'OK, are they staying for dinner?' I ask.

'God no!'

'Thanks.'

The Blanchard-Caffertys arrive customarily late for drinks and decide to stay for dinner too. It's actually not Martin and Clarissa, but Martin's brother Jeremy (Jezza to his intimates) and his ghastly wife Julia. The whole family is late for everything, something to do with their ill-disguised contempt for anyone who doesn't have a share of their genes – which is pretty much everyone since, for generations they have been very wary of sharing genes outside the immediate family.

Their contempt for us is further compounded by the fact that we work for a living in something as tawdry as hospitality.

'They're just trade,' one of the B-Cs was once overheard as saying, conveniently oblivious to the fact that what is left of their family fortune is founded on slavery.

Well I don't like to harp on about it, but our house is still bigger than theirs and they know it. And it's not falling down.

Needless to say the Blanchard-Caffertys fail to acknowledge either Wendy or myself as anything other than staff so Wendy takes the initiative by grabbing Julia's hand in a hearty handshake. 'How lovely to see you, are you well?'

Julia looks almost ready to wretch.

'Ignorant bitch,' says Wendy as she returns to the kitchen.

Dinner is almost ready and both of us, in chef jackets, go into the library to see our guests.

Chlamydia is clapping with delight, 'You're not the chefs?' she squeals.

'Well unless we're dressed like this to extract your teeth I think we probably are,' I reply.

'Oh you're soo clevvaar. How priceless, what a wheeze.' The whole experience is clearly way outside her comfort zone, having never encountered Heston Blumenthal or Gordon Ramsay anywhere near their own restaurants, let alone mingling with the guests, and she just becomes shriller and shriller.

Wendy turns to me, 'I don't know about wheezing, but I'm gasping for a drink,' and we retreat to the relative sanity of the kitchen.

Dinner goes well. Quentin gets ridiculously drunk and regales the table with tales of his happy days at prep school with one or other of the Blanchard-Cafferty brothers. 'Got buggered senseless by the prefects, didn't do me any harm.' If there's some debate about that, nobody's about to start it here.

Chlamydia doesn't say or eat much at all. Apparently she has issues with duck. It seems she's happy for Quentin to blast them out of the sky (Clam doesn't shoot of course, she's happier sitting in someone else's Range Rover leafing through the latest copy of *Hello* skillfully concealed inside the pages of *Tatler* or *Country Life*) but she can't stomach it on the plate. 'Don't worry,' she says, 'I've eaten the salady bits and half a new potato, they were delish and I'm absolutely stuffed.'

Another guest who, while not involved in the shooting, has obviously loved being caught up in all the pretentiousness has eaten everything and has her own way of telling us how good it was. 'You're so brave doing duck, people who don't know what they're doing so often get it wrong.'

Between dessert and cheese Quen, Chlam and their new found allies disappear, leaving the other half of the table looking a little shell shocked but ultimately relieved. We decide to sit down with them for cheese.

Quentin spots this and comes through from the music room.

'Aren't you going to come and sit with us?' he asks indignantly.

Before we have a chance, our other guests answer for us, 'No, they're not.'

Of course, this widening customer base means that we do find the cash to knock through to the Orangery but unfortunately the builder we found has had an accident banger racing and has apparently broken every bone in his body.

It's jolly inconvenient and the prospect of being knocked through and connected by Christmas evaporates, particularly since the only replacement builder we can find is the one who renovated the Stable House and set a new record for the length of time taken to plaster four walls.

The progress of Mum's house move is, by contrast, much less troubled but for one thing: she is still hospitalised. So her entire move is being orchestrated in her absence. This presents a unique and totally unexpected problem. The NHS simply cannot process the circumstances of a patient entering hospital living at one address and then changing address while there, to one in a completely different region of the country. It falls to a consultant who has a friend in the Freeman Hospital in Newcastle to pull some strings to navigate the problem and ensure that Mum can have continuity of care and not have to re-enter a new system and start all over again from the beginning.

In the end she is transferred by NHS taxi (because to travel with us she would have to be discharged from the system and then be re-admitted which we are told is inadvisable, and I am inclined to agree) and is allocated a bed in a cottage hospital in Alston. I imagine an NHS trolley following the taxi up the M6 carrying Mum's impressively thick patient notes and only later do I realise what wishful thinking that really was.

The move to Alston, England's highest, most isolated and, for nine months of the year, almost inaccessible, market town at the very top of the Pennines, is clearly a decision made by someone with no grasp of geography armed only with a map and a pin. That it has retained its cottage hospital is testament to just how out of the way it is and its only proximity to us is that it is in Cumbria, but only just.

Nevertheless, when we get word that she has arrived we bundle the children into the car after school and drive the 50 minutes across the moors to the hospital. It's early November and there is already snow on the ground up here and it's not long before Oliver has worked Emily into a frenzy with the suggestion of wolves around every bend.

It is truly desolate but Mum is not bothered. 'Anything is better than another day in that filthy hospital in Bristol,' she says. True, it's clean and the staff are a delight. She is in good spirits, joking and making a valiant attempt to engage with the children who have yet to get past the fact that she is an old lady in a hospital that smells of convalescence and palliative care.

'How long will she be here before she can go home?' I ask the sister, or matron or whatever cottage hospitals have.

'A week or so. She's made a good recovery so we're just monitoring her really. It's a long way to travel and we've just got to make sure her temperature and bloods are stable.'

'She's asked for fish and chips, can we get her some?'

'Well we don't really allow food to be brought in but as long as you keep it in her room it'll be OK. From what I've heard about her case it sounds as if she deserves it.'

So we welcome Mum to Cumbria with a fish and chip supper, all perched on her bed in Alston, a million miles from anywhere but a step closer to what we all hope will be a better quality of life and a chance to build some new bridges.

As we leave I reassure her that she'll soon be in her new house which is all newly decorated and full of her stuff.

'It's cold up here,' is all she says.

'It's not cold in here though,' I reply.

'It is,' she says and begins to shiver, 'pass me my jumper.' And as we leave she is wrapping herself up in anything she can find to keep warm.

CHAPTER TWENTY

Against all the odds and almost without us noticing, so consumed are we with Mum's predicament, our builder finds time to extend the existing two inch connection between the Stable House and the Orangery into a full blown opening in mid-December. It's nowhere near a fully functioning doorway, rather a ragged hole in the wall with a step ladder spanning the eighteen inch change in floor levels but nevertheless we feel we at last have room to breath, swing a cat and, most importantly, store all our family junk.

'Just like ordinary families,' observes Oliver when, a few weeks after we have moved the sitting room and dining room into the Orangery, he opens a cupboard and a whole assortment of unrelated paraphernalia including a tennis racquet, a game of scrabble and one of Wendy's bras comes tumbling out.

Oliver is frozen as if the cups of the bra at his feet are poised to morph into two gargantuan jaws and take off his fly-half's kicking foot in one bite.

I want to remind him of more innocent times when, on seeing his mother for the first time wearing a thong he carefully examined her apparel and remarked, with a genuine note of warning, 'Mummy, your bottom has eaten your pants.'

'Ooh, I've been looking for that everywhere,' Wendy says excitedly when she sees the disgorged contents of the cupboard and she's not referring to plans for a game of scrabble.

We are planning to have the kitchen next to the dining room but this involves moving the Aga from upstairs in the Stable House to downstairs in the Orangery. Although this is referred to as an internal shift by the Aga engineers (and inexplicably but happily costs a fraction of the price of moving it to another building, even though the process of dismantling and rebuilding is exactly the same), there is still a four month waiting list so for now the dining room and the kitchen are some fifty metres apart and on separate floors.

Despite these unconventional domestic arrangements the family is happy which is some consolation for what turns out to be a lousy Christmas and New Year.

Following her transfer to Alston, Mum had started running a temperature and by the weekend a fever had set in. She was transferred to the Freeman Hospital in Newcastle where more tests were carried out. Her condition deteriorated and the doctors seemed baffled.

A few days before Christmas she is lying in an isolation ward semiconscious. We are told there is nothing more that can be done other than to make her comfortable. It's a euphemism I will hear again. But for now we are confused and upset. How can somebody go from eating fish and chips to being on death's door in a matter of weeks without any sort of explanation?

She is in an isolation room in the department for infectious and tropical diseases. On other doors read notices such as 'Malaria', 'Hospital acquired infection', and 'Yellow Fever'. I wouldn't wish any of those on my mother but at least the occupants of those rooms and their families know what's wrong with them and presumably have some hope of a cure. On Mum's door the notice simply reads 'non specific'.

'Why is she here if you don't know what's wrong with her?' I ask a junior doctor who is clearly sleep deprived.

'It's just a precaution, we have run every test we can think of for infectious diseases and she is clear but she is still displaying all the symptoms,' he says.

But I remain suspicious. 'Symptoms of what?'

'A non specific bacterial infection.'

'You mean like MRSA?'

'No, sir, non specific. She is being treated with intravenous broad spectrum antibiotics and now we must just wait for an improvement.' We are being fed lies from a well-rehearsed script.

But there is no improvement. On Christmas Eve we take the children to visit her with her presents and while we are there she becomes feverish and disorientated. The staff do what they can which isn't much and by the time we leave she has no idea what day it is, where she is or who we are. The children sob quietly for most of the journey home. Wendy and I can find nothing to say to each other. Between Christmas and New Year I spend every afternoon at the hospital holding a one way conversation. Occasionally there are moments of lucidity but on the whole she is not there in the room. It's as if she has gone elsewhere.

On New Year's Day I am called in to see the doctors who tell me that I should probably prepare for the worst as there is simply nothing else they can do.

'She's a fighter, your Mum.'

I want to scream, 'I know she's a bloody fighter, I just don't know what she's fighting for other than this living hell.' And I prepare myself and the rest of the family for what seems like the inevitable.

Yet, against all the odds, she pulls through and at the beginning of February she eventually steps over the threshold of her new house in Barnard Castle, three months after she bought it.

As spring draws on we await with rapt anticipation the date of the Cumbria Tourism awards night. Wendy has bought a new frock which leaves me just enough to treat myself to some new socks and pants to go with my well worn dinner suit. In order to get into her new frock, Wendy has also invested in some special underwear. I am unsure of the technical specifications but I am assured by Wendy that, rather like scaffolding on a building site, without the undergarments the whole structure of the outfit will fall down.

So it doesn't go down well when, having arrived at the hotel in Kendal where we are to spend the night I unpack the car to discover that I have left the bag containing all our toiletries, my socks and pants and the special underwear at home. In my mind's eye I can see the bag sitting at the top of the stairs.

Wendy has already gone inside to check in.

'Um, there's been a bit of an administrative cock up,' I begin to explain.

Wendy turns to look at me as if she already knows what's coming so there's little I can do to sugar the pill. 'Someone's left the bag behind.' It isn't the right phraseology.

'Someone?' she shrieks, 'someone is a fucking idiot.'

As if with a death wish I then make things worse, 'well you didn't notice...'

The next few minutes are consumed in a frenzy of recriminations and flying scatter cushions before I suggest that we calm down and get ourselves to Marks & Spencer before it closes.

'They won't have the right stuff,' she complains.

'Rubbish,' I say more confidently than I feel, 'they must be experts in providing women with odd shapes to look good.' And once again I realise I've made matters a whole lot worse.

M&S does come up trumps and, suitably scaffolded, Wendy agrees to accompany me to the awards after all where we win Cumbria Tourism Guest Accommodation of the Year.

It isn't until we return to our hotel that we take a good look at what we have won. The award trophy is made of a large hunk of slate which I fancy may come in useful at a later date for mending the roof. For now though, I secret it away out of sight because it's rather heavy and has sharp edges and I don't want it flying across the room in my direction in the morning when Wendy discovers that her change of clothes are also in the bag with the special underwear.

In the weeks that follow our award success we receive much welcome attention from the press but also a lot of unwelcome attention from advertising executives. One such call catches me on a particularly bad morning. I have used up my daily quota of charm on some, frankly, undeserving guests and there's nothing left for anyone else.

'I'm calling from the *Borcestershire Courier* to offer you a heavily discounted opportunity to advertise in our publification'

'I beg your pardon?' I can hardly believe what I've just heard.

'We are a weekly publification...'

OK that's enough. In common with most businesses we get innumerable unsolicited sales calls every day, and a good many of them are from newspapers and magazines: *The South East Wiltshire Weekly Wurzle*, *The Cumberland Gurner*, *The North Somerset Scrumpy Press* and the *Yorkshire Yawner*. I have every sympathy for the poor souls at the other end of the telephone. I used to write for just such worthy oracles of local information and debate and I know how difficult it is to cajole local advertisers to believe in a newspaper. So I can feel the desperation that must be filling the ad sales department when the advertising manager announces that the paper is doing a feature – or an advertorial – on a holiday location 250 miles away and everyone is to get as many advertisers on the hook as possible. A fair few of the sales team will be spotty youths fresh out of school, either of their own volition or because they've been asked to leave, so the only way the campaign is going to work is to issue a script and drum into them that this must not be deviated from. And this is where the fun begins.

I want to say that I don't think the script says 'publification' but as it's such a priceless imprecision I'm encouraging him to repeat it. Of course, in interjecting and asking questions unexpectedly I try to throw him completely off script, adding to the sport.

'I'm sorry, can you just repeat the name of your title. And what are you, daily, evening...?' But he's not phased yet.

'*The Borcestershire Courier* is a weekly free publification and we reach 550,000 readers each week.'

'What! How many?'

'550,000 and they are only ABC1 readers.' Now this conversation did really take place, I have changed the newspaper name to save some blushes and a possible court case, but suffice to say that the county served by this illustrious free rag which is claiming more readers than *The Times* does not even have 550,000 inhabitants and, other than a handful of cider magnates, a paucity of ABC1 locals.

'How do you work that out?' I'm intrigued.

'Because we are a free paper we have a very high pass-on rate.' I should say, and imagine copies of the *Borcestershire Courier* being couriered twice round the globe each week to reach the 530,000 expat sons and daughters of Borcestershire who no longer live in the county but must live in rapt anticipation of news from the shire.

Oh, but there's no stopping him now, 'Due to the current climatic recessionary climate we are having,' he is either abandoning the script in desperation or he has lost a contact lens and is trying to carry on manfully, 'high end holidays are a thing of the past and high disposable income families are looking to the UK for their quality destination breaks.' No, he's sticking to the script, it's just that he wrote it himself.

'Having seen your advertisement publificated in the *Westmorland Whinger* you have been identified as a prime business to appear in our publification where we are doing a feature on the Lakes Valley District Park and the Yorkshire Dales and Moors National Park.'

At this point I'm so excited at the opportunity I blurt out, 'how much do you want for this?'

'Because we only have a few spaces left,' yeah, right, 'we can offer you a matchbox sized ad in full monotone for £23.75.' I wonder whether each copy of the courier comes with a free magnifying glass but guess not if it has got to reach such a vast global audience within a week, so ask if there might be a slightly larger size ad available. Of course, I am not hopeful as the deadline is tomorrow and there is only limited space left.

'Well, I can do a quarter page for £50, a full page for £100 or the whole newspaper is yours for £250.' OK, so it's a buyer's market, 'is there any free editorial to go with that?'

'I think the feature has already been written.' Yes, and I'm sure it is a very well researched travelogue on what to do and where to go in the land of the Lakes Valley and the Yorkshire Dales and Moors.

'I'm sorry Damien,' I don't know that's his name but it's a fair guess, 'we just don't do local press advertising, it doesn't work.' I'm sure I hear the sound of his head crashing onto the desk and a slight whimper at the end of the telephone and wish there was something I could do.

'Damien, do keep in touch and let us know of any other upcoming imaginary land features,' I add encouragingly. 'We'd be especially interested in Mystery tours of Mordor or Short breaks for Hobbits in The Shire,' but there's no reply. Of course, for all his incompetence and inappropriately channelled enthusiasm, Damien is far less irksome than the other kind of ad sales rep: the one who wants to be your friend or treats you as if he already is.

'Hi, is that Simon?' I agree cautiously.

"It's Steve here from IveGotALoverlyPlaceToStay.com. How are you doing today?'

'Bugger off.'

'That's great. How's the weather with you, we've got a nice bit of sunny weather/snow/it's a bit blustery/a freak heatwave and people are dying (delete as appropriate). I've got news of an offer that will turn your business around.'

'There's nothing wrong with my sodding business.'

'Oh, so you're fully booked for the next eighteen months?'

'No, and I don't want to be, I'd be in a straitjacket if we were.' But Steve isn't listening and has no idea what sort of outfit he's trying to sell his decidedly dodgy website to. I'm inclined to judge websites by their name now, without even looking at them if they sound ridiculous as most increasingly do, as all the best domain names get used up. SeasideAccommodationNotQuiteByTheSeaButWithAVeiwOfIt.com, ReallyVeryNicePlacesToStay.com, TieTheKnotUpTheDuff.com, MarryYourBoyfriend.com all smack of desperation and so do the people employed to flog them.

Which brings me back to Steve. 'I can guarantee you fully booked rooms once you've taken a listing with us. I know you run a quality establishment, it looks amazing and I only wish I could afford to come and stay,' OK, now I'm really aggravated.

'I'm not interested.'

'Well, can you afford to say that Simon, me old friend? We have our sales manager, Kevin, in your area this afternoon at 2.30, can I ask him to call in and see you?'

'No.'

'Well he'll be in your area tomorrow, or Thursday if that suits.' What the bloody hell has he done, pitched a tent at the top of the drive? Are we being web-stalked?

'No no NO NO!'

'Well I appreciate you're busy running your fantastic property and next time Kevin is in your area, perhaps he can pop in.'

Well he'd better make an appointment, I think to myself, and I'm going to be ready for him with my own script. Better give Damien a call back for a few tips.

We are riding high. The new living arrangements are working well, Mum is settled although still in constant pain, the root cause of which nobody seems to be able to get to, and the award seems to be bringing us plenty of new guests. We are also enjoying the company of a new cat. Harry has replaced Sooty, our trusty, long suffering black moggy who died earlier in the spring. He was nineteen.

Harry is white. Totally impractical for the country but somewhere back in the mists of time a gullible daddy promised his daughter a white kitten. He is also long haired, although in our defence he wasn't meant to be since both his pedigree parents are short haired.

'It's a throw back,' says the breeder without any offer of compensation. He is adorable but he's still a cat. And Emily has announced that she has saved enough pocket money for two pet mice.

A seven-year-old daughter does indeed have a hypnotic effect on her father. I am powerless to resist and before I know it we have our names down against two white mice at the pet shop. Now mice and hotels are rarely a happy combination. And the combination of mice, a hotel and a young cat is asking for trouble.

I try one final appeal to Emily's logical side in explaining that the natural order of things will not bode well for the longevity of the mice. I share my feelings that mice have been elevated beyond pet status and now many have an eminently more noble calling living in labs with human organs such as ears growing on their backs but I'm not getting through. So I share with her the story of the field mouse which Harry brought into the entrance hall of the castle a few weeks ago just as an American family was arriving.

'Oh how adorable your pet mouse is, it's so tame, it let me stroke it and it hardly moved,' says one of the parents of the visiting family to Wendy.

'Gross,' mutters one of the teenagers. Wendy mutters something inaudible as she has no idea there was a rodent lurking inside the front door. On examining the creature more closely she discovers that Harry has indeed brought in a live mouse that seems quite tame. It is making no effort to seek sanctuary behind the skirting or under the furniture, just quivering quietly. And this is hardly surprising as, from the stairs comes a howl of horror from another of the Americans at the discovery of the poor unfortunate mouse's two hind legs on the carpet. Gross indeed.

But Emily is unmoved and the mice come home. They have a smart new cage which she has bought with her own pocket money. They have food, a little plastic house with a chimney stack (although when I ask Em if they also have two armchairs and forks for toasting muffins on the fire she fixes me with one of those glares reserved by daughters for their fathers which says 'weird', 'old', 'fart' and 'locked up' all in one) and a wheel with an irreparable squeak as a constant reminder to them and us of the purgatory of life as a captive mouse.

They are to live in Emily's bedroom and seem quite settled and contented in their new abode. However, after a couple of nights, the mice's living arrangements are under review. 'They stink,' Emily wails. She is beside herself as they are staying up most of the night taking turns on the wheel of purgatory and Harry has worked himself in to such a frenzy over the fact that there are two ready meals fresh for the taking in the house that he has taken to spraying Emily's bedroom door with essence of pure excitement. 'That stinks too,' she howls.

The mice are relocated to the utility room on the understanding that Emily can bring them into her bedroom for playing with.

A few days on, all seems to have calmed down, except Harry. It's Friday teatime and a wedding party are arriving. I check the children are settled and poke my head into Emily's room. As I open the door, Harry shoots out and there is a scene of carnage and devastation. The cage is on it's side, there is bedding and food everywhere and in the middle of the carpet one mouse is twitching, the other is trying to get somewhere, anywhere, yes, you've guessed it, on just one pair of legs.

I run to the castle front door where Wendy is greeting guests and I half hide behind a tree and gesticulate wildly in her direction, imitating a mouse with fingers for whiskers, bearing my teeth and simultaneously drawing a slit across my throat. She fails to understand what I am trying to say but does understand that this sort of behaviour is not good for business and hurries everyone inside. Finally, after what looks like a rather apologetic explanation of her husband's erratic temperament to the guests, she comes out and I explain that she must distract Emily and stop her going into her bedroom while I clear up the scene.

What happens next then descends into true farce. When Emily eventually discovers what has happened she first says she hates the cat, then she hates us for having bought the cat, then she says she hated the mice anyway because what she really wanted was a pony and only agreed to the mice because there was no pony in the shop and then she declares there must be a funeral at once. Memories of the moles flood back.

This is quickly arranged. A hole is dug, the mice are popped in and I'm just about to cover them over when Emily says 'there must be some singing Mummy.'

Mummy looks at me, I just lean on my grave digger's shovel and she sighs the sigh of a mother who knows she must do whatever it takes for the good of the family. So she obliges with what she later claims was the only thing she could think of and across the lawn drifts a moving rendition of *Ave Maria*. I lower my gaze into the grave to pay my last respects to two mice and a pair of legs and Emily sprinkles a few daisies in for good measure. When I look up the entire assembly of wedding guests is pressed against the drawing room window and in front of them all, sitting on the window seat, is Harry and I swear he's smiling.

Chapter Twenty One

In keeping with Wendy's mantra that 'we'll find the money some-where', we find money from somewhere to take on a management cou-ple for the summer season. It's a huge leap of faith since until now we have directly controlled everything ourselves.

The decision does not go down universally well with our existing staff until we point out that the alternative is that they can share overnight cover, stay up until the last drunken wedding guests have gone home or to bed, have no more flexi-time through the school hol-idays and work every other Sunday. Val in particular is uneasy about the regime change, fearing that her military efficiency in the house-keeping department will be compromised.

So when Owen and Debi arrive in mid-May they are greeted with open arms by us, if not with open hearts and minds from the rest of the team. Owen is a chef whom we first encountered on a skiing hol-iday two years ago. He looked after us admirably and we were partic-ularly impressed by the way he re-used ingredients each night to make his budget stretch while not compromising on quality.

Together with his fiancée Debi, they are in charge of the day to day running of the castle for the summer. We plan to have a summer to ourselves. They are soon dubbed the mini-mes.

Unfortunately our plans for a long hot languorous summer of being cooked for and looked after hit a fundamental snag. It is neither hot or languorous. In fact it is the wettest, coldest summer since records began – and in Cumbria that is pretty damned wet and cold.

We do get away for a holiday in Spain however, and have the luxury of a whole fortnight off while remaining open for business. It's a first, and although the rest of the summer is pretty much a washout, we do at least enjoy being cooked some sublime lunches and dinners.

I take full advantage of my new freedom by beginning to, as Wendy describes it, 'put myself out there.' I attend a couple of tourism conferences and, on the back of our award success get elected onto the management committee of the tourist board. I secretly suspect that Wendy has her own strategy for enjoying her time while we have Owen and Debi looking after us and the castle (we both know we can't afford the luxury permanently) and part of it is to get me out of her hair.

But, beyond the walls of our castle, outside the bubble we have created, there's a storm brewing. The stock market has gone into free-fall and there is talk of a global recession. Consumer confidence is taking a bashing, ostensibly at the hands of the press which seems to have no idea what it is talking us into. Our experience with foot and mouth disease tells us that where the press is feeding frenziedly a crisis is sure to follow. We are nervous and so, clearly is our bank manager as he has requested a review meeting; something we have never before had to endure.

He is, apparently, keen that we should be getting the very best from what the bank has to offer. In truth, I think he has been charged by his superiors to keep an eye on us because we are part of a 'high risk industry'. His visit takes the guise of a 'mid-term annual health check'. As we sit down to discuss our finances over tea and delicious buns made by the chef I am sure the bank manager is now going to tell us we can't afford, I start by telling him there is absolutely nothing unhealthy about our finances. The overdraft is buoyant and we have been doing our bit to help the Chancellor stave off a recession by keeping up spending.

This is, predictably, greeted with a blank expression. The man is, in fact rather blank by nature, a cross between Frank Spencer and Mr Bean. He calls himself our relationship manager but hasn't done a thing to manage our relationship, other than to make it worse. Wendy can hardly stand to be in the same room with him and he makes me nervous, not because I am afraid of him, but because he is so inept I don't know what is going to happen next.

Nerves can lead to inappropriate behaviour. At a garden party we held last summer to celebrate ten years at the castle he was the only one who got his car stuck in the mud and as I pulled him out I joked that he should work harder, get a promotion and get himself a four wheel drive company car. This did not go down well and I dug a deeper hole by suggesting that the rescue was surely worth a favourable renegotiation of our overdraft terms. I'm not sure who was more relieved to be out of that field.

So, today I am on especially good behaviour.

'Do have a bun,' I implore, 'they are freshly baked.'

'No, I am on a diet,' he replies.

'Really, I thought you'd lost quite a bit of weight,' I say encouragingly, although he clearly hasn't.

'No, it's a gluten free diet, baked goods play havoc with my...'

'Well, so down to business,' I intervene and I decide his bun in my mouth as well as my own is the safest alternative to putting my foot in. It's a turgid meeting, rather like his digestion, as I knew it would be. He produces an agenda with headings such as 'business review', 'what the bank can do for you' (which is nothing more than a sales pitch for insurance - got it, investments - nothing to invest and pensions - plan to be looked after by the children beyond 50), and 'how can we improve our service?'

Luckily at this point in the proceedings I'm still scoffing buns and am unable to express my true sentiments so the meeting closes minus my thoughts on how to better manage relations between the bank and its customers which would start with him being out of a job. I let out a sigh of relief as he begins to pack away his papers but, horror of horrors, he begins a feeble attempt at small talk.

This is accompanied by a sudden smell of dog dirt. Surely it can't be... No, no amount of drivel can smell that bad. But I am conscious that the smell, which is coming and going, is definitely real. I surreptitiously check the soles of my shoes.

Then after a further five minutes or so I spy on the carpet beside the bank manager's foot a mouldering dog turd. This isn't a normal addition to the fixtures and fittings, but a Labrador in her dotage has her lapses. It looks quite dry and has blended well with the pattern on the carpet but is perilously close to the bank manager's right foot.

I wonder whether moving on to the sofa next to him and shuffling him along might work but decide this could go horribly wrong and that his ideas of our bank/customer relationship could be completely screwed. With a rare sense of empathy he has judged by the way my gaze is darting between him and the floor, that I am losing interest and picks up his briefcase.

It's upside down and all the contents fall out onto the floor.

In a mortifying slow motion split second he scoops all his papers up off the floor and stuffs them in to his case and when I look again there is no sign of the offending package.

And in a moment of pure comic irony, he turns to me and says, 'well thank you, I think that has been very comprehensive, I'm quite sure we shan't have any unpleasant surprises in the coming year as a result of today's meeting.'

I'm speechless. As we walk towards the front door, Wendy approaches from the opposite direction to say goodbye and I'm mouthing behind the bank manager's back 'dog shit' and pointing to the briefcase.

She fails to understand and assumes I am sharing with her my thoughts on the meeting.

'May I just use the facilities?' he enquires and puts down his case while he finds the lavatory. Quick as a flash, I'm delving inside, leafing through the papers in his case.

'What the hell are you doing?' asks Wendy.

'Dog's mess, Holly's poo is in the bag.'

'What? How did Holly get in the bag?'

'Oh don't be ridiculous, he picked it up by mistake.'

'How can you pick up a dog turd by mistake, what on earth are you talking about?'

I can't find it and too soon he's back and away. As soon as the front door closes I sprint to the music room and by the time Wendy has caught up with me I'm on all fours with my head under the sofa.

'Thank God!' I exclaim, 'the shit's still here'.

'No', says Wendy, 'he's just left, look he's getting into his car. You're not making any sense, Simon.'

'Not the bank manager, you fool, the turd,' and I point it out.

'Time to change banks,' I say.

'Before the shit hits the fan,' remarks Wendy and we both dissolve on the sofa.

We are feeling exposed. Although the business is good, we have, again, over extended ourselves with the renovations of the Orangery and two full time salaries. The economic forecast doesn't look good and neither do our forward bookings. We are sent into a further spin when we get news that the Coach House behind the castle, the ideal family home we never had, is back on the market.

'I don't believe this,' Wendy says with more than a little note of exasperation. 'Why couldn't this have happened last year?'

Whilst the Orangery and Stable House combined have afforded us some of the extra space we needed, the children's bedrooms are small and there is still little privacy as it is an integral part of the castle. But for now all we can do is watch prospective buyers of the Coach House come and go as the house itself taunts us daily. Viewings are few and far between as the global recession takes hold and we suspect the house is seriously over-priced.

'What will be will be,' says Wendy, more calmly that I expect.

Sarcastically, I ask, 'Is this another of your mantras along with "we'll find the money somehow"?' She just looks at me and smiles.

I cannot see how the Coach House is within our grasp. There is a strong business case. The room revenue we'd get from our quarters would more than cover the repayments on a new mortgage. But bank lending criteria have tightened requiring us to find a minimum 40 per cent of the purchase price. The value of what savings we have left has been decimated by the global financial crisis and we are now having to find the sodding school fees out of castle income which itself looks as if it might fall off the edge of a cliff any day.

It's not a pretty picture and every day I walk past the Coach House, as I must, I find myself turning my head away and literally giving it the cold shoulder.

By winning the Cumbria Tourism award we go forward to England's North West Regional Tourism Awards. The do is a big jamboree in Liverpool. Wendy is sceptical that we have any chance, I am quietly confident but am far too afraid to admit as much. This time we have managed to pack all the correct clothes and we are staying with a very good friend who plies us with champagne before we set off for St George's Hall, Liverpool's answer to the Albert Hall.

We find our seats at the end of a row.

'That's it, we've won,' I tell Wendy.

'What do you mean? How do you know?'

'We're at the end of a row so we can get to the stage easily,' I reason.

'Simon, practically half the audience is at the end of a row.'

Our category is first up. The flamboyant interior designer and TV celebrity Laurence Llewelyn-Bowen is compering and Wendy is suddenly excited that she might get a kiss. 'If we don't win, I'll collar him later,' she promises herself.

'Just don't show him your shoes,' I whisper, remembering our first awards ceremony.

After what feels like an interminably long stretch of lame jokes, it's time for the awards to be announced. On comes the trophy and the gold envelope and the nominees are read out, with pictures for each looming far too large on screens at either side of the stage.

We are squeezing each other's hands so hard it hurts because we both know that of all the years to win a regional award, with all the extra publicity that comes with it, this is the one.

'The winner is...'

And we know that if we win this we will be finalists at the national tourism awards too.

'The winner is...'

'Oh Christ, how difficult is it to open a sodding envelope?' I whisper.

'Augill Castle!'

Wendy screams. I punch the air. Everyone claps. There's loud music. The cameras find us and now I can't stop myself grinning and I hate how I look when I'm grinning especially when it's twelve feet wide on a big TV screen.

And then we're back in our seats. We have our award and our certificate but I can't remember collecting them, I can't remember anything except what bloody hard work the last eleven years have been. And I think, 'we deserve this.'

'I got a kiss off Laurence,' Wendy sings for the rest of the night, the award in one hand and champagne in the other. There are plenty of canapés and nibbles circulating but she eats nothing as she refuses to put down either the trophy or the bottle. I just get hammered.

When we wake up next morning there are three in our bed. Wendy, me and between us a twelve inch high lump of crystal with our name on it.

CHAPTER TWENTY TWO

Despite the doom and gloom thrown at us via every conceivable channel of communication, by Christmas it becomes clear that the world has not stopped turning, there is not mass unemployment and citizens of the western world are not taking up arms against each other to protect their own property.

Mum is better than she has been for some time, she is happy in her new home, although she is now confined to a wheelchair for any journey longer than 25 yards.

At the end of August we took her to Paris to celebrate her 70th birthday. It is somewhere she has always loved and she was thrilled to be back there with the four of us. Since moving into her new house in the spring she has made some effort at reconciliation with Oliver and Emily but they remain wary of her. Children are seldom at ease around old people they do not know intimately and she forfeited that intimacy too many years ago.

But in Paris we had a blast. There were many times when I would have happily pushed the wheelchair down the steps into the River Seine, incumbent included. Paris is not a city designed for wheelchairs and there is little concession anywhere in the city for them. Mum made a sterling effort to get out and walk when she had to but at the bottom of the Eiffel Tower as she was easing herself out of the chair I pushed her back down, perhaps a little too hard. 'Sit down and don't move,' I hissed. I had spotted an opportunity to dodge the August queues for the lift and I was quite happy for anyone to think she had lost all use of her legs.

After returning home she engaged the services of a cleaner. Wendy had offered on several occasions to help out with housework, shopping and any other chores but Mum was adamant that she could cope and wanted to remain independent with just a little help here and there. Naively and with the trust that should exist within a family but rarely, in reality, does we took her at her word. It would turn out to be one of our biggest mistakes.

Heartened by her spirit which had recovered in spite of her on-going pain we are all looking forward to Christmas in the sure knowledge it is going to be a whole lot better than the last.

By midday on Christmas Day I am nursing a bleeding cheek and a bruised eyebrow having sat on the sofa next to Wendy while she gets to grips with the latest family diversion – the new Wii. I am happily enjoying a modest second glass of something bubbly, watching the others play a game of virtual baseball. All of a sudden Wendy's arm flies back in my direction, the handset she is clutching escapes her grasp and hits me square on the left temple causing my right cheek to collide violently with a champagne flute I was already manoeuvring towards my mouth.

The real tragedy of course, is that the Bollinger is now all down my front.

The day had started unusually with Oliver tumbling into the room at ten past six with two mugs of tea and a torch. The tea was part of the bargain of us getting up when he did, but the torch? 'Well I couldn't find the light switches and it's still very dark,' he explained.

Luckily he is easily persuaded to go back to bed and we all eventually wake up at a very respectable 9.30.

We warned Mum that we wouldn't be down much before nine and she had stoically said she would occupy herself until we surfaced. Oliver reports back that she is, in fact, still snoring. She maintains that when he took her in her tea she was on the lavatory. We all decide it's a clear case of mistaken bodily functions and move on.

Santa has been and eaten the mince pies that the children left out. Rudolph has had half of the apple and the milk is gone. This is a relief as we'd forgotten to arrange this consumption before going to bed but it turns out that Mum had been peckish first thing and, on her way to the kitchen had discovered how thoughtful we had been in leaving her something to stave off the thirst and hunger while she waited for us to surface.

The fire lit, and everyone in their place, present opening begins. Emily shrieks with delight at a High School Musical something or other. Mum asks where we get such things. We remind her that is Santa's department. She looks blankly into her own stocking. Later she grumbles because someone has bought her a hairdryer. 'I didn't want all these attachments. Look at my hair, what do I want a volumiser for?'

'Well you don't have to use the bits, do you?'

'Waste of money.'

Later Mum complains about the children weeing on the toilet seat. She seems not to relate this indiscretion to her own involuntary releases of wind and belching between mouthfuls of Christmas dinner which we all feel could be more easily controlled.

'Any more sprouts?' she asks.

'No,' comes the chorused family response. Luckily she is now too infirm to reach the kitchen quickly for further investigation. After lunch we allocate her a downstairs bedroom so she can relieve herself a) without having to walk so far, b) so she does not have to suffer the inconvenience of mopping up the results of a ten-year-old's inability to aim in all the excitement of his new Wii and c) because frankly we've already had enough of her complaining about the distance to the lavatory and the frequency with which she has to go since she was put on a new regime of water tablets by the doctor which seem strong enough to drain the Nile.

'Have another sherry mother.'

'Do you think I should?'

'Do you feel alright?'

'Marvellous.'

'Fabulous – dry or medium?'

'Sweet please.'

'We haven't got sweet.'

'Oh, I'll have a Baileys then please, but just a small one.' As I go to the bar she calls after me, 'Don't water it down with too much ice.'

And so the day goes on in much the same was as Christmases for years gone by.

That is except having got over the children's noisy battery operated toys, we are now serenaded to the constant hum of Mum's massage cushion whose vibrations are pulsing through the wooden floor convincing us that a delivery lorry must be coming down the drive.

Having managed to replace the obligatory Christmas phone calls with texts, Wendy has now invested in a webcam and a Skype account which brings with it its own set of technological problems.

Eventually we get Auntie Gloria in Devon at the other end, who, because she had a webcam before everyone else in the family, is an expert – even though she can't work out much else.

It's a pretty good picture, with Auntie's scalp just visible in the bottom left hand corner of our screen. And there's a bonus – Great Auntie is there too, having had to stay a little longer than usual after lunch because of a bilious attack brought on by a heady mix of Brussels, chicken livers and Quality Street toffees. This has given her the perfect opportunity to say thank you for the lovely chocolates we sent her, although obviously she'll be saving them for the New Year. But she doesn't get much of a chance for thanks as Auntie can't see us.

'I can't get your picture.'

'Well we can see you, so Happy Christmas.'

'There's no need to shout Wendy, just speak normally,' I suggest.

'But I can't see you. We're not getting a picture.' Auntie says.

'Yes, but can you hear us? We're all here.'

'Stop shouting, Wendy.'

At this point five of us are flicking our gaze demonically between the pictures of Auntie and Great Auntie on the screen, the hideous spectre of our own five faces jockeying for position in a second box and the camera itself perched on top of the computer screen, wondering who or what we should be looking at, while at the same time holding a natural conversation.

'I can hear you, but we can't see you.' Then Auntie, who you will remember is the techno wizard in these matters says, 'We'll only be able to see you when you take the cover off the camera.'

'Thank you for the lovely chocolates Wendy, they really are...'

'Auntie do be quiet they can't hear us.'

'Yes we can hear you, you just can't see us,' Wendy is still shouting and starts fiddling with the camera to see if there is a cover.

And from the other end, 'We'll try again tomorrow,' declares Auntie.

'Thank you for those wonderful choc...' and the screen goes blank. It is soon after this unsuccessful dalliance with technology that we unwrap the Wii, and the rest is history.

As the New Year dawns so does the realisation that something is terribly wrong at school. Oliver is due to take his entrance exams for senior school but he is struggling to keep up with his classmates.

To be honest, he has always struggled and at the end of every year we have questioned whether he should be held back, whether he is getting the right support, whether he should be making better progress. And every year we have been assured that all is as well as can be expected for a child with dyslexia.

But all is not well and at the end of January, just three weeks before the exams, his class teacher telephones us to say he has grave concerns about Oliver's ability to gain a place at senior school.

'Grave concerns?' I ask incredulously, 'and you're telling us this now because...?'

'He just isn't equipped to pass the exam.'

'And whose job has it been to equip him?'

We are totally floored but are given every assurance by the headmaster that Oliver has as good a chance as anyone. We have no real choice but to trust him and in doing so override our own instinct to withdraw him from the exams.

When I confide in Mum that I am seriously concerned about Oliver's schooling and that, as a separate issue, Emily seems to be far from thriving, she simply says, 'I'm sure you'll do what's best.'

I feel my fingernails digging deep into my palms.

I: 'Could she not understand, after all the lost time, that I needed more from her than that?

'The fact that I was confiding in her clearly showed, didn't it, that I had no idea what was best. Didn't she have a single word of advice to try to help me?'

He: 'I don't think she did. I don't think she even heard what you'd said.

'Her mind was elsewhere. Had already drifted to another place, perhaps?'

I: 'Well I can see that now, but still I was angry.'

He: 'I hope that anger subsides in time because it'll destroy you otherwise.'

I: 'I'm less angry with you now.'

He: 'Hmm, I wonder. Maybe a little less angry with yourself.'

The week before Oliver's exams we are at a school quiz night in the new school hall. We are surrounded by parents we haven't sought out and teachers with whom, apart from our child's education, we have nothing in common and with whom we are also seething. It's a dismal evening but it's about to get a whole lot worse.

Just as we're nearing the end of the celebrity picture round my phone rings. I assume it to be the childminder who must be having more fun then we are. It's Mum's cleaner telling me that Mum has been rushed into hospital, 'by ambulance,' she adds with a little more relish than is decent.

'Again?' I retort which doesn't go down well and is followed by an exchange which culminates in me saying that I don't appreciate being told by my mother's domestic help how to manage my relationship with my mother. I go back into the school hall, quickly explain what is happening and I'm on my way to the hospital. Again.

On the thirty minute journey to Darlington I find myself, for perhaps the sixth time, rehearsing what I shall say at Mum's funeral. It's without emotion because I have been here before.

Ahead of every major operation, following several relapses, I have prepared for her death. But every time I do it, I think of something different to say. Sometimes when I've held her hand after an operation, it's all the good things she did for us as children, at other times when she has complained of the pain it's been impatience and frustration. But tonight it's angry things: the thoughtlessness of her timing, the selfishness of her illness, her heartlessness at making me feel so guilty if I'm not there for her every hour of every day. Yes, tonight I'm angry.

'Why? Because she telephoned the cleaner instead of me. Because we allowed her to become reliant on paid help. Because we trusted her when she told us she didn't need us. Because we should have known she needed us. Because she has been more well in the last month than she has been for years and suddenly that is snatched away from her, from all of us.

Half an hour later I am standing in the corridor outside Mum's room. 'Wait please while we clean up,' says a nurse in the broken English which seems to have become the principal language of the NHS. When eventually I am allowed in Mum is looking peaceful and my anger dissolves because, somehow, this time I know there is going to be no further need to rehearse.

She opens her eyes and, after what seems minutes, focuses on me. 'I'm so sorry,' she whispers.

'Sorry for what? You' don't have to be sorry.'

'You've had to put up with all of this. I didn't want it all to be like this.' She reaches out into mid air, her hand searching and I know she is looking for mine. I take her hand and we sit in silence, she drifting in and out of sleep, me honing that eulogy and wishing I could think of anything but that. But I can't so I stop trying.

'You thinking about what to say at my funeral?' The question startles me and I'm unsure what I should say, but she is wearing a little smile. 'It's bright in here, can you switch off the big light?' I go to switch on the bedside lamp but the bulb is blown and without it the room is too dark.

I tell the nurse at the desk and ask her if she has a new bulb. 'I can't get a bulb until the morning when maintenance comes in,' and I'm instantly angry again.

'My mother is dying and you can't even be bothered to find a light bulb to help her feel more comfortable. Pathetic.'

Mum says she doesn't mind. She doesn't want to make a fuss. So we sit in the dark with the door open to the corridor.

'Your father used to use that word a lot, pathetic,' she says.

'I know, he used to use it about me.'

'Oh he wasn't so bad,' and after a short pause, 'I don't want anymore Simon, I don't want anymore of this. You won't let them poke and prod me anymore will you? Enough now.'

'I know,' and I squeeze her hand. 'I love you, you know that,' I whisper for fear anyone else might hear.

'I know, lovvie, I love you too.' We talk about many things and many people for what feels like many hours. Maybe it's less but eventually we're done talking. We never let go of the other's hand and she drifts back into a sleep that seems so much more peaceful than she's had for several years.

By four in the morning I decide to go. As I gently pull my hand away from hers she stirs.

'I'm going now, got to get some sleep, get the kids to school and then I'll be back.'

'Don't rush, I'm fine. Thank you for being here, you know, through it all. Love you.'

'Love you too.'

'We'll talk some more tomorrow, have a good old laugh like we used to.'

'Yeah,' we'll talk and laugh again tomorrow.'

At home I ring round the family because I don't want them to think I had the monopoly on the final laughter, although I know they will think just that.

The next morning there is no more talking, no more laughing. Her face is contorted in pain. She is grasping at her hospital gown then rolling from side to side repetitively like a caged animal at the zoo.

I grab her hand to stop her and try to make eye contact but there is nothing there to make contact with and I think, 'shit, why didn't I bring her a decent nightdress.' I lean into her. Her face feels clammy against my lips, colourless and waxy.

> I: 'I remember that once before, when I didn't get down from London in time to see you before you died. They called me once you'd gone. I was pissed off about that, still am because I thought I needed to say goodbye so I went to the mortuary and there you were, all waxy and your lips were sealed up. I was angry they made me have to do that.'

Hours pass. My brother is there, and Mum's brother too. The doctor calls me out of the room and tells me that there is nothing else to be done. 'We are just making your Mum comfortable now.' That same old euphemism again.

I return to Mum and the other two have both gone out for a coffee or a cigarette and we are alone.

I lean close to her and hold her tight. 'You can go now Mum, it's alright, no-one wants you to fight anymore, it's time to go.' I don't think she really squeezes my hand but I like to believe she does.

I: I don't think she needed my permission but maybe I needed to give it anyway. She didn't say anything but she definitely mouthed your name..

'It could be a few hours, it could be a few days, we can't know,' is all the doctors will say.

I don't know if it's true for everyone but even though I've said everything I want to, even though I know she almost certainly doesn't know I'm there and even though it's the most hideous ritual to have to endure I cannot bring myself to leave her bedside.

By eight o'clock it has started snowing hard and I tell myself that the children and Wendy need me. In truth, it's me that needs them. I am on my way out. A nurse catches me before I leave, 'she's a fighter, your Mum.'

'You'll call me if there's any change? I don't want her to be alone.'

The next morning the snow has closed all the roads across the Pennines and we are snowed in. Mum is hanging on. 'No change,' is my brother's fulsome report.

He rings me again at three to tell me he's going home to get a shower and change. 'She'll only be on her own for an hour or so.'

Fifteen minutes later the hospital rings and she's gone. I wasn't there. Nobody was there. She died alone.

I: 'And I'm angry all over again. Why?'

He: 'Because you know she waited until nobody was there? Do you remember how you found her on the edge of our bed that morning you arrived after I died? The blood soaked sheets screwed up in her lap? How she sobbed in your arms? She'd seen death and she didn't want you to see it. She didn't want you to see her die.'

I: 'But I had. I'd seen her die slowly piece by piece, year on year and she denied me the last piece.'

He: 'It wasn't yours to deny, it was hers. It was her last shred of dignity to be able to die alone.'

Chapter Twenty Three

Four days after Mum's death, Oliver sits his school entrance exams. He knows nothing of our concerns or of those voiced so tardily by his class teacher. In his mind he has always worked to the best of his ability, risen to the challenge of extra lessons manfully and received nothing but praise from each of his class teachers for his positive attitude. He's a good sportsman and he is popular. In his mind he has nothing to worry about.

Afterwards he merely says of the exam, 'It was alright, can I go and play at Jack's?' It would have been unfair to have put any more pressure on him to expand further.

Wendy has been furious at Mum all week. 'How dare she die now just as Oliver has this to face. Selfish to the last.'

I know she doesn't really mean it but she is feeling the same frustration as me. The demands of the rest of the family to get the funeral sorted out; their expectation that they will all be staying at the castle despite the fact it is half term; our inability to do any of the normal formalities such as register the death or collect her personal belongings from the hospital because we are snowed in.

Nevertheless we manage to arrange a funeral for the following week, ten days after Mum died.

'It's a bit soon isn't it,' asks one never very close aunt, 'where is the funeral going to be?'

'Darlington.'

'Will we follow the hearse from the castle?'

'No, it's 45 miles away.'

'Isn't there anything closer?

'No, we live in the middle of the country,' and I want to add, 'unless you want to build a pyre out of some old tyres in the field behind the castle.'

In order to yield to my family's demands that they should be able to stay at the castle for two nights as 'it's far too far to be expected to come for just one,' we have to ring a handful of guests to cancel their bookings. Some are as tactless as the relatives.

'I'm afraid it's due to unforeseen circumstances,' Wendy begins, attempting to remain calm.

'What sort of unforeseen circumstances?' is the standard reply. 'What sort of thing closes a whole hotel?'

'I'm very sorry, I'm sure we can arrange a preferential rate for you to re-book.'

'But it's half term, we wanted to come this week, our children have been looking forward...'

'My husband's mother is dead.' And with that Wendy puts an end to the conversation.

Happily, and not for the first time, our friends provide the support so lacking from some other quarters.

The funeral goes much as funerals go.

I am the only one willing or capable of reading out the eulogy, now so well rehearsed in my mind over two or more years. I press others to contribute with readings and Mum's sister agrees to do one but in the absence of willingness by any of her other direct family, Wendy does the other. We are all far more affected by the emotion of the day, particularly Oliver and Emily who cannot be sure whether they are crying for a lost someone they only half knew or a lost future someone they were getting to know.

For my part, I find myself, to keep my composure, focussing on mundane things, many of which are redolent of my father's funeral and my grandmother's, both at which I was the reluctant chief mourner: How small the coffin is, surely a whole person, their life and influence cannot fit into such a small box but I suppose when we are just a shell, devoid of animation, we take up less space; how feebly everyone sings; how much more macabre it is to watch a coffin disappear behind a curtain than to see it lowered into the ground; what will we do with the ashes?

I: 'And it isn't until later on that the real emotions come tumbling down on top of me and I'm surprised by what they are. There's no regret. But there is humiliation that I have let my parents die; disillusionment at the frailty and weakness of you both not to be able to live a full length life; personal affront that she, and you, should leave us to fend for ourselves.'

'Puzzled sadness because if we were ever given the chance to set a plan for life in stone, it wouldn't be this way.'

He: 'And anger? Does that anger that you have so often spoken of feature in there too?'

I: 'It might have done once. But this was the last page of a final chapter of a book. And the new book was about going it alone and not hoping for something, someone that wasn't going to deliver.

'No more disappointment, no looking back in anger any more. Rather the chance to look forward to posterity and protect it from the damage of the past.'

A few days after the funeral we receive a letter from the school.

"Oliver has not performed well in the entrance exams...."

The letter goes on to tell us that Oliver can only progress to senior school if we are prepared to pay almost double the day pupil fees for a boarding place.

'But I don't want to be boarder,' Oliver protests. He'd been trying it at prep school for a couple of terms and hated it. 'Please, Mummy... Daddy. Please will you talk to them, I don't understand, I've done everything I've been asked to. Have all my friends got places?'

Our half term has just begun, but we telephone the school, sure that there will be someone who can explain how such a desultory letter can have been sent out without any effort at further communication.

'It is half term you know,' barks the unfriendly headmaster's secretary, 'nobody will be able to talk to you until school resumes next week. The headmaster has been very busy.'

'Excuse me, we're talking about our son's future,' but she's not interested. After all, it's not her job, compassion.

Perversely, here is a battle I feel I can relish. I am an angry man. I always will be. But if I have no parents to be angry with anymore, let me vent my rage at another target. This, I tell myself, is a fight worth fighting and an anger worth feeling.

In the months that follow we exchange increasingly heated correspondence with the school in which we accuse them of a failure of their duty of care, a systematic breakdown of communication and incompetent teaching and monitoring that can allow a child to progress (the word is used with some irony) through school to then be unable to pass its own internal exams. In turn, the school labels Oliver a low performer, asserts that he has a better chance of success as a boarder than a day pupil and resolutely refuses to acknowledge that it has got anything wrong, academically, pastorally or professionally.

Friends, many of whom have children at the school, question the logic: 'If there's a place in the classroom for Oliver as a boarder, the same place must exist for him as a day boy... it's extortion... It's immoral.'

Needless to say the school does not have the pleasure of either of our children on its roll past the end of the summer term.

The school debacle does at least give us reason not to dwell on Mum's death and by April it is easy to think that we have got over it, having for so long been prepared for her demise anyway. I have not cried for her and wonder whether I ever shall.

On April 23 we are invited to the National Railway Museum in York for the national Enjoy England tourism awards. For the castle it is just about the biggest thing that can happen. We offer all of our staff the chance to join us at the awards dinner but only three take us up. It is significant that they are our three longest serving employees, Faye, Esther and Val. It is no exaggeration that without these three we would never have reached such heady heights.

As well as the staff we have brought along some good friends who started out as guests at our very first Christmas to share in our hoped for success and have seen the whole thing evolve with us.

But lest we should get too excitable, as already seems to be the case as Wendy chases the waiter with the canapés and then doubles back after another waiter carrying champagne, Andrew, our dear friend, adds a bit of North Yorkshire reality to bring us down off cloud number nine.

'So what are we here for exactly?'

'Andrew!' rebukes his wife, Alison, 'they're finalists for a national award.'

'Aye, very good,' he pauses, as if weighing up his options, 'Champagne!' It's a rare moment of exuberance from such an inveterate Yorkshireman.

To get as far as the national finals is an achievement in itself, having had to have won a local and regional award and then to have been shortlisted as a finalist. And we've been mystery shopped for all of them.

I give the staff a pep talk along these lines before dinner is served telling them how proud we all should be and whatever the result we are already winners. I don't believe a word of it, of course, and neither do they. It's all bullshit and we all know that we'll be mightily pissed off if we walk out with anything other than the gold award.

I'm sorry to say that Wendy has again been out buying shoes especially for the occasion and is again very proud of them. Half way through dinner I turn to tell her something and she's disappeared. She has spotted Neil Morrissey (who is here because apparently he runs a pub which is up for an award) on a neighbouring table. Surely she doesn't think he's going to be interested in her shoes. Luckily her mission is marginally less embarrassing: she's collecting an autograph for her 'friend'.

Eventually, after what seems like hours of eating and drinking, oh the hardship of it all, the awards begin. Our category is near the end which helps to build the tension and it gets too much for Wendy who decides to order two further bottles of champagne.

'If we win we'll share it, if we don't we'll just get plastered.' She's ever practical.

The comedian Michael McIntyre is the evening's compere and at least his jokes are very funny. Also, at what looks like just a shade over five feet he's not on Wendy's radar for a congratulatory kiss. She's got her eyes on the chief executive of Cumbria's arch rival tourist board, Yorkshire and sees him as a much more challenging quarry.

As our category's nominees are announced we must endure something even worse than last time on the big screen, a promotional video. Did ever thirty seconds feel like three hours? We look haggard beyond our years and I sound like the only gay on the fell.

But that is all forgotten when Augill Castle's name is read out.

There is dancing afterwards and as Wendy and I hold each other I am overcome. It's all I can do to make it to the edge of the dance floor before I fall to my knees. I am sobbing for Mum, for you, for Mike, for all those who should have been there to share the moment.

We don't share the champers and do get plastered. The award itself, which can be best likened to a large Babybel cheese now has pride of place in the hall at the castle. I suspect that eventually, just as another award trophy found a new lease of life as an olive dish, the Enjoy England award will one day make a superb doorstop but not until we have stopped basking in its glory which won't be for some considerable time yet.

The award, of course, transforms our business and we enjoy our busiest summer so far.

In September the children start back at the village from where Oliver was originally removed. In the intervening years there's a new head teacher, new staff and new governors. His previous reception teacher is still there and Oliver is delighted to be back under her watchful eye.

Some parents make a point of telling us how brave we are to admit things went wrong and bring them back but we just say that you do what's best for your children, regardless of your pride.

We have managed to get Oliver into primary school to repeat year six rather than sending him straight to secondary school because the county's educational psychologist agreed that he would benefit from repeating year six, something his old school repeatedly said he didn't need.

By Christmas both children are thriving in a way we've not seen for several years and only now does the head teacher admit that she had been fearful for Oliver's well being when he first arrived. 'He was a broken child,' she tells us, tearfully.

'It's only when you see them happy,' I reflect with Wendy as we watch them run into school, 'that you realise how unhappy they were before.'

That our relief is palpable is made all the more so by the release from the burden of the school fees. The last payment leaves our bank on the same day that the children start their new school. It would not, however, be the end of our dealings with their old school.

If 2009 goes down as anything other than a year most of us would probably like to forget, it'll be the year I become web savvy and 2010 is planned as the year it all comes together.

Tourism is now all about branding, image management and digital marketing. At a tourism conference in the summer we are told that again and again and I feel terribly old fashioned holding on to the notion that, included somewhere in that mix ought to be customer service.

I feel befuddled when the presentation moves on to how to reach our desired audience. Out of nowhere comes talk of social networking, Facebook profiles and fan pages, getting bloggers onside, twitter feeds and tweets. I do, in all fairness, already know about Facebook, although I am ashamed to say that the first time I actually looked at it was when Wendy's 63-year-old aunt Gloria (who'd already unsuccess-fully tried to introduce us to Skype and video telephoning last Christmas) showed me her profile. But twitter feeds? It sounds like something you put out for the birds in winter.

Luckily help is at hand. Our host, who has one of those faces which is not quite familiar enough to be recognisable even though he clearly believes he is fabulously famous, explains that we (he must mean all of us collectively, although I note he is a good fifteen years my senior) are internet immigrants meaning we grew up in a world before instant broadband access, WiFi, Google, Digg, Flickr and YouTube whereas younger adults and our children – the markets of the future – are internet natives. It's an idea that speaks for itself, but still doesn't explain the nature of twitter feeding.

Back home I decide to do some research of my own. I start by ask-ing one of our girls at the castle, who is at university and should sure-ly know all about modern forms of communication. 'Are you twitter-ing and can I have a look at your tweets?'

Well, what does a twenty-year-old girl do if her boss, who is tech-nically old enough to be her father, catches her late at night and asks to see her tweets?

'I beg your pardon' she says, backing away slowly but purposefully. 'Twittering, what's it all about?'

'Umm, is Wendy around?'

No luck there then. It turns out she too has never heard of Twitter and once the true nature of my enquiry is explained her complaint of inappropriate behaviour is withdrawn. So, I look it up on Google which is, of course, what I would have done first had I been an internet native.

Two days later, I'm twittering like mad to anyone who'll listen and picking up followers like they're going out of fashion. It's social networking and I've also got myself a Facebook account. I haven't felt so with it since I got an ipod for Christmas two years ago, but that feeling soon faded after I had to ask another younger person to help me download tunes and since she went off to university I haven't added another song. It's not because I can't, it's because it doesn't come naturally.

Now, emboldened by my new hip online status, I ask one of our even younger employees if she'd like to be my friend on Facebook. But the look I get in return leaves me in no doubt that I have failed to grasp the intricate etiquette that goes with social networking.

'No way,' she says, 'my mates would crucify me.' This seems a little harsh but I feel grateful at least that she has sweetened the pill as her usual response would have been something more like 'oh my God that would make me want to vom.'

So I am now the proud owner of a Facebook account with one friend on it (and I am his only friend too – make up your own mind if that makes us both less or more sad or maybe just ultra cool).

Happily Twitter appeals to a more eclectic bunch of nerds and on my Twitter account I am following 129 other twits and being followed by 30. I guess Twitter or tweet heaven is when you are being followed by more twits than you are following so there's something to aim for.

But that's all three months ago, which in digital marketing is a lifetime. Since then things have evolved. Everything steps up a gear after I attended a digital marketing exhibition in London in September.

My befuddlement at the Yorkshire conference is nothing compared with how I feel as I hear about natural search, organic optimisation and viral email campaigns. I check to make sure I haven't stumbled into a health food conference by mistake. Natural, organic, viral? What about probiotic? Are these all types of yoghurt?

As the day goes on I hear talk of ensuring the quality of your creative, return on investment, routes to market and just as I think I know what's going on things turn athletic with mention of bounce rates and landing platforms.

I'm about to give up, having finished off a goji berry and pomegranate smoothie with kangaroo dropping booster for stamina at the juice bar (exhibition centres have come a long way too) when I spy an arrow pointing upstairs to 'The Google University'. In one hour confusion turns to enlightenment as two guys tell us about pay-per-clicks, Google Adwords and how the whole thing works and there's a sudden realisation that marketing is still marketing. It's based on common sense and anticipating how your customers are going to find you and trying to reach them before the competition does.

New words, new methods but the same old strategy.

I can see that a similar enlightenment is dawning for a significant proportion of the other delegates too.

And customer service? Well, of course, once you've got the customer hooked, you've still got to meet their expectations and that's still the hardest bit which no amount of digital trickery will change.

I return to the castle sure in the knowledge that the only thing more organic than our search engine optimisation is the yoghurt we serve at breakfast.

Chapter Twenty Four

It is a year since Mum died, since we became orphans. But we don't feel sorry for ourselves. Her illness which dragged on for so long also dragged her down and the people who loved her. It was a source of negative energy. Since she went so many positives have happened, so many doors have opened that it is hard to deny that there are forces other than ourselves influencing the direction of our lives.

Whether or not I believe that, I do understand that it is still what we do with the opportunities we encounter that really matters.

The children continue to thrive at school, we enjoy the freedom from the shackles of the school fees, the business continues to buck the general recessionary trend and the Coach House remains for sale. Having discounted it a hundred times, we agree to make a tentative offer to buy our first real family home.

The couple who moved in the same year that Mum moved away haven't talked to us for the last four years. Relations were never good after one of Holly's puppies ran under the wheel of their car back in 2003. But communication broke down completely after she shouted at the children for making too much noise and accusing them (which vicariously criticised us) of being out of control. The children were horrified and I was forced to present our neighbours with an ultimatum.

'I will keep my children under control, if you will keep control of your temper.'

It takes us six weeks to summon the courage to approach them about a possible sale, convincing ourselves that they so hate us they will do anything to prevent us getting our hands on what we so obviously need.

In the end I send Wendy over to sound them out whilst inventing something pressingly urgent to attend to. I offer my support by suggesting that if things go OK, she should telephone me and I will come and join her. She mumbles something about trousers and balls.

It isn't long before the telephone rings. Apparently our neighbours have been wracked with guilt about the parlous state of our neighbourly relations but have not known how to make amends, being convinced we hated them for even being there in the house which, they said, should so obviously be ours.

In any event, we are presented with a golden opportunity to acquire, if not the house of our dreams, as to be honest, we probably wouldn't have given it a second look as a house in its own right, certainly a house we've dreamt of. And acquire it we do, with a deposit which takes up every last penny of the old school fee fund, together with a lot of wrangling with the building society and the bank, a rescheduling of our business debt, and a new personal mortgage. But what makes it all add up is a small but crucial loan from Wendy's stepmother.

We move in on 3 February 2010. As we exchange a kiss on the threshold, Wendy whispers, 'I told you we'd find a way.'

Ten days later half term is in full swing and we are once again fully booked with children (whose parents see the chance of a quiet child-free day in the Lakes) clamouring for places on our Little Augill Cooks cookery school.

Wendy would rather be hanging her new curtains and unpacking boxes than teaching children to cook this week. In fact she says she'd rather be watching paint dry. I tell her not to be so miserable and she says, 'You do it then.'

'Can't,' I reply, 'I've got painting to do.'

In reality I'd just scare the children half to death so Wendy has no choice as our relief cookery teacher is on jury service. Wendy considers, momentarily, telephoning the Lord Chancellor or whoever is in charge of such things.

'Aprons on, hands washed and hair tied back please.' Wendy begins as she means to carry on – always with a firm hand which has certainly never done me any harm.

Eight eager youngsters are awaiting instruction on how to make pasta, various sauces to go with it, tiramisu and maybe a few sweet things to take home at the end of the day.

Wendy knows she's in for a challenge. Six of the children are seven and one has smuggled in his little sister Amy who is only five.

'I know you don't really take under sevens but she's no trouble,' pleads her mum. We heard that one too many time about dogs before banning them from the castle. But Wendy can see the fatigue in her face and relents.

'Now we have a busy day ahead so let's get cracking.' Ten minutes in, Wendy knows she's going to need a stiff drink by four o'clock.

'We're going to start by making pasta. Who has made pasta before?' Eight hands shoot up.

'Oh, OK,' Wendy is slightly taken aback, 'well who can tell us how it's made then?'

Joshua is quick to share his knowledge. 'You boil some water and open the pack and pour it in.' The others nod sagely in agreement.

'OK, well that's sort of right but today we're going to make it right from the start. Does anyone know where pasta comes from?'

A casual observer might predict the trap Wendy has just walked into. 'Asda!' exclaims Eloise excitedly.

'No,' frowns Freya, 'Waitrose and Mummy says it has to be fresh, not dried muck.' Joshua looks slightly crestfallen and declines to share the origins of his family's pasta rations.

'Italy,' Wendy interjects, 'Italy is the country where pasta comes from.'

There's a brief pause for thought, then, 'well if we're making pasta then it won't be coming from Italy will it? It'll be coming from England.'

Wendy chooses to ignore the source of such intelligent logic and moves on. 'OK, English pasta. Flour, eggs, olive oil...' moments later there are flour, eggs, olive oil in various piles on the table, on the floor and on Amy's head.

'She's annoying me,' protests her brother, 'I didn't want her to come, Mum made me bring her.'

'Never mind, everyone continue mixing together your ingredients and I'll help clean Amy up and perhaps we can find her Mum.'

No chance, Amy's Mum legged it out of the door before the kids had even put on their aprons so Wendy promises she can be her special little helper for the rest of the day. Four o'clock can't come soon enough but seems a hell of a long way off.

'Joshua, we don't do that in the kitchen do we? Go and wash your hands.' Clearly Joshua had in mind his own recipe for pasta verde.

Then there's a wail from Amy who has fallen off her footstool and is sitting under the table in a pool of egg.

'Come on Amy, let's get you cleaned up. Again.'

The doorbell rings. Could it be Amy's mum, returning wracked with guilt? But as I approach the door I know that it's not just Wendy who will be reaching for that drink at four o'clock.

'Hello Miss Hunt,' I enthuse, 'what brings you here?' I hope she doesn't see the panic etched on my face.

'I'm here to do your unannounced environmental health visit and I noted that you're also due for a health and safety inspection.'

'Lovely, shall we go to the office?'

'Shall we start in the kitchen?' and she's already pulling on her white coat.

'Children, Wendy, this is Miss Hunt, the environmental health inspector.' The children seem non-plussed. Wendy, I'm sure is holding back a tear of despair.

'Are you a doctor?' asks Freya, checking out the white coat. 'Have they food-poisoned somebody?' Wendy whimpers.

'No, I'm not a doc...'

'Joshua, I've told you not to do that. We've got to eat this pasta for our lunch, now go and wash your hands. Welcome, Miss Hunt, to our Little Augill Cooks children's cookery school.'

'Thank you, do carry on, I shall just observe if that's OK.'

Twenty minutes later ribbons of tagliatelle are finally rolling out of the pasta machines, Joshua has had to wash his hands for a third time and is on a final warning to improve his personal habits and Amy has decided to stay under the table with a copy of *The Rainbow Fish* for company.

Miss Hunt seems happy with proceedings despite having been quizzed by Freya who tells her that her Mummy says there are far too many busy-bodies and do-gooders trying to tell us all what to do. 'Is that what you are?'

Later Miss Hunt takes it upon herself to inspect the kitchen and homes in on a two foot long wooden spoon.

The children are making the sauces to go with their pasta and one of them has cut their finger with a knife and got garlic in the wound. As I am calming the hysterical patient Miss Hunt brandishes the spoon at me.

'This is not acceptable Mr Temple-Bennett, it's cracked and the cracks can harbour germs.'

'Oh don't worry about that, Miss Hunt, it's called Baboushka (Babs for short) and it's only used for disciplining the children.' In response to a raised eyebrow, I quickly add, 'our children, only our children.'

I think Miss Hunt is computing the potential combined hazard of a bacteria infected spoon which has been in contact with naughty children's backsides and in the event she simply says, 'perhaps it would be best kept away from the other utensils.'

A very reasoned response in the circumstances.

After a look at the other parts of the kitchen Miss Hunt declares herself happy and asks if we can just complete some paperwork and go through our health and safety risk assessments before she leaves.

I can hardly bear the thought of health and safety on an empty stomach and suggest that since the children are just about to sit down and eat their pasta she must join us.

She shoots a glance at Joshua and then at the hand washbasin. 'Erm, I think I need to be at another appointment shortly so we probably need to wrap things up, perhaps we could save the health and safety until another time.'

I'm almost ready to embrace Joshua and his tasty nostrils, and wonder how we can orchestrate his return next time the inspector calls.

By the end of the spring term Oliver has improved his reading age from what was 8.6 when he left his old school to 11.6, exactly matching his chronological age. He has worked tirelessly and cheerfully with his teachers, in the relaxed, less pressurised environment of a small village primary school, to achieve so much more than at his old school. Oliver is starting to realise his full potential.

With the evidence we need it is time to take the old school to task.

'We need closure,' I tell Wendy, 'and this is our chance.'

'We need closure on a lot of things,' she replies wistfully, 'but I agree. And this might just help us do that.'

Incredibly, with prep school fees for two children already running at more than some families' annual household incomes, the learning support that Oliver received cost extra.

We decide that in order to draw a line under the whole sorry business once and for all we will ask for those extra lesson fees to be refunded. If we are honest with ourselves we don't hold out much hope but we feel that if we are to tackle the school governors effectively we should have a clear objective.

A date for a complaint panel meeting is set and we ask Oliver's present teacher Jenny who has worked with him every day on a one-to-one basis and is a dyslexia specialist to accompany us to the meeting as our expert witness. But we don't tell the governors she is coming.

As we are ushered into the meeting, the panel of governors and the bursar, who is already wrong-footed by the unannounced appearance of our expert witness, are sitting behind a long table. They have chosen a room with all the trappings of public school. Panelling worn to a warm patina, garnished with old school photographs of sports teams, ex-headmasters and archive images of the school in years gone by. If we are meant to be in awe, it hasn't worked. We have seen it all before after school matches, concerts and plays when parents are invited to stay for a cup of tea and a bun as a flaccid thank you for our children's talent, but more importantly our cash.

Neither do we appreciate three chairs sitting in the middle of the room facing the governors. I had anticipated this and told Wendy and Jenny that if they tried to intimidate us this way we should simultaneously pull the chairs up to the table, place our hands in front of us, look them straight in the eye and begin.

With Jenny's help we present a strong case arguing that the school let Oliver down by not providing him with the appropriate support for his needs. The governors make a feeble attempt to argue their corner but on the whole they are like rabbits startled by headlights. An hour later the three of us are back on the sunlit school forecourt.

'That couldn't have gone much better,' we all agree.

We had been promised a letter within a week and it arrives seven days after the meeting. Wendy opens it and begins to read.

But I stop her, 'Never mind what the letter says, look. Look on the back.'

She turns the letter over and pinned neatly to the back is a cheque for the full amount of the learning support fees over four years. The letter states clearly that there were shortcomings in Oliver's support provision, in the school's communication and that the school will undertake to learn from these failings.

As if his achievements to date aren't sufficient, it's the final boost of confidence Oliver needs and he visibly pulls himself up tall and pushes back his shoulders at the eventual realisation that his feelings of failure were not of his own making.

With the best team of staff we have ever had in place we decide we will make the most of an opportunity for a two week summer holiday.

'The cheque from the school will help pay for it,' Wendy says when I voice concern about the cost. In typical fashion, and this may have something to do with our inexorable wallowing in a mire of debt, we have an innate propensity to allocate sums of money to more than one use simultaneously.

'Haven't we already spent that on the new mattresses and some sofas for the Coach House?'

'Some of it, don't worry, I have it in hand.' And I say no more since I stopped worrying about how Wendy manages the finances a long time ago. Head. Bucket. Sand.

'You know,' I say one evening in late spring, 'we still haven't decided where to go for our holiday.'

'No, have you given it any thought?' asks Wendy in a particular I-can't-be-expected-to-do-everything sort of way that she reserves for times when she feels I'm not pulling my weight.

'Well, actually, yes.'

'OK, book it, I'll go along with whatever you decide.' And so I do.

Given that it's hard fought-for money and the whole process from which it has resulted has had a pivotal role in the evolution of our family life, I book a holiday to include four nights at Les Mimosas in Roquebrun. I tell Wendy only that we are going to Northern Spain and Southern France. If she suspects, she doesn't let on.

Our week in Spain is also a return visit to an old haunt and we instantly unbend to the laid back beachside pace of life, untroubled by the need to find our bearings in a new place or to hurtle here and there trying to make the best of everything on offer. Here it is: just half a dozen restaurants, the beach and the sea.

In common, I suspect, with many hoteliers, and without needing to go into the finer detail of why, we do not go out of our way to be sociable when we are on holiday. If we are feeling talkative it is our choice and we certainly don't go in for casual conversation with people we haven't sought out.

In fact we actively create an exclusion zone around ourselves which can range from spreading our detritus far and wide in all directions on the beach to scowling menacingly at anyone who dares make eye contact in bars and restaurants.

In short, we just want to be left alone. The only exception to this hallowed rule is other people in the same business with whom we may be staying and with whom we are likely, though not always guaranteed, to have something in common.

So, imagine our horror when, as we are quietly tucking into sardines, from around the corner comes an all too familiar voice. Bernard and Sheila have been regular guests at Augill Castle for a decade. Their company is always entertaining on our home turf (admittedly sometimes enjoyed from a distance) but they are definitely not the sorts whose company we would seek out away from the castle.

Wendy's face drains of colour as Sheila is heard to shriek, 'Bernie just look at the sea, it's sooo bluuuuuuue.' As she rounds the corner it's a wonder she can tell where the sea starts as she is wearing sunglasses that cover the entire upper part of her face. The rest of her is bathed in colours so lurid they eclipse everything else including poor Bernard who is dressed in his customary beige.

'What the bloody hell do we do, they're coming this way,' mouths Wendy.

'Mummy!' Emily admonishes sternly.

'Stay calm,' I reassure, 'they might not notice us.'

But, 'Notice who? Who's coming? What's going on?' interjects Oliver loudly just as they are rounding the corner and the game is up.

'Oooh Bernie, I don't believe it, look who it is.' To be fair, Bernard (who once confided in me after his fifth pint of local ale that he loathes being called Bernie and would have probably spilled plenty more about what he doesn't like about Sheila had the Dirty Ewe continued to flow that evening) shoots us a silent but heartfelt apology but does nothing to stop Sheila drawing up a chair and planting herself at the corner of the table.

'Well what a lovely surprise,' says Wendy.

'That's not what she said just now,' adds Oliver in his best stage whisper and I kick him a little too firmly, rocking the table and sending the wine bottle toppling in Sheila's direction. But Sheila is a pro and in a single movement she's grabbed the bottle, a glass and is pouring herself a drink. 'Yes, lov-er-ly.'

'Ooh help yourself why don't you,' continues Oliver. Emily nearly chokes on a sardine. Bernard is helpless.

After a little small talk, I'm willing her not to ask where we are staying.

'So where are you staying?' Her enquiry is greeted with frantic glances around the table and Oliver says 'oh in a completely different resort. Miles away, we're just here for the day.' That's my boy!

'Oh so are we. We are on a coach tour with Saga. Bernie's reached a certain age you see.'

'Really Bernard, we'd never have guessed...' Oh God, this is getting too much. Even the grilled sardines are making a bid to return to the sea.

'It's sooo reasonable and such a lov-er-ly bunch of people,' adds Sheila as she lets out an ear piercing shriek followed by what sounds like a mixture of whale song and donkey braying.

'Wendy, I think she's having trouble breathing, an asthma attack or something,' I try to say subtly, though goodness knows why given the company. I fancy she may be choking on an olive or perhaps, if there's any justice, our wine.

'Sheila, are you OK, is anything wrong?' asks Wendy in her best if-only-I-really-cared tone.

'No,' says Bernard, 'she's laughing. Sheila does enjoy a bargain.'

'What, like half of our wine?' asks Oliver.

'Shut up.'

But Oliver won't, 'I'm only saying what everyone else is thinking,' and Bernard chuckles.

Sheila recovers her composure and in between glugs of our white Rioja Gran Reserva, which she charitably pronounces to be a decent drop of plonk, continues, 'So where did you say you were staying? Wouldn't it be a scream if it was on our itinerary! We could all do lunch or something.'

I try to deflect that enquiry, more alarmed about the nature of 'or something,' imagining she might be scheming to get us all smuggled onto a Saga excursion to the local ceramics works or perhaps an eel farm followed by a menu degustation of eel cooked twelve ways. 'Well, what places are on your itinerary exactly?'

'Oh I don't recall, Bernie deals with all that.'

'Oh we're heading south and your resort is north of here unfortunately,' he adds helpfully.

'Is it, I don't remember...'

'Yes dear, they did say, now come on or we'll be late for the bus and we don't want to miss the botanical gardens.'

'Ooh no, we're planning a Mediterranean style sunken garden so I'm looking for some tips.'

Everyone, even Oliver, refrains from commenting on the dubious suitability of a subtropical garden in Lancashire.

'Thanks for the drink, lov-er-ly to see you, what a thrill, we'll have to compare holiday snaps when we next come up to "le chateau Augill."'

We are left in stunned silence as she totters around the corner saying to Bernard, 'such a lov-er-ly family, it must be such a thrill for them to meet people they know away from the castle. They can really be themselves when they're not all on show.'

'If you say so dear.'

The next day we leave for Roquebrun.

Love for a place is as random as love for another human being. There are undoubtedly thousands of both in the world with which each of us could fall in love. But we have neither the opportunity or the capacity to encounter even a fraction of those possibilities and so it is only from the people and places which fate throws our way that we can make our life choices.

With people, if we are lucky, love can last a lifetime by embracing each others passions, celebrating their strengths, accepting their weaknesses and growing together. But it takes hard work and commitment from both sides.

With places, love is simpler. We can still revel in their qualities and accept their shortcomings but, unlike another person, places are static. We may change but they are more inclined to stay the same, waiting, uncomplaining, for us to return and welcome us with the same embrace.

Unlike a human being, a place won't turn its back on you if you've been unfaithful, won't shut you out if you've stayed away too long. A love affair with a place can only be broken by us, the place will always stay loyal until we decide to return.

Wendy has clearly guessed our next destination and she's as excited as Emily with a new pet.

It takes us just two hours to drive across the Pyrenees and as the disembodied voice of the satellite navigation system announces, 'in 500 yards your destination is straight ahead,' neither of us can conceal our excitement. As we cross the medieval bridge into the village the evening sun has turned every house a burnt orange and the smell of the surrounding forest hangs heavy and seductive in the air.

The children are quite at a loss as to why we should be so excited. But they know this is the place where we were engaged, where we made some of our biggest decisions, where Oliver took his first faltering steps and Oliver is concerned that these memories should not result in any sort of embarrassment.

'You're not going to cry or anything, are you Mummy?'

'Oh of course not,' Wendy assures him. But even she's not sure of that. When we pull up outside the house nothing has changed apart from the colour of the front door.

Wendy can't help herself. 'There's such a lot of us in this place and it's just the same, like it's been waiting for us.'

'Oh God she's crying,' Oliver says.

'Gross,' adds Emily.

We are greeted by Jacqui and Martin to whom Sarah and Denis sold Les Mimosas. Any reservations we might have had about our place falling into the wrong hands quickly evaporate. They clearly love this place and its simplicity too.

Inside the curved handrail on the grey stone staircase is still the same battered green, there are the floor to ceiling doors and windows still with their peeling paint, so much less important to touch up in the dry heat of this part of France. We show the children the terrace with its canopy of wisteria and grape vines.

'This is where you learnt to walk Oliver.'

'Great. Whatever.'

But Emily is happy, she has found a cat.

'That's Coco,' shrieks Wendy, 'she was here when we first came.'

'Must be pretty old then,' Emily observes.

The village too seems to have stood still, as if waiting for our return.

Over the following few days we introduce the children to some of our favourite restaurants, including the one where I produced our engagement ring over cheese.

'Just don't cry or make a scene, OK?' Oliver pleads.

On returning to the *chambre d'hôte* that evening we are invited by Jacqui and Martin to join them for a drink and we share stories of how we all came to be where we are.

'Perhaps we can do some business, sharing recommendations,' Wendy says.

'But we're selling it,' Jacqui replies. 'It's time for a change. We want to go back to England.'

Suddenly we are young and impetuous all over again. Our old dream rekindled but still with not a spare penny to our names save for the stones and rubble of a castle in Cumbria, where the only sun is what's left over once the rest of the world has had theirs, and Wendy's ever present optimism, 'we'll find the money somewhere'.

We have our own separate family house now. After twelve years we have just started to chip away at our debt rather than adding to it. Why are we here, now, dreaming all over again a dream that was almost lost when we have worked so hard to build what we have got into a dream itself?

For the first time since we bought the castle we are truly happy and settled as a family.

But perhaps it is only when you are truly happy and settled that absolutely anything is possible. And we talk long and hard into the night because, as with most grand plans, the ideas form before the practicalities have ever been worked out.

He: 'It's quite a story.'

I: 'Yes, more than a story, a journey really.'

He fixes me with a gaze the intensity of which I can hardly recall but which echoes of something from my childhood.

He: 'Do you really believe you needed me to achieve anything different from what you have done on your own, with a good woman at your side?'

I: 'You had a good woman, Mum was a good woman, I see that now.'

He: 'She was a good woman but I wasted her. She was never at my side. I kept her one step behind me. She didn't know how to be anywhere else but one step behind, she saw you and Wendy together ahead of her and she realised she couldn't be part of it. She gave up trying to be part of it.

'You and Wendy, you're strong. You were too strong for her. That's no criticism. But she had to leave, you see that now?'

I: 'I understand better.'

He: 'Are you still angry?'

I: 'No Dad, I'm not angry now, just sad. Sad that I could never prove to you I was capable of being the son you wanted. More than the son you wished for, I think.'

He: 'I'd agree with that. You're twice the son I could have wished for. But I don't feel sad, not for you.'

I: 'Not for me? But you are sad. I can see it in your face.'

He: 'For Oliver and Emily. I would have enjoyed them I think.'

I: 'They would have enjoyed you. They wouldn't have seen the drinking, the arguments. They would have seen the Sunday lunchtime Grandad; the barbecues on the hills Grandad; the passing half pints of shandy out of the pub window Grandad; the silly games at Christmas Grandad; the tea and toast in the morning Grandad.

'They would have seen all the best bits of you that I forgot about because I was too busy being angry.

'So I'm sad for that too. I'm sad that they didn't get to have you as a Grandad. And I'm sad that I let myself forget all the times you were my Dad.'

He: 'Be proud of who you are, Simon. Be kind to those you love and *never give your children cause to forget who you really are. Do that, and you'll be more than twice the son I hoped for and a better man than I was.*

'I'm proud of you, son. And I love you.'

There's a long pause. There can't be any touching hands, no hugging now. Anyway, that's not in either of our natures. Now there's just a companionable silence. It suits us both.

I: 'Yeah, thanks Dad. You too.'

POSTSCRIPT

The story continues. Much has and continues to change, but in a frenetic world it is reassuring to know that the Augill magic lives on.

Find out more at: www.stayinacastle.com

About the Author

Undressed for Dinner was inspired by Simon's blog about family life in a country castle at:

www.simontemple-bennett.com

Simon was born in North London and moved with his family to Somerset aged three. He attended Taunton School where he did enough to get by and Bournemouth University where the beach was always more tempting than the library.

After graduating with a BSc in Food and Catering Management he worked in various capacities in hotels in the Channel Islands, London, Sydney and Perth, Western Australia.

On his return to England he took a post-graduate diploma in journalism and worked as a reporter on evening newspapers in the East Midlands for two years before marrying Wendy, buying a share of a restaurant in London's Mayfair and moving to West London, all in the space of a month.

Simon now lives at Augill Castle in Cumbria' Eden Valley with Wendy, their two children, Oliver and Emily, a cocker spaniel called Maisie, a cat called Luther, several chickens, a turkey and six goats.

He is a director of Cumbria Tourism, a governor of two schools and a dedicated supporter of Penrith RUFC.

www.stayinacastle.com

REVIEWS

'This is neither advertised as a business book or meant to be a business book. With that said, it is one of the best business books you will ever read. Ever wanted to start a business? Read this first. You will cry, you will laugh (hard), and you will think twice about the work ahead of you!

'I woke up on my 50th birthday in the most amazing of places, Augill Castle, in northern England. We found stayinacastle.com online and fell in love with the place; its history, the family, the dog, and the chickens. Owner Simon Temple-Bennett released a book about their experiences turning this deserted castle into an award-winning hotel. The book is charming, hysterical at times, and eye-opening about what it takes to create and maintain a successful business.'

Dayna Steele,
motivational speaker and author of the
101 Ways to Rock Your World Series

'A story with something for everyone - a great read.'

Eric Robson, broadcaster and publisher

'Simon writes in a fluent and easy style which is a pleasure to read. I had difficulty putting his book down!

'He weaves his tale with a great deal of literary competence. I thoroughly enjoyed reading this often amusing, sometimes poignant but always interesting and chatty book.'

Keswick Reminder

R EAD M ORE

Simon Temple-Bennett

STOP FOR BREAKFAST

Stop For Breakfast continues the story of a family trying to lead an ordinary life in an extraordinary place. With the loss of Simon's mum, two teenaged children vying for ever more attention, a financial climate gradually suffocating them and their dream French home back on the market the couple feel the draw of the southern sun strengthening by the day.

In desperation, they start a smallholding with near disastrous consequences, expand beyond their already exhausted means while their efforts to remain sane are thwarted by ridiculous bureaucracy and government jobsworths. It's a gentle, humorous and self-deprecating take on mid-life, parenting of teenagers and self-employment and the ups and downs of having to deal with all of them at once.

Order your copy now by visiting your local bookshop quoting ISBN 978-1-910237-21-2

www.hayloft.eu